A CHOICE COLLECTION OF NEW SONGS!

" Here's the Sea, the o-pen Sea; Alice
    Gray;
  I'd be a But-ter-fly ;
Mis-sle-toe Bough ;" thus through the
    streets
  His bal-lads he will cry.
" Here's the last grand collection
  Of new songs—quite a heap,
Three yards long—a penny the price—
  Which surely is won-d'rous cheap."

A Touch on the Times

Songs of Social Change 1770-1914

Illustrated with Old Photographs
Edited by Roy Palmer

Penguin Education

Designed by Arthur Lockwood
Pictures researched by Angela Murphy

460712152 PQ

Penguin Education, A Division of Penguin Books Ltd,
Harmondsworth, Middlesex, England
Penguin Books Inc, 7110 Ambassador Road, Baltimore, Md 21207, USA
Penguin Books Australia Ltd, Ringwood, Victoria, Australia
Penguin Books Canada Ltd,
41 Steelcase Road West, Markham, Ontario, Canada

First published 1974
This selection copyright © Roy Palmer, 1974
Introduction and notes copyright © Roy Palmer, 1974
Adaptations of tunes and texts © Roy Palmer, 1974

Filmset in Monophoto Bodoni 135 by
Filmtype Services Ltd, Scarborough
Printed in Great Britain by Fletcher & Son Ltd, Norwich

Contents

Introduction   page 8

Part 1   *The Times are Altered*

The Road   22
The New Navigation   28
Humphrey Hardfeatures' Description of Cast-Iron
    Inventions   31
Johnny Green's Trip fro' Owdhum to see the Manchester
    Railway   34
Navvy on the Line   40
The Navigators   42
A New Song on the Opening of the Birmingham and
    Liverpool Railway   46
The Cockney's Trip to Brummagem   50
The Wonderful Effects of the Leicester Rail Road   52
The Jolly Waggoner   56
The Railway Whistle or The Blessings of Hot-Water
    Travelling   59
The Scenes of Manchester   62
Oldham Workshops   65
Gorton Town   68
The Dalesman's Litany   71
Liverpool's an Altered Town   73
I can't find Brummagem   78
My Grandfather's Days   83
The State of Great Britain or A Touch at the Times   88

Part 2   *Stirrings on Saturday Night*

Saturday Night   92
Sheffield's a Wonderful Town, O   95
The Rigs and Sprees of Leeds Town   98
The Rigs and Fun of Nottingham Goose Fair   102
Country Statutes   105
Truro Agricultural Show   110
The Bullard's Song   112
The Toon Improvement Bill or Nee Pleyce Noo ti Play   120
The Bonny Gray   123
The Football Match   125

Part 3 *On Monday Morning I Married a Wife*

The Rambling Miner 130
The Weaver and the Factory Maid 133
Dashing Steam-Loom Weaver 135
Poor Man's Work is Never Done 138
Washing Day 142
Fuddling Day, or Saint Monday in answer to Washing Day 144
Coulter's Candy 148
The Skeul-Board Man 150
The Captain's Apprentice 154
Cholera Humbug or The Arrival and Departure of the
    Cholera Morbus 156
The Barnsley Anthem 160
The Lasses' Resolution to Follow the Fashion 162
The Tea-Drinking Wives 166
A Drop of Good Beer 168
A Word of Advice 172
London Adulterations or, Rogues in Grain, Tea, Coffee,
    Milk, Beer, Bread, Snuff, Mutton, Pork, Gin, Butter, etc. 175
A Chapter of Cheats or The Roguery of Every Trade 179
How Five and Twenty Shillings were Expended in a Week 183
Belly and Back 188
Tally Man 190
Wife for Sale 196

Part 4 *Time to Remember the Poor*

The Rambling Comber 200
The Miseries of the Framework Knitters 204
John o' Grinfield 207
Birmingham Jack of all Trades 210
The Tradesman's Complaint 214
New Dialogue and Song on the Times 218
What Shocking Hard Times 223
The Shurat Weaver's Song 226
Poor Frozen-Out Gardeners 230
Cowd Stringy Pie 234
The Rest of the Day's your Own 236
The Buffalo 240
Botany Bay 242
Jim Jones 244
Curly Williams 246
Wakefield Gaol 250

New Bailey Tread-mill   254
Durham Gaol   257
A Dialogue and Song on the Starvation Poor Law Bill,
    between Tom and Ben   260
The New Gruel Shops   264
New Song: 'To Hereford Old Town'   268
The People's Comic Alphabet   270

Part 5 *The World Turned Upside Down*

The Colliers' March   274
The Rights of Mankind   278
Watkinson and his Thirteens   281
General Ludd's Triumph   286
Hunting a Loaf   289
A Radical Song   294
A New Song on the Peterloo Meeting   296
New Hunting Song   299
The Chartists are Coming   302
The Best-Dressed Man of Seghill or The Pitman's Reward for
    Betraying his Brethren   306
Striking Times   309
The Cotton Lords of Preston   313
The Lock-Out   316
Happy Land   318
The World Turned Upside Down   321
Poor Man's Heaven   324

Sources   328
Photographs Source List   334
Select Bibliography and Discography   340
Index of First Lines   350
Acknowledgements   352

Introduction

During the war [up to 1815] it was his [the ballad singer's] peculiar province to vend his half penny historical abridgements to his country's glory; recommending the short poetic chronicle by some familiar household air, that fixed it in the memory of the purchaser. . . . No battle was fought, no vessel taken or sunken, that the triumph was not published, proclaimed in the national gazette of our Ballad-singer. . . . It was he who bellowed music into news, which, made to jingle, was thus, even to the weakest understanding, rendered portable. It was his narrow strips of history that adorned the garrets of the poor; it was he who made them yearn towards their country, albeit to them so rough and niggard a mother.

Douglas Jerrold, 1840

The eighty-eight items in this collection are of several kinds: folk songs from the oral tradition (seventeen), songs written by entertainers and writers (nineteen), and broadside ballads (fifty-two).

The smallest number of songs come from the oral tradition – that is, they are songs which have been passed down by word of mouth from generation to generation. Historians have sometimes dismissed oral tradition as unreliable, and so in some ways perhaps it is. But in other ways there are few more reliable ways of finding out about the past: here after all is the real voice of the people who lived in the past. There is a sort of timelessness in folk songs even when they deal with particular historical events. A Board of Education 'blue book' of 1805 recommended the use of folk songs in schools as providing an 'expression in the idiom of the people of their joys and sorrows, their unaffected patriotism, their zest for sport and the simple pleasures of country life'.[1] Partly true. The 'unaffected patriotism' can include powerful anti-war songs, the 'simple pleasures of country life' include a great many erotic songs and also bitter complaints about the hardships and the quality of life.

Of the composed songs included, many were written by songwriters well known in their own day, at least in their home towns. Such were Joseph Mather (1737–1804) of Sheffield, John Freeth (1731–1808) of Birmingham, Ned Corvan (1830–1865) of Newcastle upon Tyne, Tommy Armstrong (1848–1920) of Tanfield and Shotley Bridge, County Durham, and Samuel Laycock (1812–1893) of Oldham. All of these wrote songs, set to current tunes, about topical issues of the day. John Freeth explained his work in this way:

My hobby-horse and practice for thirty years past have been to write songs upon the occurrence of remarkable events, and nature having supplied me with a voice somewhat suitable to my stile of composition, to sing them, also, while their subjects were fresh upon every man's mind, and being a Publican, this faculty or knack of singing my own songs has been profitable to me; it has in an evening crowded my house with customers, and led me to friendships which I might not otherwise have experienced. Success naturally encouraged me to pursue the trade of ballad-making.[2]

John Freeth

Ned Corvan

Tommy Armstrong

Samuel Laycock

Freeth was of humble origin, Mather worked in the cutlery trade, Armstrong was a miner, Laycock a power-loom weaver. Their songs reflected the ideas and aspirations of ordinary people, in a clear and immediate fashion. There was a close and affectionate relationship between such song-writers and their audience.

Finally, there are the broadside ballads. These were not new in the nineteenth century: they date back to the mid-sixteenth. They were sold in the streets, at fairs and at markets by vendors who would sing out their ballads in order to attract a crowd. John Aubrey, the antiquarian, describes in *Brief Lives* how the eccentric Richard Corbet (1582–1635),

> After he was Doctor of Divinity . . . sang Ballads at the Crosse at Abingdon on a market day. He and some of his Comrades were at the Taverne by the Crosse . . . The Ballad-singer complayned that he had no custome; he could not put-off his ballads. The jolly Dr putts-off his Gowne, and putts-on the Ballad-singer's Leathern jacket, and being a handsome man, and had a rare full voice, he presently vended a great many, and had a great audience.[3]

The complaining ballad singer at Abingdon was of the same kind as the one who attended Weobley Fair in Herefordshire in the late nineteenth century crying 'A song, a song, a song for a penny! As large as a barn door and not quite so thick!'.[4] A number of old people still living remember such singers, or were told about them by their parents. For example, an old lady from Stow-on-the-Wold in Gloucestershire learned the following from her father who was a young man in the 1870s:

One penny only. The life, trial and execution of Charles Peace, the Blackheath burglar, a remarkable but cruel and wicked life. Read how he acted as sidesman in his parish church, in the darkness of the night committed burglary. Read how he shot the policeman. How, when in custody, he plunged through the railway carriage. How finally he was condemned to death and led to execution. How he died on the scaffold, hung by the neck until he was dead. Only one penny, only one penny.

She explained: 'After any particular crime which resulted in the death of the criminal it was customary for broadsheet doggerel to be hawked around the streets by itinerant vendors, accompanied by a dolorous chant. One concerning Charles Peace was the last heard.'[5]

Sellers of broadsides did not confine themselves to gallows literature, nor did they only operate in the country. Hogarth's pictures of the London streets frequently show ballad singers. Mayhew's

'Old Sarah',
the hurdy gurdy
player
from Mayhew

gallery of street musicians and hawkers includes chaunters, running
patterers and long-song sellers. A writer in the *National Review* for
1861 speaks of

> Those two somewhat shabby companions, with voices of brazen
> twang, walking slowly down the sides of some quiet but not
> out-of-the-way thoroughfare, their hands filled with broad-
> sheets, their eyes keenly glancing round for every possible owner
> of a spare half-penny, and making the whole neighbourhood
> ring with their alternate lines and joint chorus of some unspeak-
> able ditty, sung to a popular air, with variations imported on the
> spur of the moment.[6]

Despite his affection for the singers – he goes on to ask, 'Alas,
where are they gone?' – the writer has little regard for their 'un-
speakable' ditties. Ballad singers were often regarded as little better
than vagrants. In Elizabethan times they were sometimes whipped
as sturdy beggars. Henry Chettle wrote in 1582 of 'a company of
idle youths, loathing honest labour and dispising lawfull trades,
[who] betake them to a vagrant and vicious life, in every corner of
cities and market townes of the realme singing and selling of ballads'.[7]
Two hundred years later (1794) it was announced in Birmingham

that 'The Officers of this Town give this public Notice, that they are come to a determined Resolution to apprehend all strolling Beggars, Ballad Singers, and other Vagrants found within this Parish.'[8]

At worst, the popular literature of ballads and chap-book tales was regarded as corrupting: 'The fears of prudent employers is directed [1796] to the troops of ballad singers, who disseminate sentiments of dissipation in minds which should have been bred in principles of industry and sobriety.'[9] At best, it was merely value-less. William Lovett, the Chartist leader, who was born in Cornwall in 1800, wrote:

With the exception of Bibles and Prayer Books, spelling books, and a few religious works, the only books in circulation for the masses were a few storybooks and romances, filled with absurdi-ties about giants, spirits, goblins, and supernatural horrors. . . . Therefore the Bible, and Prayer and hymnbook, and a few religious tracts, together with fragments of an old magazine, and occasionally one of the nonsensical pamphlets described, were all the books I ever read till I was upwards of twenty-one years of age.[10]

Others took a different view. Thomas Holcroft:

> Even the walls of cottages and little alehouses would do some-
> thing [for literacy]; for many of them had old English ballads,
> such as *Death and the Lady*, and *Margaret's Ghost*, with lament-
> able tragedies, or King Charles's golden rules, occasionally
> pasted on them. These were at that time [Holcroft was born in
> 1745] the learning, and often, no doubt, the delight of the vulgar.[11]

John Clare, the poet, came into early contact with chap-book
romances and ballads. His father was a reader of 'the superstitious
tales that are hawked about the streets for a penny', and also a
singer of ballads.[12] Clare's work was profoundly affected by the
popular ballads, and he almost shares the attitude of 'the common
people' who 'know the name of Shakespeare' as a poet, 'but the
ballad-monger who supplys hawkers with their ware is poets with
them & they imagine one as great as the other'.[13]

Broadside material is enormous in quantity and astonishing in
variety. Many hundreds of thousands of broadside ballads were
printed and sold during the nineteenth century alone. A small
printer in a small town, Ford of Chesterfield, issued 139 broadsides,
some in more than one edition, with a total of 282 titles; Catnach of
London is said to have sold as many as two and a half million
copies of each of two broadsides, in 1848 and 1849, which dealt
with spectacular murders. Material was reprinted from many
different sources: recitations, poems, glees, sentimental and popular
songs, traditional folk songs. Much was specially written, on topical
themes. 'The ballad-singer, with his rough broad-sheet, travelled
. . . over the whole surface of man's life, political and social.'[14]
Notable events, battles, disasters, sport, fashion, crime, taxation –
one could continue almost endlessly – all these were covered by
hack writers, who were paid a shilling a ballad. Although they wrote
to order, the broadside writers were often extraordinarily skilful in
capturing the ear of the public and in appealing to the popular
taste.

Many ballads, however, were composed by non-professionals.
Frank Peel wrote:

> There are evidences that the Luddite rebellion was not destitute
> of poets who celebrated in rough but vigorous rhyme the progress
> of the triumphant croppers in their crusades against the machi-
> nes that robbed their children of their food; or appealed solemnly
> to the God of Heaven to smite with swift vengeance the oppres-
> sors who despised the cries of the poor and needy and ground
> them down to the dust.[15]

A Catnach broadside

THE
NEW TIMES.

Printed by J. Catnach, London, and Sold by W. Marshall,
Lawrence-Hill, Bristol, at whose Shop Travellers can
be supplied with a better assortment of Sheets,
Songs, &c. than at any other in Bristol

—————o————o—————

YE working men where'er ye dwell, lend an attentive ear,
　While I in humble verse relate the suff'rings you endure,
Well may the industrious artizan the loss of trade deplore,
For such distress on English ground was never known before.

The masters all the country round begin to see that they,
Unless a remedy is found, must fall to want a prey,
Look where you will the scene is bad and all things at a stand
Which makes the wise men wonder where the mystic scene will end.

In Spittlefield the weaving tribe no comforts now enjoy,
Some thousands there as we are told the masters can't employ
In London too the plague is felt which makes the Cockneys start,
To think that they for want of trade with all their goods must part,

They straightway leave their home and friends & flock to country towns
But there they find with great surprise that sore distress abounds,
'Tis then to crave the charity with tardy steps they go,
Ashamed to begs afraid to steal, their harts is fill'd wit woe.

In Manchester some thousands there are cestitute of work,
Within the fields, the streets, and lanes these men are seen to lurk
Some of their families are large which makes them daily grieve,
To hear their children cry for bread when they have none to give.

The Coventry ribbon weavers have nothing for to eat,
In Leicester town the stocking men now from their frames retrea.,
In Nottingham the working tribe their wages run so low.
They can't their families maintain, which fills their hearts with woe

TRIPE

AND

Cow Heels.

THE tories in Dudley have cast in their mites,
In order to sup of rich cow heel and tripes;
A supper was granted,—to gain votes for *prize*,
Whilst the BUTCHERS their *bellies & pockets* did rise.
> Each proud upstart tory was top full of glory,
> Whilst filling his belly with tripe.

A number of voters did get very mellow,
Took *six* pounds a-piece at the *Hearty good Fellow*,
No whigs were permitted to come near their bounds,
Or taste of their tripe at the *Old Hare & Hounds*.
> Each proud upstart tory was top full of glory,
> Whilst filling his belly with tripe.

At the cross and the gate, *some* numbers did meet,
And the *tail*-or declar'd that the cabbage was sweet,
Says he gentlemen I will keep a close guard,
Should it come to a fight, I'll draw *bodkin & yard*.
> Each proud upstart tory was top full of glory,
> Whilst filling his belly with tripe.

Still after all this, if the truth I must tell,
This tailor for profit would *trick* you an ell ;
For the sake of sweet *cabbage* he'll caper and spurn,
And his *coat* and his breeches for profit would turn.
> Each proud upstart tory was top full of glory,
> Whilst filling his belly with tripe.

When Campbell comes forward for roast beef he'll call,
And the tripe and cow heels shall be stewd for St—
The whigs shall be powder'd upon the same day,
And all kinds of music so sweetly will play.
> Each proud upstart tory was top full of glory,
> Whilst filling his belly with tripe.

In Dudley they crown'd him, so firm and so true,
With lawrels, and flags, and ribbonds true blue!
To finish my song, and *complete* it withall,
Success to bold Campbell, and down with St—
> Each proud upstart tory was top full of glory,
> Whilst loading his *stomach* with tripe.

16

Forty years after the Luddites, the same spirit and the same practice was noticed among the soldiers during the Crimean War:

> The singing of old songs, catches, glees and choruses, forms a principal feature of the amusements of the Camp . . . once or twice I heard some original and extemporaneous verses, *apropos* to the time and place, to our Government at home, to our Generals at headquarters, to the Czar in his palace, and to Johnny Russ in front.[16]

In the 1880s, it was 'still quite a usual practice in Shropshire to "make a ballet" [ballad] on any passing event of interest'.[17] One man 'used to think the verses over in his mind when he was going with the horses, and when he got home at night he would put them down'. Non-professional ballads would sometimes find their way into print, perhaps because a ballad seller heard them sung, memorized or copied them down, and took them back to his printer.

In the industrial areas, strikes often produced ballads, which provided a cash income for the strikers, who hawked them round the district and also further afield:

> So with our ballad's we've come out,
> To tramp the country round about,
> And try if we cannot do without
> The Cotton Lords of Preston.[18]

The ballads were also a means of communication, in a tradition which George Orwell noticed more recently (1936) in Spain:

> At that time revolutionary ballads of the naïvest kind . . . were being sold on the streets for a few centimes each. I have often seen an illiterate militiaman buy one of these ballads, laboriously spell out the words, and then, when he had got the hang of it, begin singing it to an appropriate tune.[19]

Pedlar of song sheets, c.1890.

17

Finally, the ballads were a means of self-expression; this was an art form truly in the idiom of the people.

As such, it is a valuable source for the historian. The importance of songs has, it seems, always been readily recognized by rulers and governments, usually by banning them rather than encouraging them. A man whistling even the tune of *Hey Boys*, the rallying song of the royalists, would have been liable to arrest under the Commonwealth for 'whistling treason'. The tune of *The Wearing of the Green* was prohibited in Ireland by the British in much more recent times for a similar reason. The songs of Theodorakis are banned in contemporary Greece because of their association with the cause of the opposition. If the very tunes of songs could be, and can be, so embarrassing, how much more so the words. On the other hand, the words could be very instructive; the *Spectator* in 1712 reported

> A certain Elizabethan Minister of State was invariably at pains to discover the drift of public opinion before embarking on any new policy, to which end, we read, 'he had all manner of books and ballads brought to him, of what kind soever, and took great notice how they took with the people; upon which he would, and certainly might, very well judge of their present dispositions and the proper way of applying them to his own purpose.'[20]

There was no shortage of ballads on historical subjects. John Aubrey tells us that:

> In the old ignorant times before woomen were Readers, ye [ballads] was handed downe from mother to daughter, &c.; and W. Malmesburiensis pickt up his history from ye times of Ven. Bede to his time out of old Songs; for there was no writer in England from Bede to him. So my nurse has the history from the conquest downe to Carl. I in ballad.[21]

Macaulay believed that ballads provided the groundwork of history. Another historian, C. H. Firth, wrote of the broadsides:

> They tell historians what was felt and what was believed by those who wrote ballads and those who bought them, show how public opinion was formed, and help to explain the growth of popular traditions.[22]

A selection of eighty-eight songs from the thousands available can only be a sample, which will inevitably reflect the tastes and interests of the editor. The items have been grouped thematically, rather than chronologically. Within each group, however, a rough chronological order has been maintained. The first section, *The Times are Altered*, deals with transport, technological change and the growth of towns. It is followed by *Stirrings on Saturday Night*, a group of ballads on popular sports and entertainment, including fairs and markets. The third section, *On Monday Morning I Married a Wife*, deals with love and courtship (mainly in an urban, working-class setting) and the problems of health, housing, education, diet and the cost of living. The tone of songs varies a great deal, from jovial to angry, from tragic to humorous. *Time to Remember the Poor*, the fourth section, is concerned largely with the dangers besetting the poor man: hard times, unemployment, bad working conditions, prison and the workhouse. In the final section, *The World Turned Upside Down*, the theme of change returns. Beginning with hunger riots of the late eighteenth century and the radical rationalist movement of the same time, this section continues with industrial and political struggle: strikes, lock-outs, trade unionism, demonstrations and the aspiration towards a better life.

As far as possible when a tune is indicated on a printed ballad (which is rare), or when it is suggested by a particular metre or a refrain, it has been used. One or two tunes occur more than once, for this reason. The problem often arises, however, that no tune is either indicated or suggested. In these cases, after the style of Orwell's Spanish militiaman, any suitable tune has been used. The marriage of a tune and a text often requires minor amendments in both. Texts have, however, sometimes been amended rather more radically, either by abridgement or by adaptation, or both. If this is regarded as cavalier treatment, I can only reply that I believe that the original consumers would have done the same. Abridgements and adaptations have been indicated in the list of sources.

The tunes are provided in order that the songs may be sung, and the full flavour of a ballad seldom emerges until it is sung. The songs may be sung individually, as illustrations to particular topics, or a group of songs (perhaps interspersed with readings from other source material) can be performed as a sort of recital on a particular theme. It is possible to make a rather more sophisticated documentary programme, using songs, narrative, dramatic interludes, slide projection and 8mm film. A further alternative is to use the songs in full-blown documentary drama.

A few of the songs are in dialect. This may prove difficult for some, in which case it is an interesting exercise to rewrite a song in a different idiom. *The Skeul-Board Man* (p.150), for example, comes out very well when translated from North-eastern into Black Country. It may also be worthwhile in some cases to remake some of the songs using contemporary terms; cast-iron, for example (p.31), might well be replaced by plastic. Another possibility is to write new songs on subjects treated by the old ones. Some of the material in the book went out of date quickly, but the main themes

– change, the environment and the quality of life – are topical today.

It is hoped that what is basically an introductory book will stimulate further interest. Any of the topics covered could be explored further in terms of song and ballad, any of the localities mentioned would yield further material. Some of this is indicated in the bibliographies and discographies at the end of the book, but much more remains to be found and explored. Broadside collections, memoirs, files of local newspapers, manuscripts, and also the memories of living people are possible sources.

Such material is important, for it gives the view of those who were sometimes inarticulate, those 'who have no memorial; who are perished as though they had never been, and are become as though they had not been born; and their children after them.'[23]

References

1   Quoted in M. Karpeles, *Cecil Sharp*, Routledge & Kegan Paul, 1967, p.59.
2   Introduction to *Political Songster*, 6th edn, 1790.
3   Ed. O. L. Dick, Penguin, 1962, p.167.
4   E. M. Leather, *Folklore of Herefordshire*, 1912, p.181 (reprinted S. R. Publishers, 1970).
5   Miss Jessie Howman (b.1884), interviewed by Roy Palmer, 11 August 1966.
6   p.398.
7   *Kind Hart's Dreame.*
8   J. A. Langford, *A Century of Birmingham Life, 1741–1841*, vol.2, 1868, p.44.
9   *Rural Economy in the Midlands.*
10 *Life*, 1869, p.17.
11 *Memoirs*, ch.15.
12 Quoted in E. Blunden, *Sketches in the Life of John Clare*, 1931, p.46.
13 J. W. and J. A. Tibble, *The Prose of John Clare*, Routledge & Kegan Paul, 1951, p.31.
14 *National Review*, 1861.
15 F. Peel, *Risings of the Luddites*, 1895, p.119 (reprinted Cass, 1968).
16 Quoted in W. H. Logan, *A Pedlar's Pack of Ballads and Songs*, Edinburgh, 1869, pp.109–110.
17 C. S. Burne, *Shropshire Folklore*, 1883, p.534.
18 See song on p.313.
19 *Homage to Catalonia*, ch.1.
20 6 October.
21 *Remaines of Gentilisme and Judaisme*, 1881, p.68.
22 *Essays*, Oxford University Press, 1938.
23 *Ecclesiasticus* 44, ix.

1

The Times are Altered

The Road

The road, the road, the turnpike road!
The brown, the hard, the smooth, the broad,
    the ever, ever broad!
Without a check, without an end,
Horses against horses on it contend;
Men laugh at the gate, they bilk the tolls,
Or stop and pay like honest souls,
Or stop and pay like honest souls.
I'm on the road! I'm on the road!
I'm never so blithe as when abroad,
With the hills above and the vales below,
And merry wheresoever I go.
If the opposition appears in sight,
What matter? What matter?
We'll soon make that all right.
What matter? What matter?
We'll soon make that all right.

I love, oh! how I love to ride
With a smiling damsel by my side, a damsel by my side,
Where every prad keeps well his pace,
Nor draws my eye from the sweet one's face.
Nought tells how goeth the time of day,
Nor why the hours so fly away.
I never heard the angry sea roar,
But I loved the dry land more and more,
And away have flown to my box and reins
For wheels and whips are my favourite strains.
On my team is all my care bestowed,
For I was, for I was
Born on the turnpike road.

The clouds were dark, and grey the morn,
In the hazy hour when I was born, the hour when I
    was born.
The guard he whistled, the coach it rolled,
And the outriders shrieked and shivered with cold,
And never was heard such a curious din

As when the road child the world popped in,
As when the road child the world popped in.
I have driven since then in fair and rough
Full forty winters a traveller tough,
With primest of cattle and carriages neat
And never had a spill or a beat.
And Death, whenever he looks for me,
Shall come on, shall come on
The road and not on the sea.

prad horse.

The road, the road, the turn-pike road! The brown, the hard, the smooth, the broad, the ev-er, ev-er broad! Without a check, without an end, Horses against horses on it con-tend; Men laugh at the gate, they bilk the tolls, Or stop and pay like honest souls, Or stop and pay like hon-est souls. I'm on the road!

After many centuries of neglect, English roads were notoriously bad by the seventeenth and eighteenth centuries. Turnpikes were stretches of better road built by private boards of trustees, who charged tolls in order to pay their expenses (and to make a profit). Turnpike Trusts, as they were called, could only be set up by act of parliament, the first one of which was passed in 1663. Between 1750 and 1790 over 1500 acts were passed and there was an enormous extension of the turnpike system, coinciding largely with the careers of three famous road builders, John Metcalf (1717–1810), John Macadam (1756–1836) and Thomas Telford (1757–1834). The period of greatest activity was from about 1790 to 1810. By 1830, over 1100 separate trusts were administering 23,000 miles of roads. Between 1750 and 1830, the travelling time from London to Edinburgh, for example, was reduced from twelve days to forty-five hours; London to York from four days to twenty hours. Incidentally, the word 'turnpike' continued to be used for certain roads in every-day speech until very recently; in fact, people of sixty and over still speak about 'the turnpike road'.

I'm on the road! I'm never so blithe as when abroad, with the hills above and the vales below, And mer - ry where - so - ev - er I go. If the op - po - si - tion ap - pe - ars in sight, What matter? What matter? We'll soon make that all right. What matter? What matter? We'll soon make that all right!

The best-known vehicle which travelled on the turnpikes was the stage coach. Spanking along at a speed of between six and ten miles per hour, it was not only the fastest thing on wheels, but a fine sight into the bargain. 'In many villages', wrote an observer about 1800, 'the children still take off their hats and shout when it passes.' There is a famous chapter about a journey on a stage coach in *Tom Brown's Schooldays*. 'Next after a fox-hunt', wrote William Cobbett, in 1816, 'the finest sight in England is a stage-coach ready to start. A great sheep or cattle fair is a beautiful sight; but, in the stage-coach you see more of what man is capable of performing.'

On the whole, however, it was the well-to-do who travelled in this way. The poor were obliged to walk, or perhaps to travel in the lumbering wagons which were primarily intended for transporting goods (see *The Jolly Waggoner*, p.56).

The New Navigation

This day for our new navigation,
We banish all care and vexation,
The sight of the barges each honest heart glads
And the merriest of mortals are Birmingham lads,
Birmingham lads, jovial blades,
And the merriest of mortals are Birmingham lads.

With rapture each heart must be glowing,
Stamps, presses and lathes shall be going;
The lads to the wharf with their lasses repair
And smile at the streamers that play in the air,
Play in the air, free and fair,
And smile at the streamers that play in the air.

Let Stratford boast out of all measure
The fruits of her mulberry treasure;
Such treasure for once may cause jubilee joys
But riches spring daily from Birmingham toys,
Birmingham toys all men praise,
But riches spring daily from Birmingham toys.

The Thames, Severn, Trent and the Avon,
Our countrymen frequently rave on;
But none of their neighbours are happy as they
Who peaceably dwell on the banks of the Rea,
Banks of the Rea, ever gay,
Who peaceably dwell on the banks of the Rea.

Not Europe can match us for traffic,
America, Asia and Afric;
Of what we invent each partakes of a share,
For the best of wrought metals is Birmingham ware,
Birmingham ware, none so rare,
For the best of wrought metals is Birmingham ware.

Since by the canal navigation,
Of coals we've the best in the nation,
Around the gay circle your bumpers then put,
For the cut of all cuts is a Birmingham cut,

Birmingham cut, fairly wrought,
For the cut of all cuts is a Birmingham cut.

This day for our new nav-i-ga-tion,—— We ba-nish all care and vex-a-tion,—— The sight of the bar-ges each hon-est heart glads And the mer-riest of mor-tals are Bir-ming-ham lads, Bir-ming-ham lads, jo-vi-al blades, And the mer-riest of mor-tals are Bir-ming-ham lads.

mulberry treasure in the grounds of New Place, Stratford, is a
    mulberry tree, said to be the scion of one planted by Shakespeare.
jubilee joys the Shakespeare jubilee, in 1769.
the Rea this river is a rather inconsequential stream, which flows
    through Birmingham.
cut canal.

In 1769, David Garrick wrote a song, *The Warwickshire Lad*, with
music by Charles Dibdin, for the Shakespeare Jubilee celebrations
at Stratford. In the November of the same year, Birmingham's
first canal was opened and a local publican and balladeer, John
Freeth, wrote a song in praise of the achievements of his native
town, using Dibdin's tune. Freeth was full of enthusiasm for the new
canal and he wrote several other songs and odes about it. Later, he
became a little disenchanted with the canal mania and wrote
Navigation; or, The Canal Fever.

The Birmingham Canal went to Wolverhampton, with a branch off to Wednesbury. It was the opening of this branch, and the arrival in Birmingham of the first load of coal, which Freeth celebrated in *The New Navigation*. The price of coal in Birmingham was halved, to 7s. (35p) per ton. The rest of the canal was completed in 1772 and its original line, which had been surveyed by James Brindley, was modified by Telford in 1824.

William Hutton, the historian of Birmingham, described the canal as a 'liquid road'. 'The boats,' he wrote, 'are nearly alike, constructed to fit the locks, carry about twenty-five tons, and are drawn by something like the skeleton of a horse, covered with skin; whether he subsists upon the scent of the water is a doubt; but whether his life is a scene of affliction is not; for the unfeeling driver has no employment but to whip him from one end of the canal to the other.'

The canal and its successors were very widely used for transporting goods, and also passengers. As late as 1849, a covered market boat plied three times weekly between Birmingham and Wolverhampton. Freeth's enthusiasm for canals seems to have been shared by many of his contemporaries. The Grantham Navigation, for example, is extolled in a song printed in the *Stamford Mercury* for 17 May 1793 and it is likely that other songs of this kind are slumbering in the files of provincial newspapers. Street songs were also produced with titles like *When Leeds is a sea-port town*, which amusingly explored the effects of canals on the cities they served.

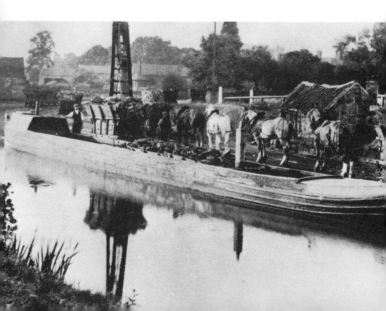

Humphrey Hardfeatures' Description of Cast-Iron Inventions

Since cast-iron has got all the rage,
And scarce anything's now made without it;
As I live in this cast-iron age,
I mean to say something it.
There's cast-iron coffins and carts,
There's cast-iron bridges and boats,
Corn-factors with cast-iron hearts,
That I'd hang up in cast-iron coats.

Iron bedsteads have long been in use;
With cast-iron they now pave our streets;
Each tailor has a cast-iron goose,
And we soon shall have cast-iron sheets.
Tommy Whalebone has grown quite a blade,
So dextrous and clever his hand is,
Swears he now shall have excellent trade
Making cast-iron stays for the dandies.

We have cast-iron gates and lamp-posts,
We have cast-iron mortars and mills, too;
And our enemies know to their cost
We have plenty of cast-iron pills, too.
We have cast-iron fenders and grates,
We have cast-iron pokers and tongs, sir;
And we soon shall have cast-iron plates,
And cast-iron small-clothes, ere long, sir.

So great is the fashion of late,
We have cast-iron hammers and axes;
And, if we may judge by their weight,
We have plenty of cast-iron taxes.
Cast-iron bank-notes we can't use,
But should we e'er prove such ninnies
A good Henry Hase to refuse,
They must issue out cast-iron guineas.

Now my cast-iron song's at an end;
I hope you'll not take it amiss, sir.
May your plaudits my efforts attend;
My heart it will burst if you hiss, sir.
I pray, my kind friends, don't say nay,
For, if I'm not out of my latitude,
Your goodness I'll never repay
With such feeling as cast-iron gratitude.

Since cast ir-on has got all the rage, And scarce
As I live in this cast ir-on age, I——
an-y-thing's now made with-out it; There's cast iron coffins and
mean to say something a-bout it.
carts,— There's cast iron bridges and boats,— Corn-
factors with cast iron hearts, That I'd bang up in cast iron coats.

goose pressing iron with elongated, S-shaped neck.
Henry Hase Chief Cashier of the Bank of England from 1807 to
1829. His signature appeared on bank-notes and his name became
a synonym for a pound note.

This song was published in 1822. At that time, cast-iron was clearly
making a big impact on the economic life of the country, but also on
its psychological outlook. The iron industry had been booming for
half a century, but the popular consciousness took some time to catch
up. Songs like *Humphrey Hardfeatures*, and others with titles like
The Cast-Iron Man and *The Steam Arm* made full use of the artistic
possibilities of the new technology and, by so doing, helped people
to accept it.

Johnny Green's Trip fro' Owdhum to see the Manchester Railway

Last New year's day eawr Nan hoo sed
Why Joan we'n bin near three yer wed
An sin the day to church I're led,
Theaw ne'er wur th'chap to treat one,
Awhoam this day aw will not stay
Awl ha me play – so aw moot say,
Theawst see th'Railway this very day,
So bless thee dunna fret mon.

Aw took an sowd me seawkin pig
For ready brass to Billy Brigg,
An looast me jacket just to rig
Me'sel in decent fettle,
Eawr Nan buck'd up ith best hoo cud,
An off we peg'd thro' Hollinwood
O'er Newton Yeoth past *Robin Hood*
An stopt at *Crown an Kettle*.

We seed sich lots o' Jerry shops,
Boh we'd na stay to drink ther slops,
Eendway we went and made to steps,
An just in toime we nick'd um,
For helter skelter, sich a crew
Wur cummin in fro Liverpoo'
Awm sure they cud no faster goo
If the devil in hell had kick'd um,

Aw shouted eawt an whirl'd me hat,
An whizz they coom at sich a bat,
Aw run so hard an puff'd an swat,
Boh aw cud naw keep with waggins,
When thinjun stopt an seet um deawn
Aw wundert wher they aw wur beawn,
They rode in callivans 'oth teawn,
Aw think to get ther baggins,

34

They coom awm sure at Leeds aw guess,
Two hundred mile it's eawr or less,
Neaw Ben, theaw loughs an winks at Bess
Becose theaw thinks awm loyink,
Theaw seed th'balloons fro Sawford goo,
Theaw seed foke run deawn Tinkers broo,
Boh it bangs um aw an th'races too –
Ecod it's next to floyink.

We seed tat coach wot Wellington
An awth greyt foke on day coom on,
They'll show it thee or any mon,
An tell thee aw ist axes.
Eawr Nan sed they'd ha sarv'd him reet,
To drag'd him on thro dry an weet,
An ridd'n him on both day an neet,
If he'd naw ta'en off the taxes

Boath Nan an me to roide had meeont,
Boh th'brass yo seen wur welly spent
So straightway up Knotmill we went,
An at th' sign oth Railway bated.
We cum by th'*Star* in Deansgate too,
An th'coachman theor look'd woeful blue,
Awm sure ther jaws han had nowt to doo,
Sin th'Liverpool Railway gated

We stopt to see that noice clock case
Leet up wi gas ith Firmary place,
A chap coom staring in my face,
An puff'd me een up fairly
Says Nan theawd best naw doot agen,
Aw gript me fist an look thee Ben.
If awd boh had me clogs just then,
Awd purr'd his ribs O rarely,

We coom straight whoam geet choilt to bed,
Aw fetch'd some beer fro th'owd *Nag's Yed*,
While Nan reach'd eawt some beef an bread
An bravely we mow'd away mon,
Its rare proime ale an drinks loike rum,
One pint a that's worth two of some
Aw had naw quite three quarts by gum
Boh me yed warch'd aw next day mon.

Aw yerd me uncle Nathan say,
They're gooink to make a new Railway,
Fro Manchester to Owdham – eh.
Aw wish it wur boh gated.
For weavers then to th'warehouse soon,
May tey ther cuts by twelve at noon,
An then theaw knows theyn save their shoon,
An not be awlus bated.

Theres weary wark ith papers – some
Say th' revolutions beawn to come,
An very loike to morn, by gum
Fo th'news is come by th' mail road
Theyn feeor eawr Nan to deeoth these chaps,
Hoo says – eh Joan awl wesh me caps,
Do thee tey down thee looms an traps
An we'n cut eawr stick bith Railroad.

Aw awlus sed yo known it too,
No mon cud tell what steam ud doo,
An if toth Owdfield lone yo'll goo
Yo'll find awm none mistaken.
Aw ne'er struck stroke this blessed day,
Aw know naw that eawr Nan'd say
Its dinner toime an if aw stay
Hool ate awth beoons an bacon.

Joan John.	*bated* took refreshment (verse 7)
seawkin pig sucking pig.	fined (verse 10).
Newton Yeoth Newton Heath.	*gated* started.
Jerry shops beer shops.	*cut* length of cloth.

There is a large group of ballads in which the hero, John o' Green-
field (or Grinfilt) sets out from his native village near Oldham to
view the wider world with innocent eyes. Johnny Green in this
broadside behaves very like his near namesake. His enthusiastic
approval was not always shared by his contemporaries. When the
railway from Liverpool to Manchester was opened in September 1830,
ordinary people appear to have been more interested in demonstrating than in admiring the railway. M. Sturge Gretton wrote

> My grandfather who was . . . one of the guests of the Liverpool and
> Manchester Railway on the occasion of the running of their first

passenger train, used to recount how the Duke of Wellington, who was also a guest, became plastered with mud in his efforts to shield the ladies from the filth that the populace, ranged along the line, was flinging at the travellers.

A Miss Fanny Kemble wrote of tricolour flags, cries of 'No corn laws', and hissing and booing.

> The vast concourse of people who had assembled [in Manchester] to witness the arrival of the successful travellers, was of the lowest order of mechanics and artisans, among whom great distress and a dangerous spirit of discontent with the Government at that time prevailed. Groans and hisses greeted the carriageful of influential personages in which the Duke of Wellington sat. . . . High above the grim and grimy crowd of smiling faces a loom had been erected at which sat a tattered, starved-looking weaver, evidently set there as a representative man, to protest against the triumph of machinery, and the gain and the glory which the wealthy Liverpool and Manchester men were likely to derive from it.

Johnny Green took the view that there was something in it for the working man after all.

The Manchester terminus from 1830 until 1844 was in Liverpool Road, where the buildings may still be seen.

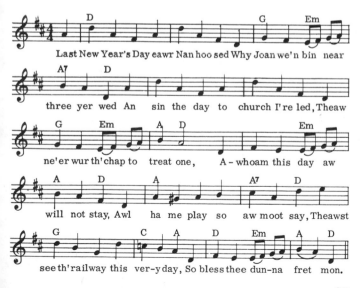

Last New Year's Day eawr Nan hoo sed Why Joan we'n bin near three yer wed An sin the day to church I're led, Theaw ne'er wur th'chap to treat one, A-whoam this day aw will not stay, Awl ha me play so aw moot say, Theawst see th'railway this ver-y day, So bless thee dun-na fret mon.

37

Navvy on the Line

I am a navvy bold, that's tramped the country round, sir,
To get a job of work, where any can be found, sir.
I left my native home, my friends and my relations,
To ramble up and down and work in various stations.

Chorus
I'm a navvy, don't you see, I'm a navvy in my prime;
I'm a nipper, I'm a tipper, and I'm working on the line.

I left my native home on the first day of September,
That memorable day I still do remember.
I bundled up my kit, Sunday smock and cap put on, sir,
And wherever I do go, folks call me happy Jack, sir.

I've got a job of work in the lovely town of Bury,*
And working on the line is a thing that makes me merry.
I can use my pick and spade, likewise my old wheelbarrow;
I can court the lasses, too, but don't intend to marry.

I worked a fortnight there, and then it come to pay-day,
And when I got my wages, I thought I'd have a play-day.
And then a little spree in High Street† went quite handy,
Then I sat me down in Jenkinson's‡ beside a Fanny Brandy.

I called for a pint of beer, and bid the old wench drink, sir,
But whilst she was a-drinking, she too at me did wink, sir.
Well, then we had some talk; in the back we had a rally;
Then jumped o'er brush and steel, and agreed we'd both
    live tally.

They called for liquors freely, the jug went quickly round, sir
That being my wedding day, I spent full many a crown, sir.
And when my brass was done, old Fanny went a-cadging,
And to finish up my spree, I went and sloped my lodgings.

---

*The original gives: 'in the town of ————', in order to leave scope for
 the singer to localize his own adventures, subject to the rhyme.
†The original gives: 'in ———— street'.
‡This name, too, would presumably have been varied.

Oh now I'm going to leave the lovely town of Bury;
I'm sorry for to leave you chaps, for I always found you
 merry.
So call for liquors freely, and drink away my dandy,
Here's a health to happy Jack, likewise to Fanny Brandy.

navvy contraction (which first appeared in 1822) for navigator.
nipper the word normally meant 'a sharp lad', but here it may
 mean one engaged on the barrow run, up the side of a cutting.
jumped o'er brush and steel navvy wedding ceremony.
live tally live as man and wife without being married.
sloped decamped, slipped away from.

The Navigators

All you that delight in the railway making,
Come listen awhile to what I do sing;
In summer time, they will use you all well,
In winter you'd best stay at home with your girl.

Chorus
That's the rule of the railway makers,
Rare, good, jolly bankers, O.

On Monday morning, it's one of our rules
For every man to choose out his tools;
And they that come first do pick out the best,
And they that come after must just take the rest.

Now when that we come to the bottom run,
We fill our barrows right up to our chin,
We fill up our barrows, right up, breast high;
And if you can't wheel it, another will try.

And when that we come to the main plank wheel,
We lower our hands and stick fast on our heels;
For if the plank does bend or go,
Our ganger on top cries, 'Look out below'.

Our master he comes with his staff in his hand;
He knows very well how to measure the land.
He measures our dumpling, so deep and so wide,
He measures it well for his own side.

Now when we are struck by the frost or the snow,
We'll blow up our mess, boys, and off we will go;
We'll call to our time-keeper, without any damp,
To give us our time before we go on tramp.

On Saturday night we receive our pay;
It's then to the ale-house we go straightway.
And each sits his sweetheart upon his knee,
And we treat them well with the barley brew.

Last Saturday night, I received my full pay;
On Monday morning, I ran away.
I buzzed up the tommy shop and stopped the score,
And swore that I'd never go that road no more.

But when several months are gone and past,
Those pretty young girls got thick in the waist.
They run to buy cradles, they learn lullabies,
And wish that they still had their dear banker boys.

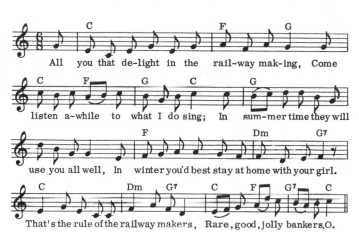

All you that de-light in the rail-way mak-ing, Come
listen a-while to what I do sing; In sum-mer time they will
use you all well, In winter you'd best stay at home with your girl.
That's the rule of the railway makers, Rare, good, jolly bankers, O.

bankers another name for navvies.
dumpling embankment.
damp rebuff.
tommy shops shops owned by the contractors, where navvies pur-
    chased food by means of tickets drawn on their wages. The word
    'tommy' is still used as slang for food.

Most of the canals and railways in Great Britain – and some further
afield – were built by the muscle and skill of navvies, with just a few
simple tools and some help from horses. Very little has survived
about the pay, conditions and techniques of the canal navigators,
but there is a wealth of material on their colleagues who built the
railways.

The navvies worked harder and played harder than most other
workers. They often lived in isolated camps, where the law reached
with difficulty. Both their work and their pleasures were often

43

hazardous. They constituted an 'anarchic elite' so far beyond the pale that a mission was set up in the 1870s to attempt to convert or re-convert them to Christianity. The navvies' achievement has been likened to the building of the pyramids. Between 1843 and 1855, for example, some 6000 miles of track were laid.

There are sentimental and bawdy songs about navvies, in which, however, the word 'navvy' is more or less interchangeable with 'miner' or 'sailor' or other folk heroes. Songs about the navvy's work and his life are very rare, which is one reason for including two of them here.

A New Song on the Opening of the Birmingham and Liverpool Railway

On the fourth day of July, I recollect well,
What bustle there was in the morning I'll tell,
With the lads and young lasses so buxom and gay,
Delighted and talking about the railway.

Chorus
You may travel by steam, or so the folks say,
All the world over upon the railway.

To view the railroad, away they did go,
It's a great undertaking, you very well know;
It surpasses all others, believe me, it's true:
There's tunnels for miles that you have to go through.

There's coaches and carts to accommodate all,
The lame and the lazy, the great and the small;
If you wish for to ride, to be sure, you must pay,
To see all the fun, sir, upon the railway.

Colliers from Hampton and Bilston likewise
And Wedgebury nailers are struck with surprise;
To see the railroad, to be sure, they must go,
Dressed up in their best, they all cut a fine show.

The cobbler left all the old shoes in the shop;
Old women on crutches were seen for to hop;
And the tailor his customers would not obey,
But rode on his goose for to see the railway.

There was fat Dumpling Bet with young Jack the
    Moonraker,
There was buxom young Kit with the butcher and baker,
And Black Sal from Walsall with two wooden legs,
To see the railroad how she trudged on her pegs.

In London, I've heard said, there is a machine,
Invented for making young children by steam:
Such dear little creatures, full thirty a day,
For young engineers to supply the railway.

Come all you young fellows and let us be free,
Again fill the glasses, now merry we'll be;
Success to all trades in the reign of our queen,
And the boiling hot water that travels by steam.

On the fourth day of July I re-col-lect well, What bus-tle there was in the morn-ing I'll tell, With the lads and young las-ses so bux-om and gay, De-light-ed and talk-ing a-bout the rail-way. You may travel by steam, or so the folks say, All the world o-ver up-on the rail-way.

Hampton Wolverhampton.
Wedgebury another name for Wednesbury.

The railway from Birmingham to Liverpool via Manchester, also known as the Grand Junction Railway, was opened in 1837. The Birmingham terminal was at Curzon Street, where part of the imposing classical station buildings still exists.

The anonymous writer of this broadside ballad, confronted with something entirely outside his experience has taken one of the songs which celebrated the goings-on at a fair as his model.

The reference to 'coaches and carts' indicates that the standards of comfort were not as good as the mood of the song might imply. Third-class travel was in open waggons. It was not until the Railways Act of 1844 that the companies were compelled to carry third-class passengers on at least one train per day in covered carriages. These trains stopped at every station and the fare was not more than a penny per mile.

The railways had an enormous impact on the social and economic life of the country, though it took some time for this to be realized.

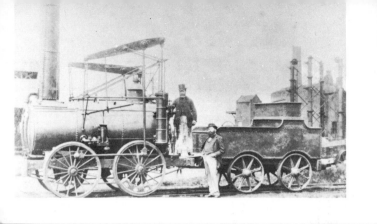

The Cockney's Trip to Brummagem

You Birmingham lads, come and listen awhile,
And I'll tell you a story will cause you to smile,
For the railroad they're going to open next spring
Will life up from London to Birmingham bring.

Chorus And sing fal the diddle lero, sing fal the diddle lay.

When the swell mob comes down, we must look out for
    squalls,
Or they'll bolt with the organ from out the Town Hall;
They think themselves clever in every feat,
But we'll show 'em one more, boys, we'll show 'em
    Moor Street.

So reckon on sport when the Cockneys come down,
For they're all very flash from the fop to the clown;
Whether tinkers or tailors or omnibus cads,
We can learn them a tune called *The Warwickshire lads*.

The Cockneys for boxing have long held the sway;
This railroad will help us to meet them half-way.
This much I can say without telling a crammer:
If they'll find the anvil, we'll find our own hammer.

They say every cock can crow on his own hill,
But they must not come here empty pockets to fill.
They may walk round our streets without trouble or pain;
They'll have something to do to walk round Hammer Lane.

We all know that London's a place of renown,
And for my own part, I will not run her down;
But I can't help thinking it'll be a queer thing
To be fighting with Cockneys in our old Bull Ring.

So now to conclude and finish my song,
May the railroad be finished before very long;
May London and Brummagem unite and join hands
And grow like the oak tree of our native land.

You Bir-ming-ham lads, come and lis-ten a-while, And I'll tell you a stor-y will cause you to smile, For the railroad they're go-ing to o-pen next spring Will life up from Lon-don to Bir-ming-ham bring. And sing fal the diddle le-ro, sing fal the diddle lay.

Moor Street site of the lock-up.

'*The Warwickshire lads*' tune by Dibdin (cf. note *The New Naviga-tion*, p.28).

Hammer Lane there is a play on words here, this being the nick-name of a well-known boxer of the day.

The line from Birmingham to London was opened in 1838, after an epic feat of construction. The twelve-hour stage-coach journey to London was halved on the train. The writer of this broadside ballad has begun to get over the amazement which characterized earlier reactions to the railways and has begun to speculate about the possibilities which were opened up.

The completion of the London to Birmingham line, in conjunction with the Birmingham to Liverpool line, permitted through traffic from London to Lancashire. The Curzon Street station in Bir-mingham was the terminal of both railways, which amalgamated in 1846 to form the London and North Western.

A first-class single from London to Birmingham cost £1 when the line opened. The company promised to 'perform the entire distance, 112½ miles, between London and Birmingham by the first-class train in five hours and thirty-seven minutes, and by the mixed trains in six hours and fourteen minutes.'

The Wonderful Effects of the Leicester Rail Road

Of all the great wonders that ever were known –
And some wonderful things have occurred in this town –
The Leicester rail road it will beat them all hollow;
And the man who first thought on 't he was a fine fellow.

No drunken stage-coachmen to break people's necks,
Turned o'er into ditches, sprawled out on your backs;
No blustering guard that, through some mistake,
His blunderbuss fires if a mouse should but squeak.

No, no, my good friends, now this rail road is finished,
All coachmen and cattle henceforth shall be banished.
You may ride up to London in three hours and a quarter,
With nothing to drive but a kettle of water.

What a beautiful sight it is for to see
A long string of carriages on the railway,
All loaded with passengers, inside and out,
And moved by what comes from a tea-kettle's spout.

And then, what a lot of employment 'twill make,
The Leicester bricklayers may now undertake
To send ready-built houses to London by steam;
No doubt it will turn out a very good scheme.

Now any old woman that has enough sense
By raking and scraping to save eighteenpence,
In service in London if she has a daughter,
She may ride up and see her by this boiler of water.

The ostlers and innkeepers and such riff raff,
The rail road will blow them away, just like chaff;
They may 'list for Her Highness, the great Queen of Spain,
And curse the inventors of rail roads and steam.

Coach horses that eat up more corn in a year
Than would maintain three parts of the labouring poor,

They are all to go to the fellmonger's yard,
Where they will be rendered into good hog's lard.

And all coach proprietors who've rolled in wealth
Must ride upon donkeys for the good of their health,
And to keep up their spirits must strike up this theme
And curse all the railroads and boiling hot steam.

Of all the great won-ders that ev-er were known — And some won-der-ful things have oc-curred in this town — The Leicester rail road it will beat them all hollow; And the man who first thought on't he was a fine fellow.

Queen of Spain Christina, on whose behalf a volunteer British force
went to Spain in the late 1830s.

Leicester had a local railway line, to Swannington, as early as 1832,
but it was linked to the developing national network in 1840 with the
arrival of the Midland Counties Railway. The ballad foretold the
fate of the stage-coach proprietors with remarkable accuracy. The
forty coaches on the run from London to Leicester all disappeared
soon after the opening of the railway.

Some of the coach proprietors tried to make a fight: like Mr J. G.
Briggs, of the George Inn, who announced firmly that he would
not 'forsake his old friends the Public, by abandoning those
roads on which his coaches have usually run, but that the same
will be continued, in defiance of the monopoly of steam and rails,
at the usual cheap and expeditious rate.' It was a lost cause,
however, and he was quickly defeated; nine years later his inn
itself was up to let' (J. Simmons, *Life in Victorian Leicester*,
Leicester, 1971, p.52).

Some coaches continued to ply on short-haul, local routes and Mr Simmons (p.48) has a photograph (above) dated about 1868 of a coach load of passengers about to depart.

The ballad was preceded by 'A Most Curious and Interesting Dialogue on the NEW RAIL ROADS, Or, the delight and pleasure of Travelling by Hot Water':

BILL Good morning, Jack. I am glad I have met with you to bid you a good-bye, for I am going away for a while for you know there is a great deal of employment going forward in making these new Railroads.

JACK Yes, Bill, the Railroads are something like the new Workhouses, make work at present for a few, and in the end be the ruin of a great many.

BILL Why, Jack, steam is all the rage, steam boats, steam sawyers, steam bakers and millers, and I expect very soon we shall have to live upon steam.

JACK No! No! Bill, you're mistaken, instead of living by steam, it will prove a great help in taking away life, and numbers will be thrown out of employment, for I cannot see what benefit we shall derive from it.

BILL Why, Jack, it may be a benefit to the town of Leicester, the London markets will be plentifully supplied with all kinds of corn, butter, cheese, eggs and stockings, and from the Seaports fish alive on the dish.

JACK Why we now see the Railroads a moving panorama of live lumber, like a string of Noah's Arks, filled with men and women, pigs, sheep and oxen carried by steam to the markets, where they will be sold by steam, killed by steam, cooked by steam, and then devoured by steam.

BILL And, Jack, it will be a fine chance for the Leicester bricklayers, they may now undertake to send ready built Workhouses by steam for the poor paupers of the different parishes from the North to the South of England; well secured with iron bars and cast iron roofs to keep them from escaping.

JACK Why they tell me, Bill, that as there are no more coach horses wanted, they will be taken to the fellmonger's yard, there to be converted into hog's lard.

BILL But what will become of the Innkeepers, Ostlers and Coach Proprietors?

JACK Become of them! Why as they have always been fond of the horse line, they may now enlist in the line of Horses of her Majesty the great Queen of Spain or ride upon English donkeys for the good of their health.

BILL Well, Jack, I must bid you good-bye at present for this job won't last always; for Shareholders, Engine scheme and all may yet be blown up by the boiler of hot water.

The ballad is paralleled in another broadside called *The Great Western Rail Road Or the Pleasures of Travelling by Steam*, printed at Cheltenham.

The Jolly Waggoner

When first I went a-waggoning, a-waggoning did go,
It filled my parents' hearts full of sorrow, grief and woe;
And many are the hardships that we do undergo.

Chorus
And sing wo! my lads, sing wo!
Drive on, my lads, I O!
For who can lead the life
Of a jolly waggoner?

It is a dark and stormy night and I'm wetted to the skin,
But I shall find contentment when I get into the inn.
Then I will sit a-drinking with the landlord and his friends.

Now summer is a-coming, what pleasure we shall see;
The small birds they are singing in every green tree;
The blackbirds and the thrushes are whistling in the grove.

Now Michaelmas is coming, what pleasures we shall find;
We'll make the money fly, my boys, like chaff before the
    wind;
And every lad shall have his lass and sit her on his knee.

But now upon the country roads, few waggons there you'll
    see;
The world's turned topsy-turvy and all things go by steam.
The public, now, they all cry out, Whatever shall we do?

The railways have taken the trade, it's worse now than
    before;
It's made it better for one or two and ruined many a score,
But I will not let my heart down, so join me in my song.

Michaelmas 29 September.

This song started life in the late eighteenth century, without its last
two verses, and is still sometimes found in the repertoire of English
country singers like Fred Jordan of Shropshire. A 'comic singer' called Paul Bedford, who used to sing at places like Vauxhall Gardens,

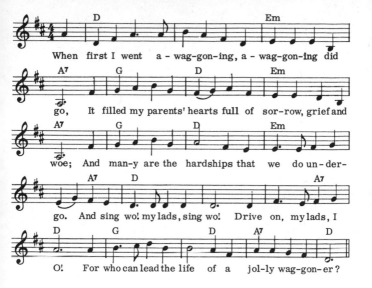

When first I went a-wag-gon-ing, a-wag-gon-ing did go, It filled my parents' hearts full of sor-row, grief and woe; And man-y are the hardships that we do un-der-go. And sing wo! my lads, sing wo! Drive on, my lads, I O! For who can lead the life of a jol-ly wag-gon-er?

added the two last verses in the 1830s. The stage waggons which the waggoners of the song used to drive had a particular place in the affections of country people:

> When the poor had to travel they used the old-fashioned stage waggons, drawn by four, six, or even eight horses, which were chiefly used for the carriage of goods. They never moved out of a walk and were in charge of a carter who usually walked beside his team. Such was the rude conveyance in which Little Nell travelled, 'comfortably bestowed among the softer packages. ... What a soothing, luxurious, drowsy way of travelling, to lie inside that slowly-moving mountain, listening to the tinkling of the horses' bells, the occasional smacking of the carter's whip, the smooth rolling of the great broad wheels, the rattle of the harness ... all made pleasantly indistinct by the thick awning, which seemed made for lazy listening under, till one fell fast asleep!' The stage waggon remained the only public conveyance suitable for the poor until the coming of the railways (E. W. Bovill, *English Country Life, 1780–1830*, 1959, pp.140–41).

FOR ALL STATIONS to NOTTINGHAM

THE NEXT TRAIN WILL DEPART AT

NOTTINGHAM. SHEFFIELD. PENISTONE.
MANCHESTER. HUDDERSFIELD. HALIFAX & BRADFORD

THE NEXT TRAIN WILL DEPART AT

THE NEXT TRAIN DEPART

STATIONS to BRACKLEY

THE NEXT TRAIN WILL DEPART AT

SCARBORO & NEWCAS

LOUGHBORO. NOTTIN
GRIMSBY & CLEE
& THE NORTH-EXPRE

DAILY
TELEGRAPH
OURTEEN PAGES
NG & SCOTLAND

SATURDAY, OCTOBER 18
THE EDUCATION BILL
DEBATE IN THE COMMONS
SIR W HARCOURT SPEECH
FRENCH SCHOOL DEBATE

The Railway Whistle
or The Blessings of Hot-Water Travelling

Of all the wonders of the age, there's nothing now so much
    the rage;
Both rich and poor seem all engaged about the Eastern
    Railway.
There's hissing here and whizzing there, and boiling water
    everywhere;
'Midst fire and smoke you crack your joke and what may
    happen no one cares,
For some blow down and some blow up, into a carriage
    haste and pop;
At the sound of the whistle off you start on the Eastern
    Counties Railway.

There's trains full half a mile in length, drawn by a fiery
    monster's strength;
Good luck to your soul, keep clear of the banks, for fear
    that you go over.
But if by chance such a thing occurs and you should roll
    among the furze,
How pleasant to be capsized thus, with pigs and passengers
    in one mess.
And while you're down in the valley below, how pleasant
    to hear the engine blow,
You mount up again and off you go on the Eastern
    Counties Railway.

But some poor simple souls may say 'tis a dangerous thing
    to travel this way;
If the rail give way or the boilers burst, there's nothing on
    earth can save us.
The money we paid from our poor pockets may send us
    in the air like rockets,
Our heads as empty as water buckets, our precious eyes
    knocked out the sockets.

But sure such people can have no sense, 'twill all be the
    same a hundred years hence,
What odds will it make, we can die but once; might as well
    be smashed by the Railway.

Farewell ye coaches, vans and waggons, farewell ye keepers
    of roadside inns,
You'll have plenty of time to repent your sins in charging
    poor travellers double.
Farewell ye blustering coachmen and guards that never
    knew how to use civil words,
You'll no more use your horns, you know, except to place
    upon your brows;
Take your lumbering vehicles off the road, neither you nor
    they were ever much good,
For how could you carry such fine, big loads, as to the
    wonderful Railways.

Let's not forget railway directors, and from all harm they
    will protect us,
They'll study never to neglect us, so dearly they love
    locomotion.
It's for our good they take such pains, and never do they
    think of gains,
And, if a few hundred should be slain, our wives and
    children they'll maintain.
Then happy and thankful may we be, such blessed
    inventions we've lived to see;
To all other travel bid for ever goodbye, but the
    wonderful Eastern Railways.

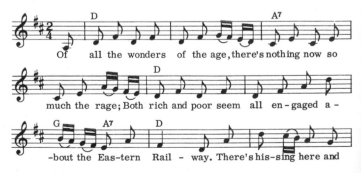

Of all the wonders of the age, there's nothing now so
much the rage; Both rich and poor seem all en-gaged a-
-bout the Eas-tern Rail - way. There's his-sing here and

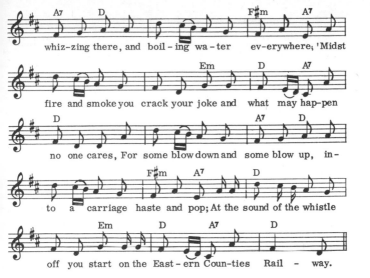

whiz-zing there, and boil-ing wa-ter ev-erywhere; 'Midst

fire and smoke you crack your joke and what may hap-pen

no one cares, For some blow down and some blow up, in-

to a carriage haste and pop; At the sound of the whistle

off you start on the East-ern Coun-ties Rail - way.

The Eastern Counties Railway was under construction during the 1840s. Navvies working on this line were involved in the celebrated Norwich election riots of 1847, when their employer, the contractor Peto, was a candidate.

The ballad is unusual in its reference to the possible disaster and death which might befall railway travellers.

The Scenes of Manchester

The scenes of Manchester I sing,
Where the arts and sciences are flourishing;
Where smoke from factory chimneys bring
The air so black, so thick and nourishing.
Where factories that by steam are gated,
And children work half suffocated,
It makes me mad to hear folk, really,
Cry, 'Manchester's improving daily'.

There's steam-loom weavers and cotton spinners
Have sixty minutes to get their dinners;
And then to make the people thrive
They're rung up in a morning at four and five.
Then if you get a drop on a Sunday
To get yourselves in tiff for Monday,
The raw lobster pops you in the Bailey,
Since Manchester's improving daily.

We've coaches now that by steam power
Will take you thirty miles an hour;
And what's still more, the devil's in it,
They killed a Parliament man in a minute.
They go so fast on iron rails, O,
To Liverpool with men and bales, O,
'Twould make either Newton, Locke or Paley,
Cry, 'Manchester's improving daily.'

We've buildings large and grand to view,
Likewise Mechanics' Institutions, too,
Where gentlemen go to learn gastronomy,
Gymnastics, optics and physionomy.
Where Doctor Lardner's LLD, sir,
A-lecturing on steam power you'll see, sir,
'Twould look better on to turn his head,
And teach poor folk to get cheap bread.

In Cromwell's days, by Fairfax led,
The men of Manchester have bled,
And what still lives to their fame and glory

Is the famous Shudehill fighting story.
But war and fighting's out of fashion,
And patriots grown quite scarce i' the nation;
All that bleed now, good people, hark it,
Are the cows and pigs in Shudehill Market.

The scenes of Manchester I sing, Where the
arts and sciences are flourishing; Where smoke from
fac-tor-y chim-neys bring the air so black, so thick, and
nourishing, Where fac-'tries that by steam are
ga-ted, And chil-dren work half suf-fo-
-ca-ted, It makes me mad to hear folk,
really, Cry, "Man-ches-ter's im-proving dai-ly."

the air so black the earlier steam engines were much disliked because
   of the black smoke they emitted.
gated driven.
tiff trim, condition.
raw lobster policeman (from its blue colour).
Bailey prison (see p.254).
Parliament man Huskisson, fatally injured at the opening of the
   Liverpool and Manchester Railway, in 1830 (see p.46).
Mechanics' Institutions the first opened in Manchester in 1825.

Lardner scientific writer, who lived from 1793 to 1859.

Cromwell's days there was a considerable amount of fighting in and near Manchester, including a siege by Royalists, in 1643–4.

Shudehill fighting story Shudehill Fight (as it was called), a series of riots directed against the high prices of food, took place in 1757. The rioters were also incensed at the monopoly of the town mills and the adulteration of flour.

The theme of pollution is again taken up in this song, which adopts a sceptical view of some of the innovations which came in the train of the Industrial Revolution. The objection to the tyranny of the clock (verse two) was very common.

A similar broadside about Birmingham is called *Birmingham Improving Daily*.

Oldham Workshops

When I'd finished off my work last Saturday at neet,
Wi' new hat and Sunday cloas I dressed myself complete;
I took leof o' my mother wi' a very woeful face,
And started off for Owdhum soon, that famous, thriving
  place,
Chorus
With my whack row di dow dow, tal la la di ral di;
Whack row di dow dow, tal de ral de ral.

When I geet to Coppy Nook, it pleased me very well;
I seed all th'town afore me of which I'm goin' to tell.
There wur coaches, carts and coal pits as throng as yo'd
  desire
And coal enough they'd getten up to set th'whole town o'
  fire.

I coom up by th' Owd Church, and I seed th' New Market
  Hall;
It looked so queer a building, I couldn't help but call.
One part of it they'd setten out wi' very pratty shops,
They'n lined it wi' cast iron and they'n built it up o' props.

To Hibbert and Platts shop then I went i'th'Lackey Moor,
And fun no little trouble to get in the lodge door;
And then, by gum, so busy, they wur at it left and right,
Un stripped in all their shirts, too, I thought they're goin'
  to fight.

Some chaps ot they cawd smiths, great bellows they had
  got,
Like foo's they blowed cowd wind to make the iron hot;
But then owd Neddy engine, I think he beats the whole,
He's fond o' summut warm, sure, for they feed him up
  o' coal.

The moulders among sand, they were making things
  complete,
Fro' a shaftin' or a fly wheel to a handsome fire grate;
Cast iron's very dear now, or it would be nowt wrong,
To make a scoldin' woman a new cast iron tongue.

65

I went to Barnes's next un just looked through some rooms,
Where sum wur making' spring frames and others power
    looms;
Some tunin' and some filin' un screwin' bolts to beams:
I reckon soon both sun and moon they'll make to go by
    steam.

I went into a weavin' shad and such a clatter there,
Wi' looms un wheels aw goin' so fast, I hardly durst go near.
Then the lasses were si busy shiftin' templets, shuttlin'
    cops,
One shuttle had like to given me a devilish slop i'th'chops.

I went to lots o' factories to see what they're about;
I couldn't get to see much there because they'd all turned
    out.
They would not gie um brass enough, as far as I could learn,
Un so th'turnouts were goin' about a-lookin' for th' short
    turn.

If th' work folk would be reasonable un th' masters be but
    just,
The turnouts will turn in and prosper all things must;
For your lasses are all pratty, your workmen rare and
    clever,
So success to Owdham Town and trade and th'working
    folk for ever.

templet contrivance for keeping cloth stretched to its proper width
    in the loom, during the process of weaving.
cops small oval-shaped bundles of cotton thread which fitted into
    the shuttle.
turnouts strikers.

In some of the ballads about railways, a remarkable freshness of
vision emerges. Here we see an innocent picture of factory life.
The railway ballads attempt to assimilate the new, partly by
humanizing it; there is talk, for example, of a machine to create
new engineers by steam power. The steam engine becomes a
'Neddy engine' feeding on coal, and the new concept is assimilated
by extension from the old. A tremendous life and energy run
through this ballad, but there is more than a hint of trouble ahead
in the reference to 'turnouts'.

When I'd fin-ished off my work last Sat-ur-day at
neet, Wi' new hat and Sunday clo-as on I dressed myself com-
-plete; I took le-of o' my mother wi' a ver-y woe-ful
face, And star-ted off for Owdham soon that famous, thriving
place, with my whack row di dow dow, fal la
la di ral di, whack row di dow dow, ral de ral de ral.

Gorton Town

Gosh, dang it, lads, I'm back again,
Though many a mile I've been;
A Gorton lad I'm bred and born,
And lots of sights I've seen.

But when I did come back again,
I nearly fell in fits,
For times and folks so altered looked,
I thought I'd lost my wits.

When I left home some years ago,
Th'owd folks had lots of trade;
Some right good jobs came tumbling in,
And every one well paid.

We'd good roast-beef and pudding,
And ale some decent swigs;
Egad! they lived like fighting cocks,
And got as fat as pigs.

But now, egad! there's none such things,
Poor folks have empty tripes;
There's no roast-beef to stuff their hides,
It's Poor Law soup and swipes.

An honest working man's no chance;
Grim want does on him frown;
I ne'er thought things would come to this,
When I left Gorton Town.

In days gone by our fine young men
Ne'er told such dismal tales;
They'd ne'er a man transported then
As far as New South Wales.

We'd honest men in Parliament,
Both Tories, Rads and Whigs;
They were not known poor folk to rob,
But now they've turned to prigs.

Our manufacturers worked full time,
Their mills were seldom stopped;
No gen'ral turn-outs were there then,
Their wages never dropped.

Those Corn-Law folks and Chartist lads
Might talk till they were brown,
Without being sent to treading-mills,
When I left Gorton Town.

In days gone by I never thought
Such days would come as these;
The lads were all as gay as larks
And wenches bright as bees.

Right merrily they jogged to th' fairs
In clogs and light shalloons;
The lasses now have grown too proud,
They look like faded moons.

The foolish frumps sport mutton pumps;
And yet, their pride to crown,
They've bustles tied behind 'em
Half as large as Gorton Town.

But, putting all these jokes aside,
We'll hope these times will mend;
There'll come a day yet when the rich
Will prove the poor man's friend.

With right good trade and fairly paid,
I dare bet thee a crown,
There'll not be such a place i' th' world
As merry Gorton Town.

Gorton now a suburb of Manchester.   *prigs* pick-pockets.
swipes weak beer.   *shalloon* kind of material.

The song was noted in 1865 from the singing of Samuel Beswick,

a nephew of the composer of the tune, and author or compiler of
the words – the late John Beswick, alias 'Parish Jack', a singer,
fluter and fiddler, in great request at 'stirs' and merry-makings,
where his vocal and instrumental services were often paid in
kind – in meat, clothes or liquor (J. Harland, *Ballads and Songs
of Lancashire*, 1875).

69

A view frequently expressed during the first half of the nineteenth century (and even later) was that the golden age lay in the past. Among historians, the debate as to the relative standards of living, before and after the industrial revolution, is still in progress.

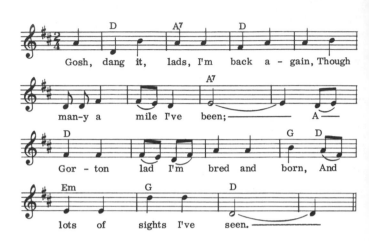

Gosh, dang it, lads, I'm back a-gain, Though man-y a mile I've been; A Gor-ton lad I'm bred and born, And lots of sights I've seen.

The Dalesman's Litany

It's hard when folks can't find th' work
Weer they've been bred and born;
When I were young I allus thowt
I'd bide 'midst royits and corn.
But I've been forced to work in t' towns,
So here's my litany:
From Hull and Halifax and Hell,
Good Lord deliver me.

When I were courting Mary Jane,
T' old squire he says, one day,
'I've got na bield for wedded folk,
Choose will ta wed or stay'.
I could na give up t' lass I loved,
So to t' town we 'ad to flee:
From Hull and Halifax and Hell,
Good Lord deliver me.

I've worked i' Leeds an' 'Uddersfield
And addled honest brass.
At Bradford, Keighley, Rotherham,
I've kept my bairns an' t' lass.
I've travelled all three Ridings round
And once I went to sea:
From forges, mills an' sailin' boats,
Good Lord deliver me.

I've walked at neet through Sheffield loyns –
'Twere same as being i' hell –
Where furnaces thrust out tongues of fire
And reared like t' wind on t' fell.
I've sammed up coils i' Barnsley pits
Wi' muck up to my knee:
From Sheffield, Barnsley, Rotherham,
Good Lord deliver me.

I've seen fog creep across Leeds brig
As thick as Bastille soup.
I've lived weer folks were stowed away
Like rabbits in a coop.

I've seen snow float down Bradford Beck
As black as ebony:
From Hunslet, Holbeck, Wibsey Slack,
Good Lord deliver me.

Well now when all us childer's fligged,
To t' country we've come back.
There's fourty mile a heathery moor
'Twixt us an' t' coilpits' slack.
And as I sit by t' fire at neet,
Well, I laugh an' shout wi' glee:
From Hull and Halifax and Hell,
Good Lord deliver me.

It's hard when folks can't find th' work Weer they've been bred and born; When I were young I al-lus thowt I'd bide midst royits and corn. But I've been forced to work int' towns So here's my li-ta - ny. From Hull and Ha-li- -fax and Hell, Good Lord de - li - ver me.

royits roots.	*coil* coal.
bield room.	*brig* bridge.
addled earned.	*Hunslet, Holbeck* villages near Leeds.
loyns lanes.	*Wibsey Slack* village near Bradford.
sammed picked up.	*fligged* left the nest; departed.

Industrialization attracted or forced many to the towns. In this case, in the old-fashioned world of the dales, the employer ('t'owd squire') still wants single farm-hands who will live in, in preference to 'wedded folk'.

Liverpool's an Altered Town

Once on a time this good old town was nothing but a
  village
Of fishermen and smugglers, that ne'er attempted tillage;
But things are altered very much, such buildings and
  Naccapolis,
It rivals far and soon will leave behind the Metropolis.

Chorus
Oh dear oh, for Liverpool's an altered town, oh dear oh.

Once on a time, were you inclined your weary limbs to
  lave, sir,
In summer's scorching heat, in Mersey's cooling wave, sir,
You'd only just to go behind the old Church for the shore,
  sir,
But now it's past Jack Langan's half a mile or more, sir.

When things do change you scarce do know what next is
  sure to follow,
For mark the change in Derby Road that late was
  Plumpton's fellow;
Now Atkins found it out so smug and changed its
  etymology,
He clapped in it his wild beast show, now it's Gardens
  of Zoology.

A market was on Shaw's Brown, and it remains there still,
  sir;
The Infirmary they have taken away and clapped on
  Brownlow Hill, sir.
There's Gloucester Street and Nelson Street have had an
  alteration,
They've pulled the most part of them down and built a
  railway station.

There's St Luke's in Bold Street, St George's in the Crescent;
St Peter's in Church Street, I'll name no more at present.

They tell the time to every one their hour that they may
    hop right;
By day they go by clockwork but at night they go by
    gas light.

The spire of famed St Thomas's, that long had stood the
    weather,
Although it was so very high, they've downed it
    altogether;
And the Old Dock, the poor Old Dock, the theme of
    many a sonnet,
They've pulled it up and now have built a Custom House
    upon it.

In former times our good old town was guarded from the
    prigs, sir,
By day by constables, by night by watchmen with Welsh
    wigs, sir;
But things are altered very much, for all those who are
    scholars,
Can tell our new policemen by the numbers on their
    collars.

In former times, if you had taken a walk through Queen's
    Square, sir,
You might have seen, if you had looked, a slashing rope-
    walk there, sir;
Yet all those things the public thought were getting very
    stale, sir,
On the rope-walk they've a market and on the square a
    whale, sir.

Not long ago our sailor swells, they were so mighty grown,
    sir,
They could not spend their evening elsewhere than the
    saloon, sir;
But things are altered very much, the saloon is gone fair,
    sir,
At every step the ladies go, policemen cry, 'Move on there.'

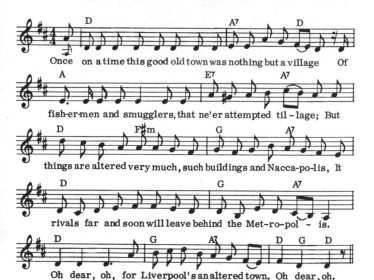

Once on a time this good old town was nothing but a village Of fish-er-men and smugglers, that ne'er attempted til-lage; But things are altered very much, such buildings and Nacca-po-lis, It rivals far and soon will leave behind the Met-ro-pol - is. Oh dear, oh, for Liverpool's an altered town. Oh dear, oh.

village something of an exaggeration, since Liverpool had 20,000 inhabitants, as early as 1746; it had, however, grown to 100,000 by 1811.

Old Church that of St Nicholas.

The Infirmary they have taken away 1828.

railway station presumably the original terminal for the Liverpool-Manchester line. (Lime Street Station was opened in 1836.) The first station for locomotives was at Edgehill, beyond the tunnel. Carriages were marshalled at Crown Street, and drawn through Edgehill Tunnel by ropes, because the original Act of Parliament (1826) stipulated that no locomotives should be allowed within the town limits.

The spire of famed St Thomas's erected 1750.

the Old Dock . . . they've pulled it up 1826.

prigs thieves.

Welsh wigs there were many Welsh immigrants in Liverpool, who evidently supplied many of the watchmen.

new policemen introduced in London in 1829 and in Liverpool in 1836.

Like *I can't find Brummagem*, this ballad is not unsympathetic towards change, though it does not lack nostalgia for the past. (Other versions dealing with Manchester and Preston were also published.)

I Can't find Brummagem

Full twenty years and more have passed
Since I left Brummagem,
But I set out for home at last
To good old Brummagem;
But every place is altered so,
There's hardly a single place I know,
Which fills my heart with grief and woe,
For I can't find Brummagem.

As I was walking down our street
As used to be in Brummagem,
I knowed nobody as I did meet:
They change their faces in Brummagem.
Poor old Spiceal Street's half gone
And the poor old Church stands all alone;
And poor old I stands here to groan
For I can't find Brummagem.

Amongst the changes we have got
In good old Brummagem,
They've made a market on the moat
To sell the pigs in Brummagem.
But that has brought us more ill-luck:
They've filled up poor old Pudding Brook,
Where in the mud I've often stuck,
Catching jack-bannils near Brummagem.

But what's more melancholy still
For poor old Brummagem,
They've taken away all Newhall Hill,
From poor old Brummagem.
At Easter time, girls fair and brown
Used to come roly-poly down,
And show their legs to half the town,
Oh, the good old sights of Brummagem.

Now, down Peck Lane I walked along
To find out Brummagem;
There was the dungeon down and gone,

What, no rogues in Brummagem?
They've taken it to a street called Moor,
A sign that rogues have got no fewer;
The rogues won't like to go there, I'm sure,
While Peck Lane's in Brummagem.

I remember one John Growse,
A buckle-maker in Brummagem,
He built himself a country house
To be out of the smoke of Brummagem.
But though John's country house stands still,
The town itself has walked up hill;
Now he lives beside a smoky mill
In the middle of the streets of Brummagem.

Among the changes that abound,
In good old Brummagem,
May trade and happiness be found,
In good old Brummagem;
And though no Newhall Hill we've got,
Nor Pudding Brook, nor any moat,
May we always have enough to boil the pot,
In good old Brummagem.

Old Church St Martin's (as opposed to the new cathedral, St
   Philip's).
the moat this encircled the ancient residence of the lords of Birmingham and was filled up to make way for Smithfield Market,
   and is shown on the photograph on the next page.
jack-bannils stickle-backs.
Peck Lane . . . a street called Moor the town lock-up, known as the
   dungeon or dungil, was originally in Peck Lane, whence it was
   later moved to Moor Street.

The song was written by an entertainer called James Dobbs and
sung by him for the first time at the Theatre Royal, Birmingham, in
1828, to the tune of *Duncan Grey*. It was issued on broadsides and
remained very popular for a number of years. Apparently it was
often sung by passengers travelling on the top of stage coaches.
A version relating to Coventry also appeared.
   One of the effects of the Industrial Revolution was the mush-
room growth of towns: the *ville tentaculaire* existed long before
Verhaeren coined the phrase late in the nineteenth century. In

79

1801, Birmingham had 71,000 inhabitants; in 1851, 233,000; in 1901, 523,000. The figures for Manchester were 70,000, 303,000 and 645,000, and for London, 957,000, 2,362,000 and 4,536,000.

Problems of pollution, excessive density of housing and the obliteration of the countryside existed long before the extreme concern of recent years. When *I can't find Brummagem* is sung in Birmingham, the audiences think it is a contemporary song.

Full twenty years and more have passed Since I left Brummagem, But

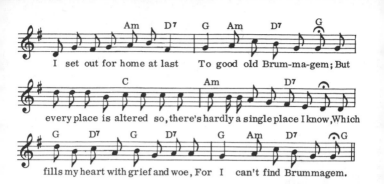

I set out for home at last To good old Brum-ma-gem; But every place is altered so, there's hardly a single place I know, Which fills my heart with grief and woe, For I can't find Brummagem.

My Grandfather's Days

Give attention to my ditty and I'll not keep you long;
I'll endeavour for to please you if you'll listen to my song.
I'll tell you an ancient story, the doings and the ways,
The manners and the customs of my grandfather's days.
The manners and the customs of my grandfather's days.

Of many years that's gone and past, which hundreds do
    say hard,
When Adam was a little boy and worked in Chatham yard,
We had no Waterloo soldiers dressed out in scarlet clothes;
The people were not frightened by one man's big, long nose.

We had not got Lord Brougham to pass the Poor Law
    Bill;
We had not got policemen to keep the people still;
We had not got a tread-mill to dance upon and grin;
Old women in the morning didn't drink a pint of gin.

If a young man went a-courting a damsel meek and mild,
And if she from misfortune should hap to have a child,
By going to a magistrate, a recompense to seek,
They'd make the man to marry her, or pay a crown a week.

But now by the New Poor Law he nothing has to pay,
Nor would he, even if he got twenty children every day.
We had not got a German queen to govern by her laws;
O'Connell had not come to town to fight for Ireland's
    cause.

A tradesman was not known to sigh, had no reason to
    complain;
Colonel Evans wasn't here to drag young Englishmen to
    Spain.
There then was none of Fieschi's gang to wheel about and
    prance;
They hadn't got the musket made to shoot the King of
    France.

In my grandfather's days, now very well you know,
They never learned to wheel about, nor learned to jump
  Jim Crow.
They walked, or rode on horseback, or travelled with a
  team;
They never thought of railroads or travelling by steam.

They travelled on the roads by day or in the morning,
  soon;
Green did not go to Holland in a dashing great balloon.
With silks and satins, women didn't decorate their backs;
The sleeves upon their gowns weren't like great 'tatoe
  sacks.

In my grandfather's days, the coats were made of cloth,
But now they're india rubber and styled a Mackintosh.
As through the streets they go along, the boys cry out quite
  pert:
'Oh, crikey, there's a swellish cove, but what a dirty shirt.'

In my grandfather's days, if a journey you would take,
The coaches ran so easy, no fear your bones they'd break;
Now we've omnibuses, patent cars and bedsteads upon
  springs,
Where children you may get by steam, such pretty little
  things.

long nose Wellington.
Lord Brougham politician (1778–1868); piloted the Poor Law Am-
  endment Bill (1834) through the House of Lords (see pp.261–2).
policemen the Metropolitan Police Act was passed in 1829.
treadmill invented in 1818 (see p.255).
German queen Victoria, who acceded in 1837.
O'Connell Irish MP who first took his seat in 1829.
Colonel Evans commanded British legion which fought in Spain on
  behalf of Christina against Don Carlos, 1835–7.
Fieschi Corsican who made an attempt on the life of Louis-Philippe
  in 1835; executed in 1836.
Jim Crow song and dance routine popular in England from 1836.
Green travelled from Vauxhall Gardens to Weilburg, Nassau, in
  1836, in a balloon.
'tatoe sacks vast sleeves were fashionable in the 1830s.
Mackintosh the word and the object became well-known in the

mid-1830s. Charles Macintosh, a Glasgow chemist, took out his patent for 'waterproof double texture material' in 1823.

omnibuses date from 1829; were originally horse-drawn.

patent cars probably steam carriage, which became fairly common on the road in the 1830s. A steam carriage operating between London and Bath in 1833 carried the legend 'Royal Patent'.

The latest of the events mentioned here occurred in 1837 and the broadside was probably issued soon after.

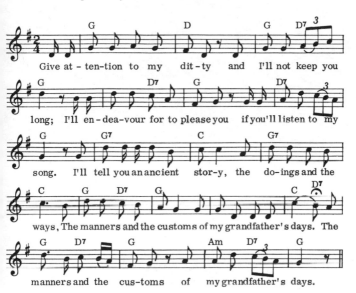

Give at-ten-tion to my dit-ty and I'll not keep you long; I'll en-dea-vour for to please you if you'll listen to my song. I'll tell you an ancient stor-y, the do-ings and the ways, The manners and the customs of my grandfather's days. The manners and the cus-toms of my grandfather's days.

The State of Great Britain
or a Touch at the Times

As old John Bull was walking one morning free from pain,
He heard the Rose, the Shamrock and the Thistle to
complain.
An alteration must take place, together they did sing,
In the Corn Laws and the Poor Laws and many another
thing.

Chorus
Conversing on the present time together they did range.
All classes through Great Britain now appear so very
strange,
That England, Ireland, Scotland, Wales must quickly have
a change.

The railroads all through England have great depression
made;
Machines of every kind has put a stop to trade;
The innkeepers are weeping, in agony and grief,
And the ostlers swear they'll buy a rope and go to felo-de-se.

The steam boats to old Beelzebub the watermen do wish;
They say they've nearly ruined them and drowned all the
fish.
Of all their new inventions that we have lately seen,
There was none begun or thought upon when Betty was
the queen.

Behold the well-bred farmer, how he can strut along;
Let a poor man do whate'er he will, he's always in the
wrong;
With labour hard and wages low he hangs his drooping
head:
They won't allow him half enough to buy his children
bread.

The farmers' daughters ride about, well-clad and pockets
full,

With horse and saddle like a queen and boa like a bull;
In their hand a flashy parasol and on their face a veil,
And a bustle seven times as big as any milking pail.

The nobles from the pockets of John Bull are all well paid;
Sometimes you'd hardly know the lady from the servant
    maid,
For now they are so very proud, silk stockings on their legs,
And every step they take you'd think they walked on
    pigeon's eggs.

As old John Bull was walk - ing one morning free from
pain,— He heard the Rose, the Shamrock and the Thistle to com-
-plain,— An alt - er - a - tion must take place, togeth - er they did
sing, In the Corn Laws and the Poor — Laws and man-y a-nother
thing.— Con - vers - ing on the pre - sent time to -
-geth - er they did range.— All class - es through Great
Bri - tain now ap - pear so ver - y strange, That
England, Ireland, Scotland, Wales must quickly have a change.

The tradesman he can hardly pay his rent and keep his
    home;
The labourer has eighteen pence a day for breaking stones.
In former days the farmer rode a donkey or a mule:
There never was such times before since Adam went to
    school.

Now some can live in luxury while others weep in woe;
There's very pretty difference now and a century ago.
The world will shortly move by steam, it may appear so
    strange,
So you must all acknowledge that England wants a change.

felo-de-se suicide.
Betty Queen Elizabeth I.
boa fur scarf.

This broadside dates from the hungry forties of the nineteenth
century.

2

Stirrings on Saturday Night

Saturday Night

Of hammers and files no more heard the din is;
Round the door of the warehouse the workmen arrange,
While the master his bankbills and snug little guineas
Is counting, or strutting about to get change.
Having reckoned, they ne'er stop, but jog to the beer shop,
Where fumes of tobacco and stingo invite,
And the oven inhabits a store of Welsh rarebits
To feast jolly fellows on Saturday night.

Chorus
Saturday night, boys, Saturday night,
What stirrings in Sheffield on Saturday night.

Now while cheerful liquor around they are pushing,
The many-mouthed chorus melodious flies,
Though oft interrupted by merchants who rush in
With 'Cockles alive O' or 'Hot mutton pies'.
Perhaps you may choose, sir, to pore o'er the news, sir,
And tell whether matters go wrong or go right:
All ranks and conditions commence politicians,
While sat in the alehouse on Saturday night.

But while o'er the tankard such fun they are raising,
Full often will fate these enjoyments annoy:
A good scolding wife puts her unwelcome face in;
An intruding guest, she breaks thus on their joy:
'So, here again, Billy, why, sure man, thou'rt silly;
'Od burn thee, come home, or I'll dit up thy sight.'
'Nay, so now, my jewel,' says he, 'this is cruel,
To begrudge one a sup on a Saturday night.'

Here maids with their baskets are to and fro walking
In shambles to bargain with butchers for meat,
While some boy ballad singer so slowly is stalking
And warbles so sweetly his lays in the street.
Here's calendars crying and people come buying,
Around the hoarse fellow in crowds – such a sight;
For, as suits your palates, confessions or ballads
Are all at your service on Saturday night.

When through the dark alleys, if slyly one passes,
What fun you may have if an ear you will lend:
Such sighs and soft wishes from lads and from lasses
Who tell their fond tale at a dark entry's end.
When he to his true-love cries, 'Polly, adieu, love',
And kisses and squeezes his lassie so tight,
She'll blushing say, 'Fie, sir,' then softly she'll cry, 'Sir,
Can't you stay a bit longer, it's Saturday night?'

Of hammers and files no more heard the din is; Round the
door of the warehouse the workmen arrange, While the
mas-ter his bank-bills and snug lit-tle gui-neas Is
count-ing, or strut-ting a - bout to get change. Hav-ing
reck-oned they ne'er stop, but jog to the beer shop, Where
fumes of to-bac - co and sting-o in-vite, And the
o - ven in-hab-its a store of welsh rare-bits To
feast jolly fel-lows on Sat-ur-day night. Sat-ur-day night boys,
Sat-ur day night, What stirrings in Sheffield on Sat-ur-day night.

stingo beer.

dit up stop up.

calendars possibly the normal meaning; alternatively, lists of offenders for trial.

A number of songs in Part One were concerned with change and growth in towns. The vigorous and swarming life of the towns existed before the Industrial Revolution, but it was during the nineteenth century for the first time that the majority of the population became town-dwellers (70 per cent in 1901, compared with 20 per cent in 1801). People were attracted to towns by the prospect of work and higher wages, but also by the wider opportunities for pleasure and relaxation.

This broadside, dating from the end of the eighteenth or the beginning of the nineteenth century, went to the tune of *Nottingham Ale* (better known as *Lillibulero*). Another version, identical except in name, refers to Birmingham; an analogous ballad about Manchester, probably to the same tune, was *Victoria Bridge on a Saturday Night*. Yet another is called *Doings on a Sunday Night*.

Sheffield's a Wonderful Town, O

Ladies and gentlemen all, I am ready at your call,
To sing a little song, and I will not keep you long,
On the sights of this wonderful town, O.
Sheffield's praise, tune my lays;
All its fame shall be named,
I'll tell, don't doubt it, all about it.

Chorus
Hey down, ho down, derry, derry, down,
For Sheffield's a wonderful town, O.

For cutlery so famed none with Sheffield can be named,
Where the people all their lives, they make razors, scissors,
     knives,
In this very wonderful town, O.
Lots of files, all in piles;
Stones go round, razors ground;
Friday quick goes boring stick;
Saturday get your pay,
Then regale yourselves with ale.

Next the market place survey when round comes the
     market day,
And there such sights you'll see that with me you will agree
That Sheffield's a wonderful town, O.
Lots of stalls against the walls;
Make your rambles through the shambles;
Beef and mutton, stuff a glutton;
Butchers cry, 'Who will buy?'
Dogs and asses, pretty lasses;
If you gain Campo Lane,
Neville's Ale, bright and pale,
You will find to your mind.

In the church-yard all the people are gazing at the steeple,
Where the man, to point the spire is each moment getting
     higher,

To amuse you in this wonderful town, O.
From the crate show his pate;
See him climb with stone and lime;
'Lord, how high', people cry;
Rather he was there than me;
Oh, by gauls, if he falls.

Last the playhouse in this street where your favourites
  you greet,
And where actors, funny folks, make you laugh with
  cracking jokes,
For the joy of this wonderful town, O.
Act away, all so gay;
Sights so funny, for your money,
Believe not me, come and see;
Bells that ring, actors sing,
Then you roar your 'encore'.

La – dies and gen – tle – men all, I am
read – y at your call, To sing a lit – tle song, and I
will not keep you long, on the sights of this wonderful town, O.
Sheffield's praise, tune my lays; Hey down, ho down,
derry, derry, down, For Sheffield's a won-der-ful town, O.

*Repeat this bar as many times as necessary.

Here are more of the diversions of the town: the Saturday night
drink, the market (one of my father's favourite leisure activities,
as late as the 1940s and 50s, was to travel seven miles to Leicester 'to

look round the market', even if he bought nothing), opportunities for bystanding, and, finally, the playhouse. In early Victorian times at least, the theatre was often rather a rowdy place. Charles Dickens went to a performance at Sadler's Wells in 1844: 'It was a bear-garden, resounding with foul language, oaths, cat-calls, shrieks, yells, blasphemy, obscenity. . . . Fights took place anywhere at any period of the performance.' Such conduct is now reserved for the football terraces.

This song, which dates from the early part of the nineteenth century, was intended to be sung from the stage. It was also published, with illustrations by George and Robert Cruikshank.

The Rigs and Sprees
of Leeds Town

You lads and lasses blythe and gay,
Just listen awhile to what I say;
If you will stay I'll not be long
To sing the rigs and sprees of the town.

Chorus
I was up to the rigs and down to the jigs,
I was up to the rigs of old Leeds Town.

Now in this town on market day,
There's plenty of farmers blythe and gay;
With pretty girls all dressed so fine,
Wearing ninepenny bustles and crinolines.

All round this spot on Saturday night,
You will see some curious sights;
There's plenty of tripe and peas all hot
And rhubarb, just a penny a lot.

The factory girls I must bring in,
They're the girls when you've the tin;
There's one I know stands here sometimes,
With hat and feather and crinoline.

From Hunslet round and every part,
There's collier chaps and their sweethearts;
They come to town on Saturday night
All for to see the funny sights.

So to conclude and end my song;
What I have sung there's nothing wrong.
It's all about the ups and downs,
Likewise the rigs and sprees of the town.

rigs frolics.
Hunslet then a village near Leeds; now a suburb.

This broadside dates probably from the late 1860s or 70s. To some
extent, Leeds still appears as the old-style market town, with the

farmers coming in on market day. On the other hand, the factory girls and the colliers are also an essential part of the scene.

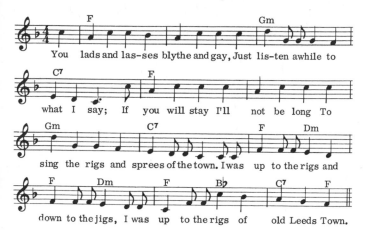

You lads and lasses blythe and gay, Just listen awhile to what I say; If you will stay I'll not be long To sing the rigs and sprees of the town. I was up to the rigs and down to the jigs, I was up to the rigs of old Leeds Town.

The Rigs and Fun of Nottingham Goose Fair

Ye lads and lasses spruce and gay, attend unto my song,
I hope you will not think it short, nor yet so very long;
It's of the rigs and fancy prigs you'll meet with I declare,
If you'll but sport an hour or two at Nottingham Goose
Fair.

Chorus
Then haste away, make no delay, to Nottingham repair,
And if you're fond of fun and glee, you'll find it at the fair.

Let people talk of times so hard, of starving and the like,
They'll find if to the fair they'll come they are mistaken
quite;
Here they may cram with beef and ham till their belly's
like a drum,
And swig such ale that ne'er can fail to send them rolling
home.

Then see what mountains of fine cheese are piled upon the
ground,
And geese with cackling music so sweetly sing all round;
And sucking pigs and turkeys invite the hungry elf,
Crying, 'Come and buy, and then pray try if you can't
please yourself.'

When evening draws the curtain and bids the day goodbye,
Why then unto the alehouses the lads and lasses fly;
And there you'll find unto your mind, what ne'er was
known to fail:
The joy-inspiring tankard, boys, or far-famed Nottingham
Ale.

But still one caution let me give, you'll like me none the
worse,
There's friendship in't if I just hint, keep an eye upon
your purse;

For there are blades of memory short, full plenty in the town,
May pop their fingers in your fob and think it was their own.

So to conclude if come you will, our fair's rare sport to see;
Enjoy your joke, laugh, drink and smoke, but keep good company.
In moderation pleasure take, you're welcome to your share,
You'll not regret you came, my boys, to Nottingham Goose Fair.

Ye lads and lass-es spruce and gay, at-tend un-to my song, I hope you will not think it short, nor yet so ver-y long; It's of the rigs and fancy prigs you'll moot with I declare, If you'd but sport an hour or two at Nottingham Goose Fair. Then haste away, make no de-lay, to Nottingham re-pair, And if you're fond of fun and glee you ll find it at the fair.

prigs normally means thieves but here, probably means dandies.
elf person (slightly derogatory).

The most famous Goose Fair in England was, and is, at Nottingham, held on the first Thursday in October and for the two following days. Not a single goose is to be seen today but at one time, 20,000 geese were driven slowly to the fair by the goose-herds, often taking weeks on the journey and stopping to feed on the way and wearing, it is said, tar and sand shoes to protect their feet.

This fair once lasted three weeks, for in 1284 a charter granted a right to hold a fortnight's fair in addition to the already established week-long Goose Fair. Both were held in the magnificent Market Place of 5½ acres. The fair is now held in the Forest Recreation Ground named after the nearby Forest of Sherwood. Since 1874 the fair has been opened by printed notice rather than proclamation.

A local legend provides an interesting story. A local farmer, through death or separation, brought up his three sons single-handed and carefully avoided their setting eyes on a woman until they were grown up. Then, bowing to the inevitable, he took them to the Goose Fair and asked them to choose whatever they liked best. The younger son's eyes lighted on three young ladies in white dresses and he asked, 'What are those things?' 'Bah,' said his father, they are nothing but geese.' 'Then buy me a goose, father,' was the reply.

(M. Baker, *Discovering English Fairs*, Tring, n.d., p.16)

The Goose Fair in more recent time figures in Alan Sillitoe's novel, *Saturday Night and Sunday Morning*.

Country Statutes

Come all you lads of high renown and listen to my story,
For now the time is coming on that is all to your glory;
For Jumping Joan is coming here the statutes to admire,
To see the lads and lasses standing waiting to be hired.

Chorus
So to the hirings we have come, all for to look for places,
If with the master we agree and he will give good wages.

The master that a servant wants will now stand in a
    wonder:
You all must ask ten pounds a year and none of you go
    under.
It's you that must do all the work and what they do
    require,
So now stand up for wages, lads, before that you do hire.

There rolling Gin the hemp will spin and Sal will mind the
    dairy
And John will kiss his mistress when the master he is
    weary.
There's Tom and Joe will reap and mow; they'll thrash
    and ne'er be tired;
They'll load the cart and do their part, so they're the lads
    to hire.

There's carter John with whip so long rises early in the
    morn;
He's always ready at his work, before day-light can dawn.
Hey up, gee wo, the plough must go, till he is very weary,
But a jug of ale both stout and stale it soon will make him
    merry.

There's Poll so red will make the bread, likewise good
    cheese and butter,
And Bet so thick will spread the rick, she's never in a
    flutter.
She'll feed the sows and milk the cows and do what she is
    able;

Although she's mean she's neat and clean, when waiting
at the table.

There's black-eyed Fan with the frying pan will cook your
eggs and bacon,
With beef and mutton, roast and boiled, if I am not
mistaken.
She'll make the puddings fat and good, all ready for your
dinner,
But if you grumble when she's done she'll cure you with
the skimmer.

The farmer's wife so full of pride must have a ladies maid,
All for to dress and curl her hair and powder it beside;
But the girl of heart to dress so smart, they call her
charming Nancy;
She can wink and blink in such a style, she's all the young
men's fancy.

And when the mop it is all o'er, you that are young and
hearty
Must take your girl all in your hand and join a drinking
party;
But when you are returning home, enjoying sweet embraces,
With love and honour spend the night at statutes, fairs
and races.

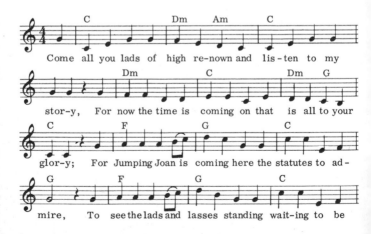

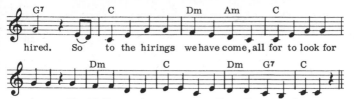

hired. So to the hirings we have come, all for to look for places, If with the master we agree and he will give good wages.

skimmer dish with which milk was skimmed; alternatively, piece of wood which was floated on top of water in a bucket to stop it spilling over when carried.

Mops and statutes were hiring fairs at which farm servants, both indoor and out, were engaged by the year. These fairs, transformed into purely pleasure fairs, still exist; they lingered in some areas until 1914 with their original function.

Thomas Hardy describes a typical hiring in *Far from the Madding Crowd*:

At one end of the street stood from two to three hundred blithe and hearty labourers waiting upon Chance – all men of the stamp

to whom labour suggests nothing worse than a wrestle with gravitation, and pleasure nothing better than a renunciation of the same. Among these, carters and waggoners were distinguished by having a piece of whip-cord twisted round their hats; thatchers wore a fragment of woven straw; shepherds held their sheep-crooks in their hands; and thus the situation required was known to the hirers at a glance.

When the bargain was struck, the labourer was given a small sum of money, known as a 'fastening penny'. There was sometimes a week's grace during which either party could repent of the bargain. If the master changed his mind, the servant might keep the advance, but if the servant did so he was obliged to return it.

With his fastening money the labourer would set off to sample the fun of the fair or to buy presents, clothes, food or drink – or ballads. These were sold in their hundreds and thousands by itinerant vendors at fairs and markets.

One who came to Weobley (Herefordshire) fair every year cried, 'A song, a song, a song for a penny! As large as a barn door and not quite so thick!' The word 'broadside' is not used by the local peasantry; they say 'ballet'. The boys never came back from the fairs without two or three 'ballets'.
(E. M. Leather, *The Folk-Lore of Herefordshire*, 1912 and 1970, p.181)

The broadside ballads sold covered an enormous range of themes, one of which was life and conditions on the land, including the hirings themselves. This particular example originally ran 'to ————— hirings we have come', so that the singer could insert the appropriate place.

Truro Agricultural Show

Good people all who hear my voice,
You now have reason to rejoice;
For off to Truro you may go,
To see the Agericultural Show.

Chorus
But* don't go kissing the girls you know
At Truro Agericultural Show.

A motley group you will see there,
Fat farmers and their wives so rare;
Their bouncing daughters neat and clean,
With a pork-pie hat and a crinoline.

From Newlyn East and St Columb, too,
There's hump-backed Jim and carroty Joe;
And a special train upon the rail
To bring all the thieves from Bodmin Jail.

They've got a band from Plymouth down,
The best that ever was in the town;
And all the gentry will be there:
It's almost as pretty at Whitsun Fair.

There's horses, ponies, cows and calves,
For Truro don't do things by halves.
There be Devon bulls, sheep, pigs and geese:
You can see it all for a shilling apiece.

There's things up there that'll make you laugh;
There's a two-legged cow and a nine-legged calf,
A billy-goat that comes from Wales
With sixteen eyes and seventeen tails.

Now all around I hear them say,
'We'll see that Show this very day;
So off we go, all in a row,
To Truro Agericultural Show.'

*This word changes to 'So' or 'And', as appropriate.

110

I'm glad you're come, I see you're here;
There's thousands come from everywhere:
Rich and poor, high and low,
At Truro Agericultural Show.

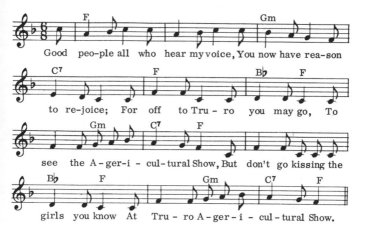

Good peo-ple all who hear my voice, You now have rea-son to re-joice; For off to Tru - ro you may go, To see the A - ger-i - cul-tural Show, But don't go kissing the girls you know At Tru - ro A-ger-i - cul-tural Show.

Though the Highland and Agricultural Society had been holding shows in Scotland for some time, the first large-scale agricultural show in England was organized by the Royal Agricultural Society at Oxford in 1839. County Agricultural Societies were then encouraged to hold their own shows, which attracted farmers from long distances and helped to promote improved methods of farming. This song dates from the 1860s. There is a good illustration of the show ground at Worcester in 1863 in John Higgs, *The Land* (Studio Vista).

The Bullard's Song

Come all you bonny boys,
Who love to bait the bonny bull,
Who take delight in noise,
And you shall have your bellyful.
On Stamford's town bull-running day,
We'll show you such right gallant play;
You never saw the like, you'll say,
As you shall see at Stamford.

Earl Warren was the man
That first began this gallant sport;
In the castle he did stand
And saw the bonny bulls that fought.
The butchers with their bull-dogs came,
These sturdy, stubborn bulls to tame,
But more with madness did inflame:
Enraged, they ran through Stamford.

Delighted with the sport,
The meadows there he freely gave;
Where these bonny bulls had fought,
The butchers now do hold and have;
By charter they are strictly bound
That every year a bull be found;
Come, dight your face, you dirty clown,
And stump away to Stamford.

Come, take him by the tail, boys,
Bridge, bridge him if you can;
Prog him with a stick, boys,
Never let him quiet stand.
Through every street and lane in town
We'll chevy-chase him up and down:
You sturdy bung-straws ten miles round,
Come stump away to Stamford.

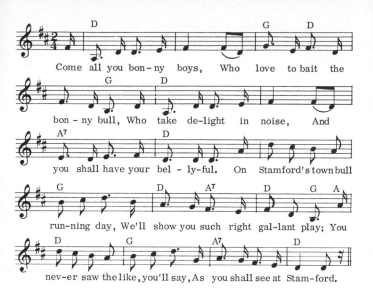

Come all you bon-ny boys, Who love to bait the
bon-ny bull, Who take de-light in noise, And
you shall have your bel-ly-ful. On Stamford's town bull
run-ning day, We'll show you such right gal-lant play; You
nev-er saw the like, you'll say, As you shall see at Stam-ford.

bullard bull-runner (see below).
Earl Warren see below.
dight clean.
bridge him see below.
prog to poke with a pointed stick.
bung-straws threshers.

THE STAMFORD BULL-RUNNING

From time immemorial down to a late period, the 13th of
November was annually celebrated, at the town of Stamford in
Lincolnshire, by a public amusement termed a Bull-running. The
sport was latterly conducted in the following manner: about a
quarter to eleven o'clock, in the festal-day, the bell of St Mary's
commenced to toll as a warning for the thoroughfares to be
cleared of infirm persons and children; and precisely at eleven, the
bull was turned into a street, blocked up at each end by a barri-
cade of carts and wagons. At this moment every post, pump and
'coigne of vantage' was occupied, and those happy enough to
have such protections, could grin at their less fortunate friends,
who were compelled to have recourse to flight; the barricades,
windows and house-tops being crowded with spectators. The
bull, irritated by hats being thrown at him, and other means of

113

annoyance, soon became ready to run; and then, the barricades being removed, the whole crowd, bull, men, boys and dogs, rushed helter-skelter through the streets. One great object being to 'bridge the bull', the animal was, if possible, compelled to run upon the bridge that spans the Welland. The crowd then closing in, with audacious courage surrounded and seized the animal; and, in spite of its size and strength, by main force tumbled it over the parapet into the river. The bull then swimming ashore, would land in the meadows, where the run was continued; the miry, marshy state of the fields at that season of the year, and the falls and other disasters consequent thereon, adding greatly to the amusement of the mob. The sport was carried on till all were tired; the animal was then killed, and its flesh sold at a low rate to the people, who finished the day's amusement with a supper of bull-beef. . . .

According to tradition, the origin of the custom dates from the time of King John; when, one day, William, Earl of Warren, standing on the battlements of the castle, saw two bulls fighting in the meadow beneath. Some butchers coming to part the combatants, one of the bulls ran into the town, causing a great uproar. The earl, mounting his horse, rode after the animal, and enjoyed the sport so much, that he gave the meadow, in which the fight began, to the butchers of Stamford, on condition that they should provide a bull, to be run in that town annually, on the 13th of November, for ever after. There is no documentary evidence on the subject, but the town of Stamford undoubtedly holds certain common rights in the meadow specified, which is still termed the Bull-meadow.

Bull-running was, for a long period, a recognized institution at Stamford. A mayor of the town, who died in 1756, left a sum of money to encourage the practice; and, as appears by the vestry accounts, the church-wardens annually gave money to aid the bull-running. In 1788, the first attempt was made by the local authorities to stop the custom, the mayor issuing a curious proclamation, stating that bull-running was contrary to religion, law and nature, and punishable with the penalty of death. The Earl of Exeter, who lived 'At Burleigh House, by Stamford town', lent his personal influence to the mayor on this occasion; but the bull was run, and both the earl and mayor were insulted by the mob. In 1789, the mayor having obtained the aid of a troop of dragoons, met the bull at St George's Gate, as it was being driven into the town by the bull-woman – a virago dressed in blue ribbons, who officiated on these occasions, and followed by the *bullards*, a name given to the admirers and supporters of bull-running. On the mayor appealing to the officer of dragoons to stop the procession, the latter refused to interfere, alleging that the people were peaceably walking on the highway. 'In that case,' replied the mayor, 'your men are of no use here.' 'Very well,' said the officer, 'I shall dismiss them.' The dismissed dragoons, to their great glee, joined the bullards, and the bull was run as usual. For a long time afterwards, the bullards received no opposition. The towns-people, delighted with the sport, subscribed for a second annual bull-running, which took place on the Monday after Christmas Day; and there were several occasional bull-runnings every year, the candidates for representing Stamford in parliament being always willing to give a bull for the purpose.

In 1831, the Conservative party canvassed the borough under a flag bearing the representation of a bull. Several clergymen and others remonstrated against this mode of obtaining popular support, distinctly declaring they would not vote, if the obnoxious banner were not laid aside. But many persons of station, and well-known humanity, defended the practice of bull-running, alleging that it was an old-fashioned, manly, English sport; inspiring courage, agility, and presence of mind under danger; and, as regards inhumanity, it was not by any means so cruel to the brute creation, nor so perilous to the life and limb of man, as fox-hunting.

In 1833, the Society for Prevention of Cruelty to Animals made its first public appearance as an opponent of the practice. One of its officers was sent to Stamford on bull-running day, and, being more bold than prudent, was roughly hustled by the crowd. This interference of the society, however well-meant, had a very different effect to that desired; instead of discountenancing the practice, the people of Stamford were thereby stimulated to support it. 'Who or what is this London Society,' they asked, 'that, usurping the place of constituted authorities, presumes to interfere with our ancient amusement?'

In 1836, the society sent several of its officers and agents to Stamford. The 13th falling that year on Sunday, the bull was run on the following day; in the evening the populace resented the interference of the society's officers, by assaulting them, and breaking some windows. At the following Lent Assizes for Lincolnshire, the society preferred bills of indictment before the Grand Jury, against eight persons, for 'conspiring to disturb the peace by riotously assembling to run and torment a bull' at Stamford, on the 14th of November previous. . . . Five of the prisoners were acquitted, three only being found guilty; these last were discharged on giving bail to appear to receive judgement, at the Court of Queen's Bench, when called upon.

The bullards, accepting the result of the trial as a victory, determined to have a grand run in 1837. Influence, however, had been brought to bear on the Home Secretary, who wrote to the mayor of Stamford, impressing upon him the necessity of taking active measures to prevent a proceeding so illegal and disgraceful as a bull-running. The mayor, accordingly, swore in more than two hundred special constables to his assistance; but their opposition being lukewarm, the bull was run with greater *éclat* than ever.

In 1838, the Home Secretary determined to put down the custom. Several days before the 13th, a troop of the 14th Dragoons, and a strong force of metropolitan police, were sent to Stamford, and a considerable body of special constables were sworn in. The commanders of the military and police, having viewed the field of action, consulted with the mayor. As prevention was better than cure, and there could be no bull-run without a bull, measures were taken accordingly. The town was strictly searched, and two bulls being found, the animals were taken and confined in an inn-yard, under a picket of dragoons. Sentries were then placed on all the outlets of the town, and parties patrolled the roads night and day, to prevent a bull from being brought in. The eventful 13th arrived, and though the streets were crowded with bullards, the authorities were perfectly at their ease. They even heard with complacency the bell of St Mary's toll the time-honoured bull-warning. But at the last stroke of the bell, their fancied security was rudely dissipated by the well-known shouts of 'Hoy! bull! hoy!' from a thousand voices; a noble animal having appeared, as if by magic, in the principal street. There never was such a run! The wild excitement of the scene was enhanced by the bewildered dragoons galloping hither and thither, in vain attempts to secure the animal. The metropolitan police, with greater valour than discretion, formed in a compact phalanx on the bridge; but the bull, followed by the bullards, dashed through them as an eagle might through a cobweb. After a run of some hours, the bull came to bay in the river, and was then captured by the authorities. An attempt was then made to rescue one of the bulls confined in the inn-yard. This led to a collision between the military and the people, stones and brickbats were thrown, and sabre cuts returned in exchange; but, on the dragoons being ordered to load with ball-cartridge, the mob dispersed. Where did the strange bull, a very miraculous animal, so miraculously spring from? This enigma was soon solved by its being claimed by a certain noble lord. He had been sending it, in a covered wagon, from one of his estates to another, and, by a 'curious coincidence', it happened to pass through

Stamford on the very day and hour its presence was required by the bullards, who, seizing the wagon, released the animal. Whether the coincidence was accidental or designed, the preceding explanation, if not quite satisfactory, produced a good deal of good-humoured laughter.

In 1839, a stronger force of military and police was sent to Stamford; every precaution was taken, yet some treacherous special constables smuggled a bull into the town, and the bullards had their last run. The animal, however, being young and docile, did not afford much sport, being soon captured by the authorities. In the following year, as bull-running day drew near, the people of Stamford began to count the cost of their amusement. The military, metropolitan police and special constables of the two previous years, had cost them more than £600 – a sum which might with greater fitness, have been laid out on certain town improvements, then much wanted. So the townsmen forwarded a memorial to the mayor, to be laid before the Home Secretary, pledging themselves that, if no extraneous force of military or police were brought into the town, nor expense incurred by appointing special constables, they, the subscribers, would prevent bull-running from taking place in Stamford during that year. The townsmen were wisely taken at their word, and there never has been a bull-run in Stamford since that time. (*Chambers Book of Days*, vol.2, 1863, pp.574–6).

The Stamford bull-running is fully treated in R. W. Malcolmson, *Popular Recreations in English Society 1700–1850*, Cambridge University Press, 1973.

STAMFORD
BULL-RUNNING.

The manly, daring, and unique sport of Bull-running, peculiar to Stamford, has been grossly, wantonly, and maliciously misrepresented by those who should be teachers of truth, and a few other persons, through a mistaken zeal, though no doubt good motives, have been induced to co-operate with them, in endeavouring to stir up a feeling hostile to the diversion,—and in a foolish handbill, mixed it up with the Election, with which it has no concern, being the amusement of the greater part of the town and unconnected with either party.

If these *would-be-humanity Gentlemen* were actuated solely by their pity for suffering animals, and not by an *impertinent interference with the Amusements of the Lower Orders*, they would begin with the cruel Sports of the Gentry, and not let the *mere running of a Bull among the people, unfettered*, having his natural weapons of defence to protect him, engross all their sympathy, when so many other objects of genteel and fashionable barbarity naturally present themselves.

Nov. 6, 1830.   F.AIRPLAY.

DRAKARD, PRINTER, NEWS AND CHAMPION OFFICE, STAMFORD.

The Toon Improvement Bill
or Nee Pleyce Noo ti Play

Noo, O dear me, what mun aw dee, aw've nee pleyce noo
   ti play,
Wor canny Forth an' Spital te, eh, man, they've tune away.
Nee pleyce ti bool wor peyste eggs noo, to lowp the frog
   and run,
They're elways boeldin summuck new, they'll spoil
   Newcassel seune.

(Spoken) Thers nee pleyce ti play the wag noo; the grund's
a' tuen up wiv High Levels, Central Stations, an' dear knaws
what else. Aw used ti play the wag doon the quay thonder.
Aw've seen me fish for days tigither. The lads ca'd me the
fisherwoman. Aw was a stunner. Aw've mony time browt up
three French apples at a time; but wor aud wife said if aw
fell i' an' gat droon she'd skin me alive when aw com heyme;
so aw played the wag doon the burn after that, but noo ti
meyke improvement they've filled it up wi' cairt loads o'
muck, to beeld hooses on; some o' wor lads an' me petitioned
the magistrators for a new play ground an' he telled us ti
gan to the boardin schuel. What an idia. Wor aud wife hes
sair tues ti raise the penny for Monday mornins the maister
seldom gets 't though, aw buy claggum wid, then the maister
hes ti tek 't oot i' flaps. But aw's broken hearted when aw
think aboot wor canny Forth wiv its auld brick walls; what
curious days aw've spent there; man, aw've seen me play
the wag for heyle days tigither, wi' maw mouth covered wi'
claggum and clarts. What a chep aw was for one hole teazer
then; mony a time aw hev fowt an hour for a farden bullocker;
aw used to skin thor knockles when aw won me beeks; aw
used ti fullock; man, what a fullocker aw was. But what's
the use o' jawin' noo, the aud gams is a' geyne. Thors widdy-
widdy-way, the morrow's the market day slyater, slyater,
comin' away, comin' away; an' King Henry's boys go round,
what a gam that was; aw used ti be King Henry. But aw'd

120

better drop off or else maw feelin's 'll set me on a bubblin for

Chorus
O dear me, what maun aw de, aw've nee pleyce noo ti play;
Wor canny Forth an' Spital te, eh, man, they've tune away.
The toon improvement's meyde greet noise, but aw heard
    my feyther say,
Thor was summick mair then little boys kept wor wise
    heeds at play;
Thor's bonny wark amang thorsels, but aw mun haud my
    jaw;
But still thor's folks 'boot here that smells the cash buik
    wiv its flaws.

(Spoken) Aw heard maw feyther tell maw muther, yen neet,
a' aboot the toon concerns – they thought aw was asleep.
Aw's a cute lad. Aw's elways waken when the tripe is fryin
for feyther's supper; aw heard him say thor was a vast o'
rates, sic as poor rates, leet rates, sewer rates; but aw think
at onny rate, thor's nee first-rate rates amang them. Noo
thor's the watch rates; thor's the pollis, noo we cannit dee
wivoot pollis but it's not fair to teyke a chep up for playin at
holes; but the magistrates isn't deein fair wiv us at nowt.
Aw's lossin' aw maw lairnin' noo. What a heed-piece aw
had at yen time, aw'd ti use the shoehorn ti put maw Sunday
hat on, maw heed gat swelled wi' knowledge se. Noo a' thor
days is geyne, so aw'll learn to chew baccy, etc, etc.

(Chorus)
Bedstocks that canny gam's noo dune, an' three hole
    teaser tee,
They've tune away wor best o' fun, so, lads, what mun aw
    dee?
Aw'll bubble tiv aw dee, begox, or teyke some arsynack;
Then corporation men may funk when aw is laid upon
    maw back.

(Chorus)

Noo a' ye canny folk that's here, just think on what aw say,
An' recollect yor youthful days, when ye were fond o' play.

Ye say yor schule days was the best, so help me in maw cause,
An' cheer poor Bobby Snivvelnose be gean him yor applause.

(Chorus)

Forth and Spital open spaces used by the children for play.
peyste eggs Pace, or Easter Eggs.
lowp the frog leap-frog.
High Level the High Level Bridge, completed in 1849 by Robert
    Stephenson, son of George.
Central Station Newcastle Central Station, opened by Queen Vic-
    toria in 1850.
play the wag play truant.
aud wife mother.
claggum treacle toffee.
clarts mud.
one hole and three hole teazer types of games of marbles.
farden bullocker the largest type of marble, which cost a farthing.
beeks 'a punishment inflicted upon the loser in a game of marbles by
    "firing" a marble at the knuckles'.
fullock to cross the line at marbles (a form of cheating).
widdy, widdy way a chasing game.
King Henry's boys go round another game.
cash book . . . i.e. some people care more for the cash book than for
    the pleasures of childhood.
vast o' rates large quantity of rates.
bedstocks form of relievo or prisoner's base (i.e. a game).
bubble cry.
tiv until.

When the Central Station was laid out, open spaces in the centre of
Newcastle were enclosed, and could no longer be used by the people
for their pleasures. Ned Corvan, a local singer and song-writer,
wrote this song to voice the popular indignation. He performed it
dressed as a small boy, and carrying a hoop.

Opposition to enclosure appears to have been more vocal in the
towns than in the countryside. Apart from this song, I know of
others opposing enclosure from Nottingham, Derby and Birmingham (relating to Sutton Coldfield). There were many manifestations
of opposition in the countryside, but I have not yet come across a
song.

The Bonny Gray

Come you cock-merchants far and near,
Did you hear of a cock-fight that happened here?
Those Liverpool lads, I've heard them say,
'Tween the charcoal black and the bonny gray.

We went to Jim Ward's and called for a pot,
Where this grand cock-battle it was fought;
For twenty guineas these cocks did play,
The charcoal black and the bonny gray.

Then Lord Derby came swaggering down:
'I'll bet ten guineas to a crown,
If this charcoal black he gets fair play,
He'll clip the wings of your bonny gray.'

Now when these cocks came to the sod,
Cry the Liverpool lads, 'How now, what odds?'
The odds, the Prescot lads did say,
'Tween the charcoal black and the bonny gray.

This cock-fight was fought hard and fast,
Till black charcoal he lay dead at last.
The Liverpool lads gave a loud hurray
And carried away the bonny gray.

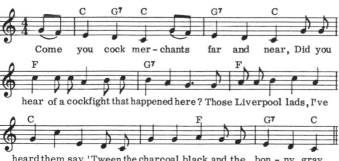

Jim Ward's Ward (1800–55) was a champion pugilist and artist. He kept a tavern in Liverpool from 1832 to 1853.

Lord Derby according to Harland, this was Edward, the 12th earl; he came from a sporting family, which gave its name to a still-famous horse-race.

Ward opened his tavern in 1832 and Derby died in 1834, which gives us a fairly precise date for the cock-fight. The Liverpool lads backed the bonny gray, while Lord Derby backed the losing charcoal black.

Cock-fighting was popular in England for centuries. During the eighteenth century it was possibly the most popular sport of all. It was forbidden by Act of Parliament in 1849.

The Football Match

It's of a football match, my boys, delightful to be seen,
And six young rippling lads who played on Salisbury Plain.
Here's health unto those rippling lads and so the game
    went on.

Chorus
You rippling lads, huzza! You're sure to win the day;
You will gain the prize and you'll carry it away.

The ball has been thrown up, my boys, the game it did
    begin;
Good Lord, how they did kick it, more like devils than like
    men:
They having such a notion in kicking it along.

The ball it being thrown up, my boys, the game it did draw
    nigh,
Young William stuck a sharp penknife into young Jackson's
    thigh.
Here's health unto those rippling lads and so the game went on.

Young William aimèd at the ball, it was his full intent;
But then he missed his aim and right through the goal he
    went.
Here's health unto those rippling lads and so the game went
    on.

This song was collected by Alfred Williams during the second decade
of this century. He comments:

> Lovers of football should be interested in this very old and
> quaint song, descriptive of a football match once played on
> Salisbury Plain. It would appear that but six players took part
> in the game, and they were dressed with ribbons and caps, or
> hats, after the fashion of the morris dancers. I do not know
> whether or not they had a referee, or whether such practices
> as that of stabbing at the ball with a knife were considered
> lawful and fair. I obtained the piece of John Pillinger, who
> learned it of his father at Lechlade, over eighty years ago (i.e.
> about 1840) (*Folk songs of the Upper Thames*, 1923 and 1970,
> p.223).

Football, in its traditional form of a mass mêlée involving large numbers of people, still exists in one or two places: at Hallaton in Leicestershire, for example, where it goes by the name of bottle-kicking. In common with other popular sports, it came under fire from officialdom during the latter part of the eighteenth century and the earlier part of the nineteenth. This is rather a sad letter from the magistrates of Kingston to the Home Secretary, the Duke of Portland, in 1799:

My Lord Duke,
It having been a practice for the populace to kick foot ball in the Market Place and Streets of this Town on Shrove Tuesday to the great nuisance of the Inhabitants and of Persons travelling through the Town and complaint having been made by several Gentlemen of the County to the Magistrates of the Town they previous to Shrove Tuesday 1797 gave public Notice by the distribution of hand bills of their determination to suppress the

Practice which not having the desired effect several of the Offenders were Indicted and at the last Assizes convicted but sentence was respited and has not yet been declared the Judge thinking that after having warned them of their situation that they would not attempt to kick again but we the present Magistrates of the Town having been previously informed it was their intention with others to kick again as on last Shrove Tuesday some days before issued hand bills giving notice of our intention to prosecute any persons who should on that day kick foot ball in the said Town and apprehending that we should find great opposition two days previous thereto addressed a letter to the Officer commanding the Cavalry at Hampton Court informing him of the Circumstance and stating that if we found it necessary we should call on him for the Assistance of the Military

On the Shrove Tuesday a great number of persons having assembled and begun to kick a ball in the market place We caused three that seemed the most active to be taken into Custody hoping that would induce the others to disperse but not having that effect we then caused the Riot Act to be read and the Mob not then dispersing but increasing in Number and threatening to Use violence in liberating those in Custody we addressed another Letter to the Officer on Command at Hampton Court requiring him to send part of the Cavalry to our Assistance but not receiving an Answer in a reasonable time one of Us went to Hampton Court in search of the Officer where it was said that Major Hawker was the Officer on Duty there but was gone from home and not to be seen nor could any Other be found who could Act and the Men at the same time kicking foot ball on Hampton Court Green

Not being able to obtain the Assistance required the Persons in Custody were rescued by the Mob as the Constables were conveying them to Prison and the Keeper was violently assaulted and much hurt If the Military had attended we should have succeeded in abolishing the Nuisance without much difficulty but not having met with such support the Game will be carried on to a greater height than it ever has been the Mob conceiving they have got the better of Us and that the Military would not attend As we apprehend that Major Hawker (having previous Notice of our intention to apply to him in case we stood in need of his assistance) ought not to have been Absent from his Post without leaving some other Officer capable of acting in his absence we think it our Duty to state these circumstances to your Grace in Order that such steps may be taken therein as the Case requires and shall seem meet and necessary to your Grace (Public Records Office, HO 42/46).

This letter is placed in context in Malcolmson's *Popular Recreations*.

Professor Perkin calls the change in attitude which led to attacks on bull-baiting, cock-fighting, popular football and other traditional customs and pastimes, the 'Moral Revolution'. He writes:

> Between 1780 and 1850 the English ceased to be one of the most aggressive, brutal, rowdy, outspoken, riotous, cruel and blood-thirsty nations in the world and became one of the most inhibited, polite, orderly, tender-minded, prudish and hypocritical. The transformation diminished cruelty to animals, criminals, lunatics and children (in that order); suppressed many cruel sports and games, such as bull-baiting and cock-fighting, as well as innocent amusements, including many fairs and wakes; rid the penal code of about two hundred capital offences, abolished transportation, and cleaned up the prisons; turned Sunday into a day of prayer for all; 'bowdlerized' Shakespeare, Gibbon and other 'obscene' classics, inhibited every kind of literature save that suitable for family reading, and almost gave the death-blow to the English stage; and generally removed from the language, except in official publications and medical literature, all words calculated to 'bring a blush to the cheek of the young person' (*Origins*, p.280).

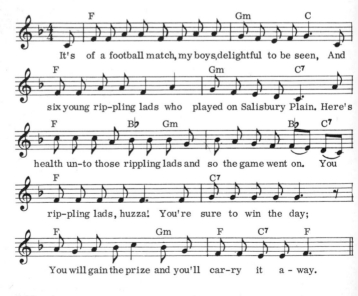

It's of a football match, my boys, delightful to be seen, And six young rip-pling lads who played on Salisbury Plain. Here's health un-to those rippling lads and so the game went on. You rip-pling lads, huzza! You're sure to win the day; You will gain the prize and you'll car-ry it a-way.

3

On Monday Morning I Married a Wife

The Rambling Miner

I am a miner stout and bold,
Long time I've worked down underground,
To raise both tin and copper, too,
For the honour of our miners.
Now brother miners I'll bid you adieu,
I'll go to work no more with you,
But scour the country through and through,
And still be a rambling miner.

The very first house I went up to,
They made me lie out in the barn;
A pretty young girl to her mother did say,
'I'm afraid you will do him some great harm.
If you put him to lie on the cold barn floor,
Where the wind and rain comes in the door;
You may pop him in my bed, mother, if you please,
For I'm told he's a rambling miner.'

It was in the morning when I rose,
I left my love a-sleeping;
I left her for an hour or two,
While I went to court some other.
If she stays there till I return,
She may stay there till the day of doom;
I'll court some other girl in her room,
And still be a rambling miner.

Now when I came to Redruth Town,
There I saw lasses plenty;
I boldly stepped right up to one,
To court her for her beauty.
I said, 'My dear, be of good cheer;
I'll never leave you, have no fear;
But travel the country through and through,
And still be a rambling miner.'

And when I came to Merthyr Town,
There I saw lasses bonny;
I boldly stepped right up to one,

To court her for her money.
I said, 'My dear, be of good cheer;
There's ale and wine and rum punch, too,
Besides a pair of new silk shoes,
To travel with a rambling miner.'

Now when I came to Callington,
I met with Captain Thomas;
I asked him for a job of work,
Which he gave me the promise.
He told me I should have a job,
To work in the shaft with pick and gad;
And good wages he'd allow to me,
For being a rambling miner.

And if you want to know my name,
My name it is young Simmons;
I've a roving commission from the queen
To court all girls who're handsome.
With my false heart and deluding tongue
I'll court them all, both old and young;
I'll court them all and marry none,
And still be a rambling miner.

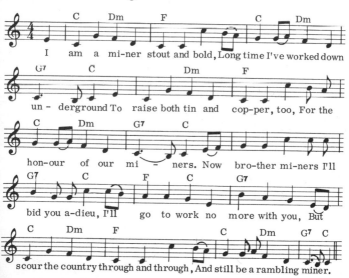

I am a miner stout and bold, Long time I've worked down
un-derground To raise both tin and cop-per, too, For the
hon-our of our mi — ners. Now bro-ther mi-ners I'll
bid you a-dieu, I'll go to work no more with you, But
scour the country through and through, And still be a rambling miner.

Redruth in Cornwall.
Merthyr (Tydfil) in South Wales.
in her room instead of her.
Callington also in Cornwall.
Captain Thomas in the Cornish mines, Captain meant manager.
gad wedge.

This song makes an interesting comment on the mobility of labour as a result of the Industrial Revolution. Our rambling miner came from Cornwall, an area in which the mines produced metals, not coal.

An excellent piece of work on the Cornish miners is J. G. Rule, *The Labouring Miner in Cornwall c.1740–1870*, Warwick University Ph.D. thesis, 1971.

The Weaver and the Factory Maid

I am a hand weaver to my trade,
I fell in love with a factory maid;
And if I could but her favour win,
I'd stand beside her and weave by steam.

My father to me scornful said,
'How could you fancy a factory maid,
When you could have girls fine and gay,
And dressed like to the Queen of May?'

'As for your fine girls, I do not care;
And could I but enjoy my dear,
I'd stand in the factory all the day,
And she and I'd keep our shuttles in play.'

I went to my love's bedroom door,
Where oftentimes I had been before;
But I could not speak nor yet get in
To the pleasant bed my love laid in.

'How can you say it's a pleasant bed,
When nowt lies there but a factory maid?'
'A factory lass although she be,
Blest is the man that enjoys she.'

Oh, pleasant thoughts come to my mind
As I turned down her sheets so fine,
And I seen her two breasts standing so,
Like two white hills all covered with snow.

Where are the girls? I'll tell you plain,
The girls have gone to weave by steam;
And if you'd find 'em you must rise at dawn
And trudge to the mill in the early morn.

I am a hand-wea-ver to my trade, I fell in love with a fac-tory maid; And if I could but her fa-vour win, I'd stand be-side her and weave by steam.

This song clearly dates from the early years of power-loom weaving when, in general, the men continued to work at home on their hand-looms, while the women and boys worked in the factories. In 1834, out of an adult labour force of some 190,000 in all textile mills in the United Kingdom, roughly 102,000 were women, the rest being men. Most of the men were young, for two reasons. Firstly, they were paid less than older men. In 1835 the rates were 4s. 10¾d. a week (age eleven to sixteen), 10s. 2½d. (sixteen to 21), and 17s. 2½d. (twenty-one to twenty-six). Secondly, the older hand-loom weavers could not or would not easily adapt themselves to working in factories. They disliked the regulation of their comings and goings by a factory bell or hooter, and resented not being able to work part-time in their gardens or small-holdings. The hardships of weavers who did not go into the factories were a national disgrace for many years, and the subject of a number of Parliamentary inquiries.

The Weaver and the Factory Maid is not, however, primarily a song of protest, but a song of love, of love in an industrial setting. The tune and most of the text (the rest being from an early ms. source) were collected in Widnes by A. L. Lloyd, as recently as 1951.

Dashing Steam-Loom Weaver

One day I got out on the spree – I fell out with my mother.
She says to me, 'We can't agree, you'd better find another.'
I said, 'My dear, yo need not fret; I'm in the humour o'
  starting;'
So then straightway out I did set, all for to seek my
  fortune.
Sing right fa looral ooral ay, sing right fa looral o,
So then straightway out I did set, all for to seek my
  fortune.

Well, when I came to Bolton Town, I met all things
  satisfactory;
I tried at many and many a loom, till I geet to weave at
  factory.
I had not long been i' th' shade before my merit took, sir,
So weel I did geet on with trade, they made me
  overlooker.

I dressed myself in clothes so fine; thinks I, I'll cut a dash
  on,
And I will geet a sweetheart too, fear I be out o' th'
  fashion.
Hoo talked to me so very fine, said hoo wur no deceiver;
Hoo said well off that we should be: hoo wur a dashing
  steam-loom weaver.

One night I cam down into t' town and didn't happ'n t'
  bring her;
I scarcely had set myself down to harken to t' *Star Inn*
  singer,
When a chap as works beside o' me – I thought him no
  deceiver –
Well he walked in and sit by me with my dashing steam-
  loom weaver.

Now first I thought to let him sup, but he put me in such
  fettle,

And so to him I bristles up to show I had some mettle.
I said, 'Thou'll leave that lass o' mine or I'll gi'e thy chops
    a driver;'
He says, 'Now dunna thee come it so fine: hoo's my dashing
    steam-loom weaver.'

And so next day to her I went to see if hoo'd a
    conscience.
Hoo said, 'Lad, rest thyself content; it's nobbut a bit o'
    nonsense.'
I met this chap the very next day, gin him o'er his chops a
    driver;
We fought a full hour up and down, through my dashing
    steam-loom weaver.

And when that we were on the ground as hard as we could
    batter,
This girl she did come walking round to see what was the
    matter.
So then I purred him o'er his mug; hoo run at him in a
    fever;
Hoo pelted at him with her clog, so I won my steam-loom
    weaver.

Now very soon we geet our friends, geet wed on Easter
    Sunday,
And wedding kept among our friends all day on Easter
    Monday.
As you may see, I geet good wage; what brass I mean to
    save, sir,
We are content as ought can be, me and my steam-loom
    weaver.

i' th' shade out of work.
hoo her.
purred punched or kicked. As late as the 1870s, purring or kicking
    matches were held in Lancashire, sometimes with fatal results.

mother. She says to me, "We can't agree, you'd better find a-
-no-ther." I said, "My dear, yo need not fret, I'm
in the hu-mour o' start-ing;" So then straightway out
I did set, all for to seek my for - tune, Sing
right fa loo-ral oo-ral ay, sing right fa loo-ral o, So
then straightway out I did set, all for to seek my for-tune.

Poor Man's Work is Never Done

When I was a young man I lived rarely,
I spent my time in grief and woe
For the want of a young wife to lie by me,
When my trouble did run so.

Chorus
With my whack fal lor, the diddle and the dido,
Whack fal lor, the diddle aye day.

Now I hired one for my constant service,
To milk my cows and brush my shoes;
Some women take delight in a deal of pleasure:
Poor man's labour is always abused.

When I come home in the morning early
To see my flock that were astray,
My wife she lay abed till noon
On the shortest winter's day.

When I come home all wet and weary,
No dry clothes for to put on,
It's enough to make a poor man crazy:
Poor man's labour is never done.

The very first year that I was married
I could not get one wink of sleep,
For all night long she kept on crying,
'Husband, do not go to sleep.'

She kicked my shins till the blood ran down 'em,
Crying, 'husband dear, my dear.'
It's very well I knew her meaning:
A poor man's labour is never done.

The second year that I was married
I had a very fine baby born.
She forsook it, I took to it,
Wrapped it up and kept it warm.

One night as I sat by the fire
She came in roaring like a gun;
In my face her fist came slapping:
A poor man's work is never done.

All young men who want to marry,
Take care how you choose a wife,
For if you meet with my wife's sister,
She'll be a devil all the days of her life.

So court them long before you marry:
Women seldom prove a friend.
Well now away with my wife and welcome,
Then my troubles will have an end.

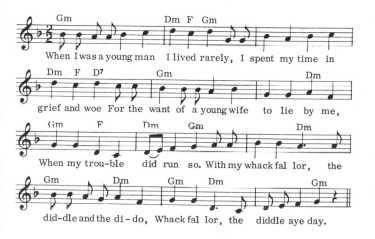

When I was a young man I lived rarely, I spent my time in grief and woe For the want of a young wife to lie by me, When my trou-ble did run so. With my whack fal lor, the did-dle and the di-do, Whack fal lor, the diddle aye day.

Washing Day

The sky with clouds was overcast, the rain began to fall,
My wife she beat the children and raised a pretty squall.
She bade me with a frowning look to get out of the way;
The devil a bit of comfort's there upon a washing day.

Chorus
For it's thump, thump, scold, scold, thump, thump away;
The devil a bit of comfort's there upon a washing day.

My Kate she is a bonny wife, there's none more free from evil,
Except upon a washing day, and then she is a devil.
The very kittens on the hearth, they dare not even play;
Away they jump with many a thump upon a washing day.

A friend of mine once asked me how long poor Kate was dead,
Lamenting the poor creature and sorry I was wed
To such a scolding vixen whilst he had been at sea.
The truth it was he chanced to come upon a washing day.

I asked him once to stay and dine: 'Come, come,' said I,
   'oddsbuds,
I'll no denial take, you shall, though Kate is in the suds;'
But what he had to dine upon in faith I shall not say,
But I'll wager he'll not come again upon a washing day.

On that sad morning when I rise, I make a fervent prayer
Unto the gods that it might be throughout the day quite fair,
That not a gown or handkerchief may in the ditch be laid,
For should it happen so, egad, I'd catch a broken head.

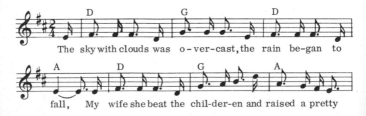

squall. She bade me with a frowning look to get out of the

way; The devil a bit of comfort's there u-pon a washing

day. For it's thump, thump, scold, scold, thump, thump a-way; The

devil a bit of comfort's there u-pon a washing day.

Fuddling Day, or Saint Monday
in answer to Washing Day

Each Monday morn before I rise I make a fervent prayer
Unto the gods my husband might from tippling keep quite
    clear;
But oh, when I his breakfast take to shop without delay,
What anguish do I feel to hear it is a fuddling day.

Chorus
For it's drink, drink, smoke, smoke, drink, drink away;
There is no pleasure in the house upon a fuddling day.

St Monday brings more ills about, for when the money's
    spent,
The children's clothes go up the spout, which causes
    discontent;
And when at night he staggers home, he knows not what
    to say;
A fool is more a man than he upon a fuddling day.

My husband is a workman good, no man can be more civil,
Except upon a fuddling day, and then he is a devil,
For should I thwart his humour then, the claret's sure
    to fly,
And I have cause to dread his look upon a fuddling day.

A friend of mine came in one day, 'twas cold and foggy
    weather;
'To comfort you,' says she, 'we'll have a drop of max
    together.'
My husband came in at the time, I knew not what to say,
But she'll not come again I'm sure upon a fuddling day.

shop workshop, factory.   *claret* blood.
St Monday see opposite.   *max* gin.
up the spout into pawn.

Each Monday morn before I rise, I make a fervent prayer Unto the gods my husband might from tippling keep quite clear; But oh, when I his breakfast take to shop without delay, What anguish do I feel to hear it is a fuddling day. For it's drink, drink, smoke, smoke, drink, drink away; There is no pleasure in the house upon a fuddling day.

Keeping Saint Monday was the practice of taking Monday off from work, or going into the shop but not working on that day. This was part of the general irregularity of working hours and weeks which appertained before the Industrial Revolution and, in some cases, long after.

There are few trades which are not described as honouring Saint Monday: shoemakers, tailors, colliers, printing workers, potters, weavers, hosiery workers, cutlers, all Cockneys. . . . Saint Monday, indeed, appears to have been honoured almost universally wherever small-scale, domestic and outwork industries existed; was generally found in the pits; and sometimes continued in manufacturing and heavy industry. It was perpetuated, in England, into the nineteenth – and, indeed into the twentieth – centuries for complex economic and social reasons (E. P. Thompson, 'Time, work-discipline and industrial capitalism', *Past and Present*, no.38, 1967, pp.75–6).

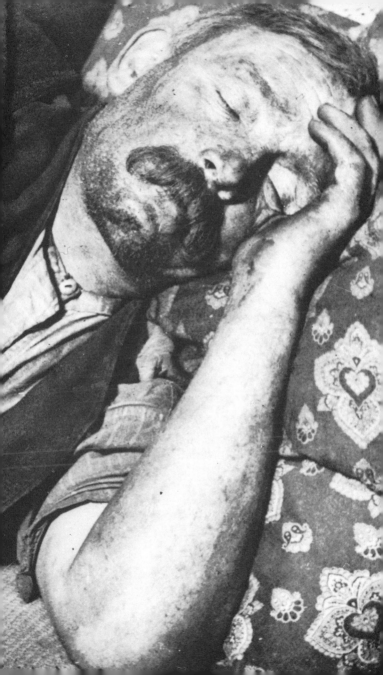

Coulter's Candy

Ally bally ally bally bee,
Sittin' on your mammy's knee,
Greetin' for anither bawbee
Tae buy mair Coulter's candy.

Ally bally ally bally bee,
When you grow up you'll go to sea,
Makin' pennies for your daddy and me
Tae buy mair Coulter's candy.

Mammy, gi'e me ma thrifty doon;
Here's auld Coulter comin' roon,
Wi'a basket on his croon,
Selling Coulter's candy.

Little Annie's greetin' tae,
Sae whit can puir wee mammy dae,
But gi'e them a penny atween them twae,
Tae buy mair Coulter's candy.

Poor wee Jeannie's lookin' affa thin,
A rickle o' banes covered ower wi' skin;
Noo she's gettin' a double chin.
Wi' sookin' Coulter's Candy.

Life is very hard, the noo,
Father's signing on the broo;
I've nae got a penny for you
To buy your Coulter's candy.

bawbee halfpenny.   *greetin'* crying.
Coulter see below.   *rickle* heap, pile.
thrifty purse.   *broo* (borough) Labour exchange.

The song was made by Robert Coltart (the Coulter mentioned),
to advertise the candy which he sold round the fairs and markets in
the border country between England and Scotland. The last verse
was probably added in the late 1920s or 30s.

Al - ly bal - ly   al - ly bal - ly bee,

Sit - tin' on your mammy's knee,   Greet-in' for a -

-nither baw-bee   Tae buy mair Coulter's can - dy.

The Skeul-Board Man

One mornin' at half-past eight, aa sais te ma bit bairn,
'On wi' yor claes an' get off to skeul, for ye knaa that aa
     want ye te lairn.'
(Boy) 'The skeul gans in at nine, an' ye knaa it's not vary
     far.'
(Man) 'Ye knaa aa like for te see ye be in time, so yor
     beuk an' yor slate's in the draaer.'

(Man) 'Get off te skeul as sharp as ever ye can.'
(Boy) 'Aa can't gan this morning.'
(Man) 'Ye cannot gan this morning. What's the matter wi'
     ye?'
(Boy) 'Aa heh the tic, man.'
(Man) 'Thor's aalways summat the matter wi' ye when ye have
     te gan te skeul. Aa divn't knaa aboot the tick. Aa cannot get
     thon mesel. If ye divn't gan aa'll be gettin' a lump o' paper, an
     at the bottom there'll be written on :

Chorus
Send yor bairns te skeul,
Learn them aal ye can.
Make scholarship yor faithful friend
An' ye'll never see the skeul-board man.

(Boy) 'Aa've been very bad for a week.' (Man) 'Wey, aa
     thowt that ye'd getten the torn;
An' if aa let ye bide at yem the day,' (Boy) 'wey, aa'll try
     te gan the morn.'
(Man) 'If ye bide at yem the day, the morn aa'll mek ye
     gan;
For ye knaa vary weel the next thing we'll get is a
     summons from the skeul-board man.'

(Man) His Uncle Jack got a summons the tother day, but the
     canny aad judge set 'im clear after he paid seven-an'-
     sixpence; an' he telt im if he didn't send his bairns te skeul,
     an' was browt te Lanchester agyain, he wad get his seven-an'-
     sixpence back – mebbe. So when he comes away he was
     singin':

(Chorus)

(Man) 'So upon that very day', (Boy) 'when aa was
  playin' at the door',
(Man) 'There was a man with a beuk in his hand, that aa
  nivver seen before;
So aa kindly invited him in, an' te taak he soon began;
An' aa soon got te knaa, by the soond of his jaa, that he
  was the skeul-board man.'

*He knocked on the door. Aa shoots, 'Come in.' In he comes.
He sais, 'Good mornin', Mister Armstrong.' Aa sais,
'Howld on, ye've getten the wrang hoose.' But he wadn't be
stopped; he sais, 'How mony children have ye got?' Aa sais,
'Man that's an impitent question!' He sais, 'Well, but
ye knaa what aa mean; aa mean how many have ye had?'
Aa sais, 'Be oot o' this, or else aa'll vaccinate ye!' So he
torned to wor Bess, an' he sais, 'What family have ye had?'
She sais, 'We had two deed, an' three alive; they'd aal
been livin', that wad be five. Are ye satisfied noo?' He nivver
said another word till he got ootside, an' he put hees fyace
against the window an' he sais:*

(Chorus)

(Man) 'Well aa axed 'im te sit doon – 'Noo aa've got ne
  time to spare;
Aa've been te skeul an' aa've looked through the beuks'' ' –
(Boy) 'An aa warrant thor's a lot not there.'
(Man) 'Ye can take ma word for the day, te the skeul ye'll
  have te gan.'
(Boy) 'Aa's sure aa will, for aa's scared to deeth when aa
  meet wi' the skeul-board man.'

*(Boy) 'He has aal the bairns in the countryside scared te
deeth, an' not only the bairns but their fathers an' their
mothers doesn't care aboot seein' 'im. He sent poor Billy
Potts a summons the tother week for their little Bob bein'
off skeul half a shift, an' fined 'im five shillings an' costs.
He's been off his meat ever since, an' that's a bad job for
him, 'cos the more he eats the more tokens he gets. Aa met
'im the tother day; aa was sorry for 'im; aal he could say was:*

(Man) 'Noo, aa want ye te gan te the skeul.' (Boy) 'Yis,
    an' aa'll aaways gan.'

(Man) 'Aa want ye te be a better scholar than me, that is,
    if ye possibly can.'

(Boy) 'If ye hadn't played the truant, when like me ye were
    young,

Ye'd ha' made better songs an' po'try tee, an' yor songs
    wad ha' been better sung.'

One mornin' at half-past eight, aa sais te ma bit bairn,

"On wi yor claes an get off te skeul for ye knaa that aa want ye te lairn. The

skeul gans in at nine, an' ye knaa it's not va-ry far." "Ye

knaa aa like for te see ye be in time so yor beuk an'yor slates in the draaer.

Send yor bairns te skeul, Learn them aal ye can. Make

scholarship yor faithful friend An' ye'll never see the skeulboard man.

school-board man see opposite.

tic involuntary movement of facial muscle.

tick credit.

getten the torn taken a turn for the worse.

Lanchester town in County Durham where court sat.

the more he eats the more tokens he gets the more he eats the more he
    earns. Tokens were discs or strips of metal or leather which indi-

cated the number of tubs of coal filled, and therefore the earnings of the fillers.

Under the Education Act of 1870, School Boards were set up which could make school attendance compulsory in their own areas. Few did this immediately, but attendance became compulsory on a national scale in 1876. Enforcement often proved very difficult.

The Beadle, vanishing figure of fun, underwent a strange rejuvenation into the School Board Man, the Attendance Officer; and how forcible and disturbing his presence was we may divine from the consideration that in Birmingham, before the Act, forty children out of a hundred, in Manchester fifty, were running loose in the streets (G. M. Young, *Victorian England*, 1936, p.116).

Despite their new title of Welfare Officer, attendance officers are still known in some areas by their old appellation, School Board Man. Many of the Board Schools may still be seen; indeed, many are still in use. There are many accounts of life in such schools (see for example, Laurie Lee, *Cider with Rosie*, and Flora Thompson, *Lark Rise to Candleford*) but few songs. *The Skeul-Board Man* was written by Tommy Armstrong (1848–1920), a miner from County Durham who was famous for his songs on topical issues.

The Captain's Apprentice

A boy to me was bound apprentice
Because his parents they were so poor;
I took him from St James's Workhouse,
All for to sail on some Spanish shore.

This boy one day he did offend me;
Well, nothing to him then did I say,
But straightway to the main shrouds I dragged him,
And I kept him there till the very next day.

His eyes and teeth did hang towards me,
With his hands and feet bound down likewise;
Then with my marlin-spike I killed him,
Because I could not bear to hear his cries.

And then my men they did reject me,
Because that I had done such wrong;
And in my cabin they close confined me
And bound me down in irons strong.

To London Town they then did bring me,
And here lay I, condemned to die;
If I had by my men been ruled,
I might have saved the poor boy's life and mine.

You sailors bold that sail down the ocean,
That have got servants, one, two and three,
I pray you never, never ill-use them,
For you plainly see it was the death of me.

St James's Workhouse at Kings Lynn.
shrouds wire ropes supporting masts.
marlin-spike pointed wooden or steel bar.

Workhouse children were frequently apprenticed as chimney sweeps
and mill-hands, though less frequently as sailors. From the age of
seven and upwards they were handed over to their masters until
they were twenty-one. They were often far away from places they
knew, and they were frequently treated with great cruelty. During

154

the nineteenth century, immense efforts were made on behalf of
child labourers, whose cause was one of the great moral issues of the
age.

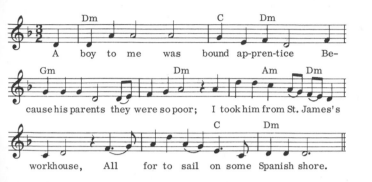

A boy to me was bound ap-pren-tice Be-
cause his parents they were so poor; I took him from St. James's
workhouse, All for to sail on some Spanish shore.

Cholera Humbug or The Arrival and Departure of the Cholera Morbus

All you that does in England dwell,
I will endeavour to please you well;
If you will listen, I will tell
About the cholera morbus.

Chorus
They tell me now it's all my eye,
No more you'll hear the people cry,
'Have mercy on me, I shall die,
I've got the cholera morbus.'

In every street as you pass by,
'Take care,' they say, 'or you will die;'
While others cry, 'It's all my eye,
There is no cholera morbus.'

If the cholera morbus should come here,
The best of clothes you then must wear;
Eat and drink, then never fear,
You'll get no cholera morbus.

They say the doctors all went round
Through every part of London Town,
But it was nowhere to be found,
It was off, the cholera morbus.

Now some do say it was a puff,
'Twas done to raise the doctors' stuff,
And there has now been near enough
About the cholera morbus.

This nation long has troubles borne,
The people have been left forlorn;
It was reported that Reform
Had caught the cholera morbus.

Now Grey and Brougham are men of wealth,
And Russell purged him well himself;
The bill is now in perfect health,
It's got no cholera morbus.

In Parliament of late did pass
A motion for a general fast;
And if it very long should last,
It may bring the cholera morbus.

Says William, we'll soon have at least
Not a fast, but a general feast;
That'll be a good receipt at least
To cure the cholera morbus.

'Twas rumoured that our king would prance
And with his queen from England dance,
And together take a trip to France,
For fear of the cholera morbus.

'I'm not afraid,' says royal Will,
'I must watch the Tories and the bill;
I'll send the villains for to dwell
Where they'll get the cholera morbus.'

It's my opinion as a man
That trade has long been at a stand;
There's thousands starving through the land
And that's the cholera morbus.

You must acknowledge what I say,
When thousands go from day to day
With scarcely food or clothing: they
May have the cholera morbus.

Pray don't be frightened, great or small,
The cholera won't come here at all;
If it does it will the Tories call,
It will, the cholera morbus.

The cholera you understand
Has took a trip right out of hand;
From here into Van Dieman's Land
Is gone the cholera morbus.

All you that does in England dwell, I will endeavour to please you well; If you will lis-ten, I will tell A-bout the choler-a mor - bus. They tell me now it's all my eye, No more you'll hear the peo-ple cry, "Have mer-cy on me, I shall die, I've got the cholera mor-bus."

cholera morbus medical name for cholera.
Reform the agitation for the reform of the franchise, which resulted in the Reform Act of 1832.
Grey . . . Brougham . . . Russell Whig ministers, who supported reform.
general fast it was suggested that a fast should take place in order to appease the divine anger which was causing cholera.
William William IV.
Van Dieman's Land Tasmania.

Trade was bad in 1829, 1831 and 1832. In October 1831, an outbreak of cholera occurred at Sunderland, and spread to London by the following January. In the same month of October, the Reform Bill was rejected by the House of Lords. It eventually became law in June 1832 after William IV had threatened to create enough new peers to force it through the House of Lords, if necessary. Such was the background to this ballad, which ingeniously interweaves the three themes of slump, cholera and reform. It probably dates from late 1831, before the arrival of cholera in London (see verse 4). The same spirit is shown in *The Cholera's Coming*, which was sung in the 1830s to the tune of *The Campbells are Coming*:

The cholera's coming, oh dear, oh dear,
The cholera's coming, oh dear!
To prevent hunger's call
A kind pest from Bengal
Has come to feed all
With the cholera, dear.

The people are starving, oh dear, oh dear,
The people are starving, oh dear.
If they don't quickly hop
To the parish soup shop
They'll go off with a pop
From the cholera, dear.

Cholera, however, was a real scourge. Apart from the outbreak in 1831–2, there were others in 1846–9 (which killed over 50,000 people), 1853–4 (over 20,000 victims) and 1865–6. Dirt and ignorance (the cholera bacillus was not discovered until 1883) made matters worse. The cholera virus was water-borne, and the spread of the disease was the direct result of impure water supplies and poor sanitation in the large industrial towns. Cholera epidemics and the panic which resulted provided the impetus for reforms, such as the Public Health Act of 1848, the first of its kind, which established local Boards of Health. Improvements in water supplies and sanitation were not quick however.

> John Bull's ear is only reached through his pocket when in a state of alarm. Cry 'Cholera!' or any other frightful conjuration and he bestirs himself. To cholera we owe the few sanitary measures now in force, but which were passed by the House in its agonies of fright. The moment, however, cholera bulletins ceased to be issued, John buttoned up his pockets tighter than ever and Parliament was dumb regarding public health (*Household Words*, 10 August 1850).

The cholera provided opportunities for typically Victorian moralizing:

> Whatever may be the cause of cholera, thus much is certain, that hitherto, almost without exception, this pestilence has been the portion of the poor, and we know that those who are in want of food and clothing most readily fall the victims of this disease. Let therefore the working man, the head of a family, reflect, that by idleness and drunkenness he not only exposes himself, but in all probability his wife and his children, to the attacks of cholera, by depriving them of the comforts and necessaries of life (from a broadsheet, *How to avoid Cholera*).

The Barnsley Anthem

We're all dahn in't cellar 'oil
Wheer t' muck slaghts on t' winders;
We've used all t' coil up
An' we're reight dahn to t' cinders.
If bum bailiffs come
They nivver will find us,
'Cos we're all dahn in t' cellar 'oil
Wheer muck slaght on t'winders.

We're all dahn in t' cellar 'oil
Wheer t' muck slaghts on t' winders;
Dooer 'oil's wide oppen as it's oft bin afooer;
Fire 'oil it's nearly reight chock full o' cinders,
An' t' waaf she's art callin' wi' t' neerbur next dooer,
'Cos we're all dahn in t' cellar 'oil
Wheer t' muck slaghts on t' winders.

We're all dahn in t' cellar 'oil
Wheer t' muck slaghts on t' winders;
T' dooer 'oil's blocked up wi' ashes and cinders.
When t' chap comes for t' rent
Will 'e be able to find us?
Ma comes wi' t' rollin' pin,
Pa wi' t' belinders,
When we're all dahn in t'cellar 'oil
Wheer muck slaghts on t'winders.

Pronunciation
find us rhymes with *cinders*.
callin' first syllable rhymes with pal.

'oil hole.
slaghts dashes.
coil coal.
bum bailiffs court officers who were usually employed to seize
    furniture and goods, which were sold to defray debts.
belinders bellows.
callin' gossiping.

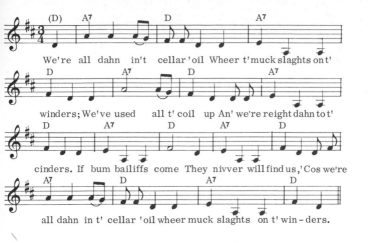

We're all dahn in't cellar 'oil Wheer t'muck slaghts on t' winders; We've used all t' coil up An' we're reight dahn to t' cinders. If bum bailiffs come They nivver will find us, 'Cos we're all dahn in t' cellar 'oil wheer muck slaghts on t' win‑ders.

This is a curious little song, still current in the Barnsley area; there are Lancashire versions too. With the immense growth of the towns during the nineteenth century, housing was an enormous social problem, as it is for that matter in the twentieth.

The Lasses' Resolution to Follow the Fashion

Good people, come listen awhile, now,
A sketch of the times I lay down,
Concerning the rigs and the fashions
That are now carried on in each town;
The lasses they have such a spirit,
They will imitate the new pride,
With bustles to wear on their hips, boys,
To make them look buxom beside.

They have a spring bow in their stays, now,
It is the old truth I do tell,
With their handkerchieves up to their chin, boys,
Which makes them all cut such a swell;
Their high chimney caps they do wear, boys,
Likewise hats with straw bound beside:
You scarce can see their pretty faces,
They are so much covered with pride.

Stuff slippers and white cotton stockings,
These lasses they mostly do wear,
With a dimity corduroy petticoat,
It is whiter than snow I declare;
With a fringe or a flounce round the bottom
These lasses they will have beside,
And a sash, for to go round their middle
And to tie up in bunches behind.

As well as the farmers' daughters
They'll powder and frizzle their hair,
And when they review in a market,
They will stare like a wolf or a bear;
With the skirts of their gowns to their armpits,
So coddy they look and so square:
They are nothing but legs, thighs and hips, boys,
And heads without bodies appear.

The servant girls follow the fashions

As well as the best in the place;
They'll dress up their heads like an owl, boys,
And will think it no shame or disgrace.
They will bind up their heads with fine ribbands,
And a large bag of hair hangs behind;
And when they do walk through the streets, boys,
No peacock can touch them for pride.

Good people, come listen awhile, now, A sketch of the times I lay down, Concerning the rigs and the fashions That are now carried on in each town; The lasses they have such a spirit, They will imitate the new pride, With bustles to wear on their hips, boys, To make them look buxom besides.

coddy tiny.

From the seventeenth to the nineteenth centuries, women's fashions of hair and costume were frequently satirized in broadside ballads. Bloomers, for example, attracted a good deal of attention, when they appeared in the late nineteenth century. Bustles succeeded the crinoline during the late 1860s. Apart from its rather gentle comments on bustles and other items of ladies' costume, this ballad is interesting because of its reference to servant girls following the fashion. Not only servant girls, but all the working classes tried to follow fashion in England, a practice which often amazed foreigners.

163

The Tea-Drinking Wives

A man that is born a husband to be,
He comes to hard fortune in every degree:
If he marries a scold, she'll plague him of his life;
If he happens to meet with a tea-drinking wife,
(If she loves tea with gin, and likewise good ale)
His nose will look thin and his cheeks very pale.

If he marries a whore, a cuckold he'll be,
So he's born to hard fortune in every degree,
For women's deceit is not hard to believe,
Since Adam's downfall by our old mother Eve.
So for to live single it's best, I declare,
Than marry a woman who drinks gin, tea and ale.

To marry a jealous one causes much strife,
So a poor man is blest that has got a good wife
That will mind her own business and sit down to spin
And do her endeavour his favour to win.
But some they are idle, the scales they are turned,
The kettle they mind but the wheel may be burned.

What a fashion it is they have brought up of late:
Over tea they will blother, they'll lie and they'll prate;
The wives of the poor they have got the best hands,
They drink tea with those that have houses and land,
For tea is their favourite and for it they'll thirst:
Their bellies they fill but their children may trust.

The ninepenny sugar is so very brown
That none but tenpenny with them will go down;
Their poor husband's labour ne'er disturbeth their brain,
Though put to their shifts this tea to maintain.
It has ruined England, it plain doth appear,
And makes country people sell butter so dear.

Tea's a poor man's downfall and woman's favourite;
These lines they are true and no one can deny it.
A man that is married, let him be content,
Because it's a folly for him to repent.

So we'll cheer up our hearts with a full flowing bowl,
And drink a good health to each married soul.

A man that is born a husband to be, He comes to hard for-tune in ev-ery de-gree: If he marries a scold she'll plague him of his life; If he happens to meet with a tea-drink-ing wife, (If she loves tea with gin, and likewise good ale) His nose will look thin and his cheeks very pale.

wheel spinning wheel.
blother to idly chatter.

Tea, introduced into England in the seventeenth century, became popular with the well-to-do during the eighteenth. Dr Johnson's addiction is well-known. Towards the end of the century, the poor began to drink the beverage, and were attacked for their extravagance in doing so. By the middle of the nineteenth century, tea was the drink of all classes, and had ceased to be worthy of comment.

This ballad dates from the earlier part of the century, when tea was still making its way. (The prices of sugar mentioned indicate a period between 1825 and 1830.) It is one of several about tea-drinking.

A Drop of Good Beer

Come one and all, both great and small,
With voices loud and clear,
And let us sing bless Billy the King,
Who bated the tax upon beer.

Chorus
For I likes a drop of good beer,
I likes a drop of good beer;
And damn his eyes who ever tries
To rob a poor man of his beer.

Let ministers shape the duty on Cape
And cause port wine to be dear,
So that they keep the bread and meat cheap
And gi'e us a drop of good beer.

In drinking rum the maggots will come
And bald pates will appear.
I never goes out but I carries about
My little pint noggin of beer.

My wife and I feel always dry
At market on Saturday night.
Then, a noggin of beer, I never did fear,
For my wife always says that it's right.

In harvest field there's nothing can yield
The labouring man such good cheer,
To reap and sow and make the malt grow,
As to give him a skinful of beer.

The farmer's board will plenty afford,
Let it come from far and from near;
At harvest time the jug will foam
If he gives his men plenty of beer.

Now long may Queen Victoria reign
And be to her subjects most dear.
Wherever she goes, we'll wallop her foes,
Only give us a skinful of beer.

Billy the King William IV.
bated reduced.

The Beerhouse Act of 1830 commonly called at the time the three Bs – Billy's Beer Bill – 'in reaction against the severity of earlier licensing policy . . . permitted anyone to sell beer on payment of a two-guinea excise fee: the result was that ordinary houses, petty chandlers' shops and mere country shacks were rapidly turned into beer houses. In Liverpool alone, fifty new beer-shops opened every day for several weeks, and over the whole country 45,000 were established within eight years. Goulborn, the Chancellor of the Exchequer, had said in moving the bill, "This measure . . . would work well. It would conduce at once to the comfort of the people in affording them cheap and ready accommodation; to their health in procuring them a better and more wholesome beverage"' (Burnett, *Plenty and Want*, p.113).

Despite the act, the consumption of beer continued to fall, until 1850. From that date it increased until it reached 34·4 gallons per head per year, in 1876, the highest figure in the century.

A Word of Advice

Come all sporting husbands, wherever you be,
In high life or low life, of every degree;
A word of advice now I am going to pen,
It's good for all sorts and conditions of men.

Chorus
Down derry down, down derry down,
Down derry down, derry down, derry down.

Some men when they're married are spending their lives
In drinking and gaming and beating their wives;
But when that the day of their bloom it is past,
It only brings sorrow and shame at the last.

To the ale-house they go without dread or fear
With a pipe and a pot of good ale or strong beer;
Though the landlord will serve you and come at your call,
When your money's all gone, he'll laugh at your downfall.

With the money you take him, he's filling his bags,
While your own wife and children are clothed all in rags;
The best roast and boiled to his table is brought
While your children and wife eat potatoes and salt.

There's the landladies also, like dolls at a fair,
With silk gown and lace cap are stuck in the bar;
Well surely it's shameful such things should be said,
While your wife has scarcely a cap to her head.

Now all the week long while you're spending your money,
They'll caress you with words that are sweeter than honey;
But when for to please them you have spent it all,
You'll find that their honey's as bitter as gall.

Strong ale at the first it was sent for our good,
To strengthen our bodies and nourish our blood;
But drink to excess, why, it must be confessed,
It oftentimes makes a man worse than a beast.

So all rakish husbands who're given to roam,
I'd have you think better for the time that's to come;
Look well to yourself, to your children and wife,
Then you may live happy the rest of your life.

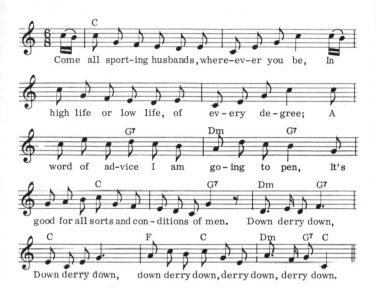

Come all sporting husbands, where-ev-er you be, In high life or low life, of ev-ery de-gree; A word of ad-vice I am go-ing to pen, It's good for all sorts and con-ditions of men. Down derry down, Down derry down, down derry down, derry down, derry down.

Within three years of the passing of the Beer Act (see previous song), the House of Commons had set up a Select Committee to investigate ways of diminishing 'the prevailing vice of drunkenness among the working classes', but it was not until the 1870s that the sales of drink were properly regulated. Even then, drunkenness continued to be a major problem in the working class for at least the rest of the century, despite strenuous campaigns by various temperance societies. The Band of Hope, the most famous of them all, was still arranging lectures for primary school children in the 1930s, as I know from personal recollection.

Part of the propaganda for temperance was broadside ballads, often melodramatic and lachrymose in tone, with titles like *The Drunkard's Child* and *The Drunkard's Farewell*. The present ballad is sensible and moderate and echoes the sentiments of many generations of working-class wives.

London Adulterations
or, Rogues in Grain, Tea, Coffee, Milk, Beer, Bread, Snuff, Mutton, Pork, Gin, Butter, etc.

Here tradesmen, 'tis plain, at no roguery stop,
They adulterate everything they've in their shop;
You must buy what they sell, and they'll sell what they
    please,
And they would, if they could, sell the moon for green
    cheese.

Chorus
Sing tantararara, rogues all, rogues all,
Sing tantararara, rogues all.

Now it is well known imitation's the rage:
Everything's imitated in this rare old age;
There's tea, coffee, beer, butter, gin, milk, in brief,
No doubt they'll soon imitate mutton and beef.

The grocer sells ash leaves and sloe leaves for tea,
Tinged with Dutch pink and verdigris, just like bohea;
What sloe poison means Slomon now has found out;
We shall all to a T soon be poisoned, no doubt.

Some grocers for pepper sell trash called PD;
Burnt horse beans for coffee – how can such things be?
I really do think those who make such a slip
And treat us like horses, deserve a horse-whip.

The milkman although he is honest, he vows,
Milks his pump night and morn quite as oft as his cows;
Claps plenty of chalk in your score – what a bilk –
And, egad, claps you plenty of chalk in your milk.

The baker will swear all his bread's made of flour,
But just mention alum, you'll make him turn sour;
His ground bones and pebbles turn men skin and bone:
We ask him for bread and he gives us a stone.

The butcher puffs up his tough mutton like lamb,
And oft for South Down sells an old mountain ram;
Bleeds poor worn-out cows to pass off for white veal,
And richly deserves to die by his own steel.

A slippery rogue is the cheesemonger, zounds,
Who with kitchen stuff oft his butter compounds;
His fresh eggs are laid o'er the water, we know,
For which, faith, he over the water should go.

The brewer's a chemist, and that is quite clear,
We soon find no hops have hopped into his beer;
'Stead of malt he from drugs brews his porter and swipes:
No wonder so oft that we all get the gripes.

The tobacconist smokes us with short-cut of weeds,
And finds his returns of such trash still succeeds;
With snuff of ground glass and of dust we are gulled:
For serving our nose so, his nose should be pulled.

The wine merchant, that we abroad may not roam,
With sloe juice and brandy makes port up at home;
Distillers their gin have with vitriol filled:
'Tis clear they're in roguery double distilled.

Thus we rogues have in grain and in tea, too, that's clear;
Don't think I suppose we have any rogues here.
The company present's excepted, you know,
Here's wishing all rogues their deserts they must have.

Dutch pink a colouring.
bohea a kind of tea.
Slomon probably one of the doctors who helped to reveal adulteration.
PD pepper dust.
over the water should go should be transported to a penal colony in
  Australia or Tasmania.
porter black beer.
swipes weak beer.

The problem of the purity of food stuffs is still with us, but at least
in recent times there have been few deliberate attempts to pass off
substitutes fraudulently as the real thing. In *Plenty and Want*, John
Burnett's social history of diet in England from 1815 to the present,

we are told that: 'Adulteration of food prevailed in the first half of the nineteenth century to an unprecedented and unsupposed extent, and had far-reaching social, economic and medical consequences.' There were complaints of adulteration in the late eighteenth century, but the issue was brought firmly forward by Frederick Accum's publication in 1820 of his *Treatise on Adulterations of Food and Culinary Poisons*. This and subsequent research revealed that: inferior bread was whitened with alum and contained pulverized gypsum, whiting and burnt bones; beer and porter contained various poisons to give strength, including sulphuric acid; ash, sloe and elder leaves were used in (or instead of) tea, while green tea was coloured with 'Dutch pink and poisonous verdigris to impart the fine green bloom'; pepper was 'adulterated with the sweepings of the warehouse floors – commodities known in the trade as "PD" (pepper dust) or, more inferior still, "DPD" (dust of pepper dust)'. The first Adulteration of Foods Act was not passed until 1860, and further acts were needed before the problems were contained. Thus, for much of the century, adulteration was a recurring issue. The present ballad dates from fairly early in the century (c.1825?).

Here tradesmen, 'tis plain, at no ro-guer-y stop, They a-
-dul-ter-ate ev-ery-thing they've in their shop; You must
buy what they sell, and they'll sell what they please, And they
would, if they could, sell the moon for green cheese. Sing
tan-ta-ra-ra-ra, rogues all, rogues all, Sing
tan-ta-ra-ra-ra, rogues all. ——

As late as 1854–5 a Select Committee of the House of Commons was inquiring into 'the Adulteration of Food, Drinks, and Drugs'. A doctor, in evidence, gave a formidable list:

> Bread is adulterated with mashed potatoes, alum, 'hards, and sometimes, though rarely, with sulphate of copper. Butter, with water. Bottled fruits and vegetables with certain salts of copper. Coloured confectionery, with East India arrowroot, wheat and potato flour, hydrated sulphate of lime; and it is coloured with cochineal, lake, indigo, Prussian blue, Antwerp blue, artificial ultramarine, carbonate of copper, carbonate of lead or white lead, red lead, vermilion, and chrome yellows, etc. . . . Coffee, with chicory, roasted wheat, rye and potato flours, roasted beans, mangel-wurzel, and a substance resembling acorns (E. R. Pike, *Human Documents of the Victorian Golden Age*, p.295).

The catalogue continued with cocoa and chocolate, custard powder, flour, gin, rum, lard, mustard, milk, marmalade, oatmeal, porter and stout, pickles, potted meats and fish, preserves, pepper, tea, tobacco and vinegar.

A Chapter of Cheats
or The Roguery of Every Trade

Attend you blades of London and listen unto me,
While I sing to you a ditty of the tradesmen's roguery;
And when you hear my ditty through you cannot fail to
    laugh,
For you lately have been bothered with a little bit of chaff.

Chorus
And they're all a-cheating, cheat, cheat, cheating,
In country and in town, in country and in town.

Now the first it is a lawyer, to bother and to jaw,
He knows well how to cheat you with a little bit of law;
And the next it is a doctor, to handle you he's rough,
He will charge you half-a-crown for six pennyworth of stuff.

The pawnbroker comes next with a ticket in his hand,
To cheat you like the devil for the interest is his plan;
The grocer sands his sugar and he sells sloe leaves for tea,
And then there's the dusty miller, where's a bigger rogue
    than he?

The next it is the butcher, all with his greasy hat,
And underneath his scale is stuck a dirty lump of fat;
Well, then there comes the baker with his alum bread and
    starch,
In the dishes hot potatoes he will not forget to search.

The cobbler mends your boots and shoes, in cold and
    rainy weather;
He will mend the sole and upper too, and all with rotten
    leather;
Now the tailor as you all do know is always full of sloth:
He will think no sin to cabbage up a yard and more of cloth.

Now the barber when he shaves you will cut you in the
    chin;
The chandler's shop will cheat you and will think it not a
    sin;

And rotten wood the wheelwright he will put into a wheel;
The blacksmith he will sell you iron and swear that it is
steel.

The hatter sells his hats and he calls them waterproof;
They are plastered up with horse-dung, it is nothing but
the truth;
The carpenter will hammer in your table broken nails;
And I know the police will very quickly pop you into jail.

The linen draper will mark up things – he knows it makes
you grin,
And he is sure enough to cheat you when his shop you
enter in;
The cheesemonger will cut his cheese, his butter and his
lard,
And cheat you with his bacon – oh, the times are very hard.

The costermonger's next, with his measures but half full;
The tater merchant washes his potatoes in a pool;
The tallow chandler cheats you until he makes you grin;
The porkman he does stuff his sausages with skin.

And there's the hackney coachman will cheat you like the
devil,
And a pretty girl will drain your money, and all the time
be civil;
Old iron shops buy stolen goods, it's true I do declare;
If a chimney sweep comes to your house he'll steal away
your ware.

Bricklayers, weavers, maltsters, will cheat you in a bother;
If a glazier mends one pane of glass he's sure to break
another;
The undertaker'll cheat you, believe me it is so;
If the body-snatchers get you, to the doctor's off you go.

Stay-stitchers, bonnet-makers, they look so very shy,
The bill-stickers sell their paper and swear it is a lie;
The coal merchants in a sack of coals will use you very
rough;
The tobacconist will sell you fine sand instead of snuff.

The next is the gin-shop, how they will take you in,

There's such a load of vitriol in a half a pint of gin;
The landlord for rent, too often he will call,
And he that gathers taxes is the greatest rogue of all.

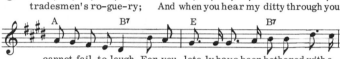

to cabbage normally, to take as a perquisite scraps of cloth left over after garments had been made; the assumption here is that unwarrantably large pieces are taken.

body-snatchers those who stole bodies from cemeteries in order to sell them to doctors for dissection; sometimes called burkers, after William Burke (1792–1829), who was hanged for murdering people in order to sell their bodies. He is, of course, commemorated in song:

To help the folk at medical school
Word is spread around.
A body nae mair than ten days' auld
Will bring in fourteen pund.
It's a terrible thing, but true to say,

In this age of grace,
A man's worth muckle when alive
But plenty when he's deid.

Chorus
An it's doon the close and up the stair,
A but and ben with Burke and Hare.
Burke's the butcher an Hare's the thief
And Knox is the man that buys the beef.

Our ballad moves on from cheating by adulterating food to cheating in general. It seems that the public for much of the nineteenth century was prey to a great variety of sharpers, cheats and confidence men.

How Five and Twenty Shillings were Expended in a Week

It's of a tradesman and his wife I heard the other day,
And they kicked up a glorious row – they live across the
    way.
The husband proved himself a fool when his money was
    all spent;
He called upon his wife, my boys, to know which way it
    went.

Chorus
She reckoned up and showed him, she showed him quite
    complete,
How five and twenty shillings were expended in a week.

There's two and threepence for house rent – attend to me,
    she said;
Four shillings always goes for meat and three and
    ninepence bread;
To wash your nasty, dirty shirt there's sixpence halfpenny
    soap;
There's one and eightpence goes for coals and tenpence
    wood and coke.

Now fourpence goes for milk and cream and one and
    twopence, malt;
There's threepence goes for vinegar and twopence
    halfpenny, salt;
A penny goes for mustard; three halfpence goes for thread;
You gave me threepence the other night for half a baked
    sheep's head.

Red herrings every morning's fivepence farthing in a week;
Sometimes you send me out for fish – you say you can't
    eat meat.
Last Monday night when you got drunk there was
    ninepence went for capers;

You'd a penny box of congreves and a halfpenny baked
    potato.

A penny goes for pepper, too, as you must understand;
Twopence halfpenny soda, starch and blue, and a
    farthing's worth of sand;
Fourpence halfpenny goes for candles; three farthings goes
    for matches,
And a penn'orth o' pieces o' corduroy you had to mend
    your breeches.

A shilling potatoes, herbs and greens; tenpence butter, now
    you see,
And sixpence coffee, eightpence sugar, and one and
    fourpence tea.
There's twopence goes for this thing and a penny for that
    and t'other;
Last night you broke the chamber pot and I had to buy
    another.

There's eightpence for tobacco and seven farthings swipes;
Threepence halfpenny goes for snuff and twopence
    halfpenny, tripe.
A penny you owed for shoe strings, down at the cobbler's
    shop;
You know last Sunday morning you'd a bottle of ginger
    pop.

Now twopence goes for blacking and eightpence halfpenny,
    cheese;
Three farthing rushlight every night to watch the bugs and
    fleas.
It cost me threepence to mend your coat when you tore it
    on a nail,
And twopence halfpenny calico to mend your old shirt tail.

'Well now,' he said, 'I've reckoned up and find without a
    doubt,
One pound four and sevenpence halfpenny exactly you've
    laid out.'
She said, 'To call me to account you never should begin;
With the fourpence halfpenny that was left I'd a quartern
    of gin.'

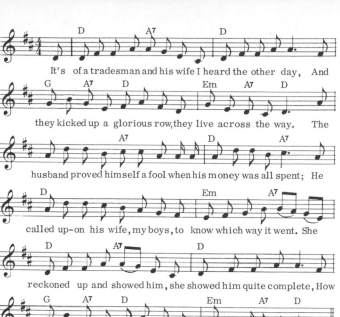

It's of a tradesman and his wife I heard the other day, And they kicked up a glorious row, they live across the way. The husband proved himself a fool when his money was all spent; He called up-on his wife, my boys, to know which way it went. She reckoned up and showed him, she showed him quite complete, How five and twenty shillings were ex-pen-ded in a week.

capers scented tea.

congreves a friction match (after its inventor, Sir W. Congreve).

swipes weak beer.

shoe strings shoe laces.

rushlight thin candle with a rush wick, made by dipping dried rushes in tallow.

quartern a quarter.

'The wage of an urban semi-skilled worker in regular employment in mid-century was around 15s. to £1 a week. . . . The "comfort line" came at something over £1 a week, depending on the size of family' (John Burnett, *A History of the Cost of Living*, 1969, p.263). The

ballad therefore probably gives the budget of a skilled worker, whose earnings (with the addition, possibly, of those of his wife and children) totalled at least thirty shillings a week. (The items listed add up not to 25s., but to 27s., and several purchases are mentioned without prices being given.)

The ballad appears to have been enormously popular. It was issued by at least four different London printers and also by others in provincial centres, including Leeds, Nottingham, Birmingham, Bristol, Preston and Manchester. There are numerous, earlier versions in which the budgets total 15s., 16s., 18s., £1.1s. and £1.2s., so apparently the ballad was updated periodically to keep abreast of the rising cost of living.

Belly and Back

A story I'm going to tell ye,
Attend and you'll hear in a crack;
It's about a man's hungry belly
Conversing along with his back.

Says the belly, 'Here, I have been fasting
For twenty-four hours or more;
And if suchlike fun's to be lasting,
Mr Death will soon open his door.'

Says the back, 'You your appetite dote on,
You're satisfied never, I think;
Don't you see that I've got a new coat on:
You can't expect victuals and drink.

'I must keep a genteel appearance,
It's useless your being so hot;
For the pocket has had such a clearance,
There's nothing for you in the pot.'

Says the belly, 'Why you have no feeling,
While at your new coat people stare,
My rumblings are loudly revealing,
There's nothing within me but air.

'You may set it down really as done, sir,
If I don't soon have boiled meat or roast,
Then both of us, sure as a gun, sir,
Must certainly give up the ghost.'

The back thought that there was no need on 't,
Cared not what the belly did say;
The effects of his taking no heed on 't
Was both of them went to decay.

Mr Death's name was soon plainly wrote on,
He nailed 'em without any rout;
Now instead of a fine flashy coat on,
They're wrapped in a wooden surtout.

The drift of my story I'll tell you,
It's plain as white is from black:
If you do not take care of your belly,
You soon will be laid on your back.

So enjoy yourselves in moderation,
Live neither too low or too high;
And then, by a clear calculation,
You'll all of you live till you die.

A story I'm going to tell ye, Attend and you'll hear in a crack; It's a-

-bout a man's hun-gry bel-ly con-ver-sing along with his back.

rout marching orders.
wooden surtout wooden overcoat (coffin).

Tally Man

It's of a buxom tally man who dwells in our town,
And every day throughout the week he always goes his
    rounds.
Last week he called on mistress Bounce and began to show
    his airs,
So she whopped him with the rolling pin and kicked him
    down the stairs.

Chorus
Little Billy out aloud does bawl, and so do Kit and Sam:
'Oh, mother, mother, shut the door, here comes the tally
    man.'

(Spoken) *'Good morning, Mrs Bounce.'*
*'Good morning, Mr Cheatem. What is your pleasure this morn-
ing?'*
*'Why, I hope you have got some money for me; I have had no
money from you for the last three weeks.'*
*'My husband declares that I sha'n't pay you a farthing for them
infernal blankets you sold me for 7s. 6d.; they are full of moth
holes, and not worth fourpence apiece.'*
'Then I shall summon you, Mrs Bounce, so here goes.'

Now it would make you laugh to see women hide away
    complete,
When'er they hear the tally man is coming down the
    street;
Some run into a neighbour's house, so nimble it appears,
While others in the coal-hole get, or underneath the stairs.

(Spoken) *'Well, my little boy, is your mother at home?'*
'No, sir, my mother has just popped out.'
'Where is she gone to?'
'Why, to the gin shop, I suppose.'
'Has she left any money for me?'
*'I don't think she has left any money for anybody; but who are
you, sir?'*
'Who am I? Why, I am the tally man.'

'Oh, if you are Mr Cheatem, the tally man, you had better cut your stick, for my father has whopped my mother with the broom-stick, for buying your rotten twopenny halfpenny calico – and mother says that you are an infernal old rogue, and I wouldn't like to stand in your shoes if father was to catch you.'

There's scarce a street in our town, let it be rich or poor,
But you may see a tally man a-knocking at the door;
It is well known to any one that's got a grain of sense,
They'll make you pay a crown for something not worth
    eighteen pence.

(Spoken) 'Dear me, Mrs Ginger, what a rumpus there is over the way at Mr Nipper's; do you know what it's all about?'
'Why, Mr Nipper, you must know, has been summoned by Mr Swindle, the tally man, for one pound nineteen and eleven pence for goods taken upon the tally by Mrs Nipper; the two Miss Nippers had a new gown each, a pair of fine stockings, a bustle, some lace caps, and some furbelows.'
'Well, I wondered, do you know, Mrs Ginger, how the devil the Nippers were so flashy. I thought they must have got their things upon the tally, or some other way, I couldn't tell how; but there it is, you see.'
'Well, I gets nothing on the tally but a little tea, and that's all sloe leaves; but the tally men are the ruination of all persons, you may depend upon it; for I know perfectly well in one street that there is many a woman that takes a tremendous lot of things unknown to their husbands, who never find it out until they are summoned to pay a pound for articles not worth five shillings.'

'Pray, Mrs Ginger, are you at home,' bawls out the tally
    man.
'No, Mr Swindle, I am not, and you must understand:
Call when you will, my husband swears, you shall not have
    a mag;
Since you've turned rogue, you took me in, your things
    aren't worth a gag.'

(Spoken) 'Is your mother at home, my little girl?'
'No, sir.'
'Where is she?'
'How should I know?'

'Why, I saw her looking out at the window, and I saw her peeping out at the door, just now; and if I am not mistaken she is gone to her uncle's to spout a shawl for a shilling that she got upon the tally for 18s. 6d. Is your father at home?'

'No. My father is gone a-hopping, and he wanted to get a donkey on the tally, but mother couldn't tell where to find the tally man.'

'Oh, he did, did he?'

'Yes, he did indeed.'

'Where is your sister?'

'In her skin, I suppose.'

'Well, my little girl, you're keen, lass.'

'Ah, as my mother says, half as keen as a tally man but not so big as a rogue. And I can assure you, somebody in a family need be a little sharp, for if every one was so silly as my mother, we should be hunted to death by tally men who would sell us their rubbish and expect elevenpence halfpenny profit out of a shilling.'

Now every day throughout the week to visit rich and poor,
You may behold the tally man a-creeping near the door.
The children will bawl out aloud, 'Mister tally man, I say;
Mother's in the station-house and father's run away.'
(Chorus)

Tally man
    an accommodating salesman who takes payment by instalments to suit the convenience of the purchaser, but who is anything but accommodating when payments are irregular. Tallymen are the cause of much misfortune to the working classes, from their high and exorbitant rates, and the temptations they offer to weak-minded women, who purchase in haste and repent at leisure (J. C. Hotten, *Slang Dictionary*, 1859, 1887 and 1972).
cut your stick go away.
furbelows flounces.
mag halfpenny.
gag lie.
uncle's the pawnshop.
to spout to pawn.
a-hopping picking hops.

The dangers and problems of hire purchase are still with us, but with increased affluence they have assumed rather less importance than they do here. The twin ogres, pawnbroker and tally man

192

remained very much a reality for working class people up to the 1930s.

Mayhew has an interesting section on 'the tally packman' (in *Mayhew's London*, 1969, a selection from *London Labour and the London Poor*, edited by Peter Quennell).

Wife for Sale

Pay heed to my ditty, ye frolicsome folk,
I'll tell you a story, a comical joke;
It's a positive fact that I'm going to unfold,
Concerning a woman by auction was sold.

There was a ship carpenter lived close to here,
Who was not as fond of his wife as his beer;
He was hard up for brass, to be sure, all his life,
And so for ten shillings he auctioned his wife.

This husband and wife they could never agree,
Because he was fond of going out on the spree;
They settled the matter without more delay,
And the day of the auction they took her away.

They sent round the bellman announcing the sale
Unto the hay market and that without fail;
The auctioneer struck with his hammer so smart,
While the carpenter's wife stood up in the cart.

Now she was put up without grumble or frown.
The first was a tailor to bid half a crown,
Who began, 'I will make her a lady so spruce,
For I'll fatten her well on cabbage and goose.'

'Five and sixpence three-farthings,' a butcher he said;
'Six and ten,' said a barber, with his curly head;
Then up jumps a cobbler and with a loud bawl,
Nine shillings bid for her, bustle and all.

'Just look at her beauty, her shape and her size;
She's mighty good-tempered and sober likewise;'
'Go on,' says a sailor, 'she's one out of four,
Ten shillings bid for her but not a screw more.'

'Thank you, sir, thank you,' says the bold auctioneer,
'She's going at ten; is there nobody here
To bid any more? Isn't this a sad job?
She's going, she's going, she's going – at ten bob.'

The hammer came down, concluding the sale;
Poor Tarry paid down the brass on the nail.
He shook hands with Betsy and gave her a smack.
And took her away straight home on his back.

The people all relished the joke, it appears;
They gave the young sailor three hearty good cheers.
He never called 'Stop' with his darling so sweet
Till he landed with Betsy right on his own street.

They sent for the piper and fiddler to play,
And they danced and they sang until it was day.
When Jack told the company 'twas time for to go,
The piper and fiddler played *Rosin the bow*.

Oh, Betsy is happy at home in the croft,
Jack boxes the compass and goes up aloft;
While roving the ocean, regardless of life,
He sings as he thinks of his ten-shilling wife.

And long may they flourish and prosper through life,
For Jack was well pleased with his ten-shilling wife.*

*Repeat the second half of the tune for these lines

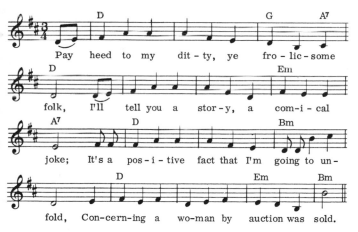

cabbage and goose (pun) cabbage was scraps of cloth accruing to tailors (see note on p.181) and a goose was a pressing iron with an S-shaped handle.

six and ten six shillings and ten pence.

Tarry the sailor.

box the compass repeat the thirty-two points of the compass.

There is a wife-selling scene in Hardy's *Mayor of Casterbridge*, but it does not give a very authentic picture of the practice. The sale of wives went on in England until at least the late nineteenth century. The sale was usually announced or advertised and the woman was ceremonially led into the market with a halter round her neck. This was not the degrading ordeal which it appears, however. Normally the marriage had broken down, the sale was by common consent, and the purchaser selected in advance. Often the three parties repaired to a public house to celebrate together afterwards, and to spend the purchase price. Divorce was only available by a special act of Parliament, which was enormously expensive, until 1857. In that year the Matrimonial Causes Act in effect brought in divorce for the middle classes (the proceedings were still expensive), but only in the case of adultery by the wife or adultery aggravated by cruelty or desertion in the case of the husband. The custom of wife selling provided a form of divorce for ordinary people.

Records of the sale of wives can be found in local newspapers, memoirs and histories, and sometimes in the memories of people:

Well now, I'll tell you how this wife selling came about. You see in the days a hundred and fifty years ago, for the poor man there was no such thing as divorce, so it became common law that he could sell his wife. Then he could take another and, although he would be committing bigamy if he married her, as regards the population and his comrades and all that, it was quite accepted that he could take another woman. Now that was the reason that you read about where a wife would be sold for sixpence. The reason was that the man who was going to have her was already selected and sixpence was merely the nominal fee.

Now in 1853 my grand-dad, he saw a woman sold at Tipton [Staffs.] and she was sold for sixpence and the bids went up by a halfpenny. And she was a poor little slip of a girl who'd been half starved. She was only twenty years of age and the chap who bought her he took her home and he said, 'I'll soon put some flesh on 'er bones. I'll feed 'er on fat baacon.' And he did. Now she became a comely little woman and had several children and I can just remember her. She was an old woman when I was a boy. Now I can tell you this, that three of her children became school teachers (Tom Langley, then aged sixty-three, interviewed by Roy Palmer, 17 April 1970).

4

Time to Remember the Poor

The Rambling Comber

You combers all, both great and small,
Come listen to my ditty,
For it is ye and only ye
Regard my fall with pity.
For I can write, read, dance or fight,
Indeed it's all my honour.
My failing is I drink strong beer,
For I'm a rambling comber.

Now on the tramp I'm forced to scamp;
My shoes are all a-tatter.
My hose unbound are to the ground;
I seldom wear a garter.
I have a coat scarce worth a groat,
I sadly want another;
But it's, oh, my dear, I love strong beer,
I am a rambling comber.

I have no watch, I have a patch
On each side of my breeches.
My hat is torn, my wig is worn,
My health is all my riches.
Oh, would I had some giggling lass
My coat all for to border
With straps and bows; I would hold those,
I'd hold them all in order.

A tailor's bill I seldom fill,
I never do take measure;
I make no debt that doth me let
In taking of my pleasure,
Nor ever will, till I grow old,
Then I must give it over.
Oh, then old age will me engage
For being a rambling comber.

A pitcher-boy I will employ
While I have cash or credit.
I'll ramp and roar and call for score,

And pay them when I have it.
For this is always in my mind,
Let me be drunk or sober,
A bowl of punch my thirst to quench.
And a quart of old October.

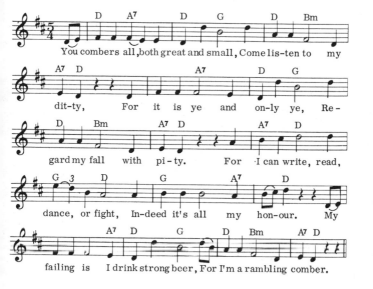

You combers all, both great and small, Come lis-ten to my dit-ty, For it is ye and on-ly ye, Re-gard my fall with pi-ty. For I can write, read, dance, or fight, In-deed it's all my hon-our. My failing is I drink strong beer, For I'm a rambling comber.

comber wool-comber.
groat fourpence.
let hinder.
October presumably, a sort of beer.

The Industrial Revolution resulted in greater mobility in the working population than ever before. Yet, paradoxically, it was the beginning of the end for many of the old itinerant tradesmen. Nevertheless, songs about supposedly free and unfettered people, like tinkers and beggars, soldiers and sailors, and even miners (see p. 130) continued to be popular. No doubt the factory worker could derive pleasure from hearing about men who were their own masters, footloose and fancy free.

The Miseries of the Framework Knitters

Ye kind-hearted souls, pray attend to our song,
And hear this true story which shall not be long;
Framework knitters of Sutton, how ill they are used,
And by the bag-masters how sorely abused.

Chorus
Derry down, down, down derry down.

They've bated the wages so low for our work
That to gain half maintainence we slave like a Turk;
When we ask for our money comes paper and string,
Dear beef and bad mutton or some suchlike thing.

Bad weights and bad measures are frequently used –
Oppressive extortion – thus sorely abused;
Insulted and robbed, too – we mention no names –
But pluck up our spirits and bowl in their frames.

Good people, oh pity our terrible case,
Pray take no offence though we visit this place;
We crave your assistance and pray for our foes,
Oh may they find mercy when this life we lose.

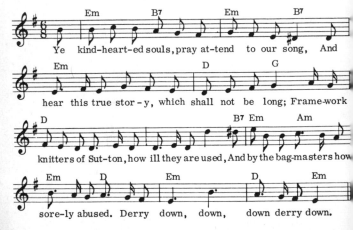

framework knitter person who worked a foot-driven stocking frame.
Sutton in Nottinghamshire.
bag-masters middlemen who supplied materials to the knitters and
   collected the finished work.
bated reduced.

Like the hand-loom weavers, the framework knitters were among
the casualties of the Industrial Revolution, though not without
protest: the Luddite outbreaks in the Midlands in 1811–12 were the
work of framework knitters (cf. song on p.289). This ballad appears
to have been a fund raiser. It brings to mind Cobbett's remark
about Frome, Trowbridge and Bradford, in Wiltshire: 'there are,
through all these towns, and throughout this country, weavers
from the North, singing about the towns ballads of Distress! They
had been going it at Salisbury, just before I was there' (*Rural Rides*,
2 September 1826, ed. G. Woodcock, 1967, p.341).

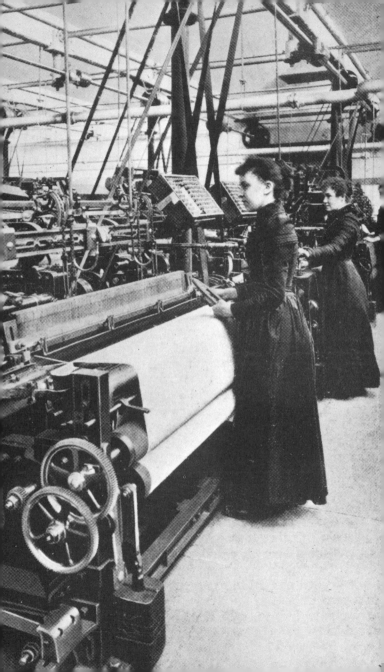

John o'Grinfield

I'm a poor cotton weaver as many a one knows,
I've nowt t' eat i' th' house and I've worn out my clothes;
You'd hardly give sixpence for all I've got on,
My clogs they are bursten and stockings I've none.
You'd think it wur hard to be sent to the world
For to clam and do best that you can.

Our parish church parson kept telling me long,
We'd have better times if I'd bùt hold my tongue.
I've holden my tongue till I can hardly draw breeoth,
I think in my heart they mean t' clam me to death.
I know he lives weel by backbiting the de'il,
But he never picked o'er in his life.

I tarried six weeks, thought every day was the last,
I shifted and shifted till now I'm quite fast;
I lived upon nettles while nettles were good,
And Waterloo porridge was t' best of my food.
I'm telling you true, I can find folks enoo,
That are living no better than me.

Now old Bill o' Dans sent bailiffs one day
For a shop score I owed him which I could not pay;
But he was too late for old Bill o' Bent
Had sent horse and cart and ta'en goods for th' rent.
We'd nowt but a stoo' that was seats for two,
And on it cowered Margit and me.

The bailiffs looked round as sly as a mouse,
When they saw all things wur ta'en out o' th' house;
Says one to the other, 'All's gone thou may see;'
Said I, 'Never fret, lads, you're welcome to me.'
They made no more ado, but nipped up th' old stoo',
And we both went wack upon th' flags.

I geet hold of Margit for hoo're stricken sick,
Hoo said hoo ne'er had such a bang sin hoo're wick.
Then the bailiffs scoured off with th' old stoo' o' their back,
They wouldn' 'a cared had they broken her neck.

They'n mad at old Bent he'd ta'en goods for rent,
They was ready to flee us alive.

I said to our Margit as we lay on the floor,
'We ne'er shall be lower in this world I'm sure;
But if we alter, I'm sure we mun mend,
For I think in my heart we are both at far end,
For meat we have none nor looms to weave on,
Egad, they're as good lost as found.'

Then I geet up my piece and I took it 'em back,
I scarcely dare speak, master looked so black.
He said, 'You were o'erpaid the last time you coom;'
I said if I was 'twere weaving bout loom.
In the mind that I'm in I'll ne'er pick o'er again,
For I've woven myself to th' far end.

Then I coom out of th' house and I left him chew that,
When thought at it again I was vexed till I sweat,
To think I mun work to keep him and a' th' set
All the days of my life and still be in their debt;
So I'll give over trade and work with a spade,
Or go and break stones upo' th' road.

Our Margit declared if hoo'd clo'es to put on,
Hoo'd go up to London to see th' great mon;
And if things wur not altered when there she had been,
Hoo swears hoo would fight wi' blood up to the een.
Hoo's nowt agen th' king but hoo likes a fair thing,
An' hoo says hoo can tell when hoo's hurt.

clam starve.
de'il devil.
picked o'er threw the shuttle; wove.
Waterloo porridge thin gruel, with a pun on the first two syllables.
flags flag-stones.
wick alive.
flee flay.
bout without.
een eyes.

I'm a poor cot-ton wea-ver as many a one knows, I've nowt t'eat i' th' house and I've worn out my clothes; You'd hard-ly give sixpence for all I've got on, My clogs they are bursten and stockings I've none. You'd think it was hard to be sent to the world For to clam and do best that you can.

Weaving was an ancient and honourable trade, much celebrated in song. The application of power to spinning machinery put the weavers' work at a premium but, when looms were mechanized, a prolonged decline set in. Hand-loom weavers in Lancashire were receiving between 19s. and 25s. a week in 1800. Despite fluctuations in between, the figures in 1814 were between 18s. and 24s. a week. After 1815, however, a rapid decline set in; by 1820, earnings were down to 8s. a week and, by 1832, to 5s. or 6s.

The ballad, which is perhaps the best of the John o' Grinfilt cycle (cf. song on p.34), was very popular in Lancashire for several decades after 1815, being frequently reprinted on broadsides.

Birmingham Jack of all Trades

I am a jolly roving blade,
They call me Jack of all trades,
I always fixed my chief delight
In kissing of the fair maids;
To Birmingham I did set out
To seek a situation,
I'd often heard folks say it was
The toy-shop of the nation.

Chorus
I'm a roving Jack of all trades,
Of every trade and all trades,
And if you want to know my name,
They call me Jack of all trades.

'Twas in the Bull Ring first I went,
There I became a porter;
I with my master soon fell out,
And cut acquaintance shorter.
In Bull Street was a pastry cook,
Dale End an undertaker,
Then I removed to Friday Street,
There set up coffin maker.

In Pinfold Street I sold rag mops,
In Bread Street was a grinder;
In Dudley Street I lost my wife,
Thank God I never could find her.
In Hill Street I sold black puddings,
In Edmund Street made mouse-traps:
At the Old Wharf I did sell coal,
In Suffolk Street made louse-traps

In Digbeth was a waterman,
St Martin's Lane a saddler;
In Ran's Yard was a slaughterman,
In Park Street was a fiddler.

In Spiceal Street I sold hot pudding,
At Friday Bridge sold charcoal;
In Philip Street sold blacking paste,
In High Street kept the louse-hole.

In Smallbrook Street made candle-sticks,
In Worcester Street a broker;
In Floodgate Street made fire-irons,
Both shovel, tongs and poker.
In Ann Street was a dialist,
Newhall Street a die-sinker;
In New Street drove a hackney coach,
In Moor Street was a printer.

In Walmer Lane, steel trusses made,
In Lichfield Street a sad shop;
In Steelhouse Lane made snuffers,
And in Bell Street kept a rag shop.
In Church Street was a silversmith,
In Livery Street made split-rings;
In Charles Street was a clock-maker,
And all such little odd things.

In Aston Street I did make glass,
In Coleshill Street a baker;
In Woodcock Street I did cast brass,
In Duke Street was a Quaker.
In the Horse Fair sold crumpets rare,
Made penny wigs in Cox Street;
At Lady Well I kept a bath,
In Hurst Street I sold dogs' meat.

At Islington I sold sky-blue,
In Smithfield was a drover;
In Stafford Street I sold old shoes,
In Bath Street was a glover.
In Loveday Street sold measuring tapes,
In Price Street bled with leeches;
In Lench Street I sold penny pies,
In York Street sold old breeches.

In Bread Street I made spectacles,
In Sand Street an engraver;

In Weaman Street a gun-maker,
In Newton Street a pavior.
In Snow Hill was a pawnbroker,
In Shadwell Street a sawyer;
In Bromsgrove Street made coffin nails,
In Cannon Street a lawyer.

In Temple Street I sold shaloon,
In Queen Street a cork-cutter;
In Colmore Street I kept a shop,
Sold bacon, cheese and butter.
In John Street I sold faggots hot,
Of which I often boasted;
And then in London Prentice Street,
Sold mutton ready roasted.

In Swallow Street made bellows-pipes,
In Wharf Street was a blacksmith;
In Beak Street there I did sell tripe,
In Freeman Street a locksmith.
In Cherry Street I was a quack,
In Summer Lane sold pancakes;
Oh then at last I got a knack
To manufacture worm-cakes.

In Wood Street I sold sand-paper,
In Buck Street I sold prayer books;
In Duddeston Street made pattern cards,
In Doe Street I sold fish-hooks.
In Ashted I made jew's harp springs,
In Thomas Street made awl blades;
So now you know the ups and downs
Of a jolly Jack of all trades.

louse-traps hats.   *sad shop* bakery(?).
louse-hole lock-up.   *shaloon* sort of cloth.
dialist maker of dials.

Birmingham was known as 'the city of the thousand trades', and
many of these are represented here. Other versions of the ballad
feature Liverpool and Dublin.

212

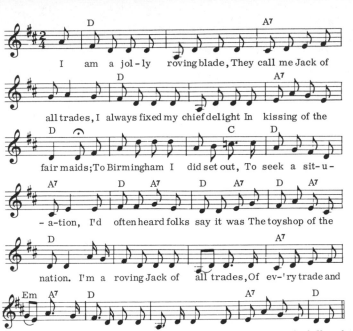

I am a jol-ly roving blade, They call me Jack of all trades, I always fixed my chief delight In kissing of the fair maids; To Birmingham I did set out, To seek a sit-u-a-tion, I'd often heard folks say it was The toyshop of the nation. I'm a roving Jack of all trades, Of ev'ry trade and all trades And if you want to know my name They call me Jack of all trades.

The Tradesman's Complaint

You Englishmen where'er you be, come list to what I say;
Our English pride in commerce now is fast fading away.
Distress of trade some thousands feel, for they know not
     where to go,
And many are forced to beg or starve for they have no
     work to do.

For many years trade has declined, but ne'er so much as
     now,
For thousands they can get no work and wages are so low;
There's spinners, weavers, clothiers, and stocking-
     makers, too,
Are wandering through the country, not knowing what to do.

In Nottingham and Manchester, in Bolton and in Hyde,
There's thousands who once worked for bread now cannot
     bread provide;
In Bury, Rochdale, Dukinfield, Stockport and Ashton, too,
Great numbers are working on short time and more have no
     work to do.

Through Lancashire and Yorkshire and all old England o'er,
Nought else but poverty does appear among the labouring
     poor;
Their bread is scarce, their clothes are rags, their naked
     skin peeps through;
'Twas different when their wage was good and they'd
     plenty of work to do.

The labourers of England once lived on pudding and beef,
But now the times are altered, which fills their hearts
     with grief;
No more the pudding and the beef their dinner tables show,
But gruel and taters are their fare now there's no work to do.

Now let us hope the times will mend, but this is vain, I fear;
Instead of better they're getting worse, each and every year.

But if the Corn Laws are repealed and we get work to do,
Then with Free Trade we will rejoice and get good wages, too.

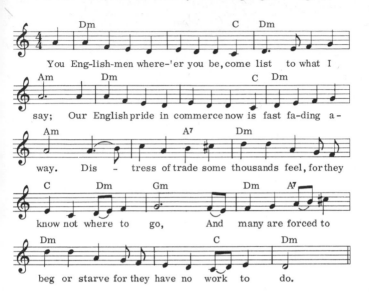

You Eng-lish-men where-'er you be, come list to what I say; Our English pride in commerce now is fast fa-ding a-way. Dis - tress of trade some thousands feel, for they know not where to go, And many are forced to beg or starve for they have no work to do.

Ballads complaining at the lot of the poor are not difficult to find.
They were published in the seventeenth and eighteenth centuries
with titles like *The Poor Man's Distress*, *The Poor Man Pays for
All*, *All Things are Dear but Poor Men's Labour*. The tradition was
continued into the nineteenth century, with titles like the *Mechanic's
Lamentation* and *The Tradesman's Complaint*. Often, the ballads
do not demand or even call for a solution, but confine themselves to
expressing pious hopes that 'the times will mend'. Alternatively, they
look back in a rather dispirited fashion to what they consider the
better days of the past. The present ballad probably dates from
between 1838 and 1842, when 'widespread unemployment existed
side by side with low wages. In the main factory areas, especially
Lancashire, wages were definitely lower in this period than they had
been ten years before, whereas the cost of living was markedly
higher' (G. D. H. Cole and R. Postgate, *The Common People, 1746–
1846* p.304). Hope is expressed in the last verse that the repeal of
the Corn Laws would help trade to revive; the popular reaction
when repeal came is voiced in the next song.

New Dialogue and Song on the Times

BILL Good morning, Jack, I'm glad to see you. What's the meaning of all these Spinners, Piecers, Weavers, Winders, Grinders, Strippers, Carders, Doffers, Stretchers, Throstle Spinners, Bobbin Winders, Frame Tenders, and all those folk that work in these places with big chimneys at top of 'um walking about?

JACK Why, if thou recollects, a few months back there wur great talk about the Corn Laws going to come off, and all those big chaps in the Parliament House, and all these Factory Lords of Lancashire, said if the Corn Laws wur repealed that poor people would get plenty of bread for little money, work would be plentiful, and wages would be a great deal higher; but instead of that, bread's dearer, wages is lower, and factories are on short time.

BILL Yes, Jack, I recollect hearing people talk about a lot of chaps that wur going to bring such times as wur never seen before, they said that Bobby Peel and Dicky Cobden, and a great many chaps was going to give us cheap bread, and they said that we should have plenty of work and get good wages for it, but I've only worked ten weeks since that corn bill as they call it passed, and I get less wages for it too, Jack.

JACK These big cotton masters of Lancashire want to drop poor people's wages, so as to accomplish it they're only working four days a week, so that when they start full time again, they can drop the people's wages.

BILL Well, but Jack, don't you know when the corn bill passed, these Masters gave a great sum of money to rejoice and have grand processions in honour of it passing.

JACK Don't you see, Bill, it is poor people that must pay for it now, for they must work for less wages, or else for short time.

BILL Yes, but Jack, there's several factories that's stopping for a month or two, and some working none at all, and a great deal breaking down; what's the reason of that, eh Jack?

JACK Why the reason of them stopping a month or two is,

they want to get rid of their old hands; so that when they start again they can have all fresh hands, and reduce their wages. As for them that are breaking down, it's a scheme they've got, it's these chaps that rejoiced so much at the time the bill passed, and they are ashamed to tell the people that they'll have to work for less wages or short time, so they are breaking down on purpose.

BILL Well, I think you're somewhere about right, Jack, for there is a deal of factory hands that are walking about and has nothing to do, so you've learnt me something, Jack.

JACK I bought a new song about these Factory Masters and their short time system, and if you'll stop you shall hear it too.

You working men of England one moment now attend,
While I unfold the treatment of the poor upon this land;
For nowadays the factory lords have brought the labour low,
And daily are contriving plans to prove our overthrow.

Chorus
So arouse, you sons of freedom, the world seems upside down;
They scorn the poor man as a thief in country and in town.

Now when the bill was in the House they said it would do good;
For the working man it has not yet, I only wish it would.
The factories they are on short time wherever you may go,
And the masters are all scheming plans to get our wages low.

There's different parts in Ireland – it's true what I do state –
There's hundreds that are starving for they can't get food to eat;
And if they go unto the rich to ask them for relief,
They bang their door all in their face as if they were a thief.

Alas, how altered are the times; rich men despise the poor,
And pay them off without remorse, quite scornful at their door;
And if a man is out of work his parish pay is small:
Enough to starve himself and wife, his children and all.

In former times when Christmas came we had a good big
 loaf:
Then beef and mutton plenty were, and we enjoyed them
 both;
But nowadays such altered ways and different is the times,
If, starving, you should ask relief, you're sent to a Whig
 bastille.

So to conclude and finish these few verses I have made;
I hope to see before it's long men for their labour paid.
Then we'll rejoice with heart and voice and banish all our
 woes;
Before we do old England must pay us what she owes.

You working men of England one moment now at-
-tend, while I unfold the treatment of the poor upon this
land; For now-a-days the factory lords have brought the labour
low, And daily are contriving plans to prove our overthrow. So arouse, you sons of freedom, the world seems upside
down; They scorn the poor man as a thief in country and in town.

piecers joined broken ends.
winders wound weft or yarn.
grinders fixed rollers of carding machine between iron rollers, which
 sharpened the pins.

strippers stripped away shoddy (waste) which accumulated in carding machines.

carders in charge of carding machines.

doffers removed full bobbins from throstle frames and replaced them with empty ones.

throstle spinners worked the mechanical spinning machine.

Bobby Peel Sir Robert Peel, responsible for the repeal of the Corn Laws.

Dicky Cobden Richard Cobden who, with Bright, formed the Anti-Corn Law League in 1838, which campaigned against the Corn Laws, in the name of Free Trade.

Ireland the Great Famine in Ireland lasted from 1845 to 1850.

Whig bastille workhouse (see songs on pp.260–265).

Despite the repeal of the Corn Laws, there was a recession in trade in 1846–7, which this ballad reflects.

What Shocking Hard Times

Good people all, both great and small, come listen to my
    rhymes,
I'll sing to you a verse or two, concerning of the times;
The butchers and the bakers they've come to one decision,
With the millers and the quakers on the prices of provision.

Chorus
There never was such hard times seen in England before.

The man who speculates in corn will purchase all he can,
He's nothing but a traitor to the honest working man;
And I am sure before the poor should have it under price,
He'd leave it in his granary all for the rats and mice.

They talk about Free Trade, my boys, but that is all my
    eye,
Their fortune it is made and banked, we may lie down and
    die;
We need not look for honesty among a lot of elves,
Free Trade is but a policy, they have it all themselves.

The farmers whistle Charley, we had some splendid crops:
Oats, taters, wheat and barley, and lots of turnip tops;
They seem to say, 'Good lack-a-day, success attend the
    Czar':
They're making money every day all by the Russian War.

The farmers, millers, bakers, too, are plucking up their
    feathers,
They are a mob, so help me, Bob, of humbugs all together;
The bounteous gifts of Providence, they do monopolize,
And rob the poor, I'm certain sure, their guts to
    gourmandize.

If I'd my way, mark what I say, I'd screw their bellies
    tight,
I'd send them off to Russia and make the tigers fight;
Sad would be their condition, they'd carry, dear oh lack,

Full seventy rounds of ammunition, stuck on the
    landlord's back.

Now go into a shambles, there's mutton and beef enough,
At seven pence a pound, you'll find it rather tough;
Come buy, come buy, it is the cry, resounds from stall to
    stall,
But when you come to eat it, keep your napper from the
    wall.

The pawn-shops they are crowded out with different kinds
    of things:
Shawls, petticoats and trousers and ladies' wedding rings;
The landlord and landlady, too, are looking fat and plump,
With her crochet knitted night-cap and a bustle on her
    rump.

The Cotton Lords of Lancashire, they think it is no more;
They say, bedad, the trade is bad, and they must have
    short time;
They eat their beef and mutton, aye, and sport about on
    Monday,
But they do not care a button if you eat brick on Sunday.

elves term of contempt.
Russian War Crimean War (1853–6).
tigers parasites.
napper head.

This ballad, which presumably originated during the Crimean War,
protests against high prices, and in so doing follows a long tradition.
It is more novel however, in its attack on the ideology (Free Trade
– and the business men – speculators, farmers, Cotton Lords) seen
as being responsible. Its tone is bitter, and far removed from the
resignation of, say, *The Tradesman's Complaint* (song on p.214).
The casual treatment of the labour force by the employers is a
particular grievance which is mentioned in the ballad. Professor
Hobsbawm comments:

> When workers lost their employment – which they might do
> at the end of the job, of the week, of the day or even of the hour –
> they had nothing to fall back upon except their savings, their
> friendly society or trade union, their credit with local shop-

keepers, their neighbours and friends, the pawnbroker or the Poor Law. . . . Skilled workers, or those in expanding industries, would probably enjoy some of the benefits of being in short supply, except in the recurring economic crises. They would also benefit from trade unions, friendly societies, cooperatives and even modest private savings. Unskilled ones would be lucky to make ends meet, and would probably bridge the empty part of each week by pawning and repawning their miserable belongings. In the Liverpool of the 1850s, 60 per cent of all pawnbrokers' pledges were for five shillings or less, 27 per cent for 2s. 6d. or less (*Industry*, p.155).

Good peo-ple all, both great and small, come listen to my rhymes, I'll sing to you a verse or two, con-cern-ing of the times; The butchers and the ba-kers they've come to one de - ci - sion, With the mil-lers and the qua-kers on the pri - ces of pro - vi - sion. There never was such hard times seen in Eng - land be - fore.

The Shurat Weaver's Song

Confound it, aw ne'er wur so woven afore,
Mi back's welly brocken, mi fingers are sore;
Aw've bin starin' an' rootin' amung this Shurat,
Till aw'm very near getten as bloint as a bat.
Every toime aw go in wi' mi cuts to owd Joe,
He gies me a cursin' an' bates me an' o;
Aw've a warp i' one loom wi' boath selvedges marred,
An' th' other's as bad, for he's dressed it too hard.

Aw wish aw wur fur enough off, eawt o' th' road,
For o' weavin' this rubbitch aw'm gettin' reet stowed;
Aw've nowt i' this world to lie deawn on but straw,
For aw've nobbut eight shillin' this fortni't to draw.
Neaw aw haven't mi family under mi hat,
Aw've a woife an' six childer to keep eawt o' that;
So aw'm rayther amung it at present yo' see,
Iv ever a fellow wur puzzlt, it's me.

Iv one turns eawt to stale, folk'll co me a thief,
An' aw conno' put th' cheek on to ax for relief;
As aw said i' eawr heawse t'other neet to mi woife,
Aw never did nowt o' this sort i' mi loife.
One doesn't like everyone t' know heaw they are,
But we'n suffered so lung thro' this 'Merica war,
'At ther's lots o' poor factory folk getten t' fur end,
An' they'll soon be knocked o'er iv th' toimes dunno mend.

Oh dear, iv yon Yankees could only just see
Heaw they're clemmin' an' starvin' poor weavers loike me,
Aw think they'd soon settle their bother, an' strive
To send us some cotton to keep us alive.
Ther's theawsands o' folk just i' th' best o' their days,
Wi' traces o' want plainly seen i' their face;
An' a future afore 'em as dreary an dark,
For when th' cotton gets done we shall o be beawt work.

We'n bin patient an' quiet as lung as we con;
Th' bits o' things we had by us are welly o gone;
Aw've bin trampin' so lung, mi owd shoon are worn eawt,
An' mi halliday clooas are o on 'em up th' speawt.
It wur nobbut last Monday aw sowd a good bed –
Nay, very near gan it – to get us some bread;
Afore these bad toimes come aw used to be fat,
But neaw, bless your life, aw'm as thin as a lat.

Mony a toime i' mi loife aw've seen things lookin' feaw,
But never as awk'ard as what they are neaw;
Iv ther isn't some help for us factory folk soon,
Aw'm sure we shall o be knocked reet eawt o' tune.
Come, give us a lift, yo' 'at han owt to give,
An' help yo'r poor brothers and sisters to live;
Be kind, an' be tender to th' needy an' poor,
An' we'll promise when th' toimes mend we'll ax yo' no
    moor.

Con-found it, aw ne'er wur so wo-ven a-fore, Mi
back's wel-ly brock-en, mi fin-gers are sore; Aw've bin
starin' an' rootin' amung this Shurat, Till aw'm very near getten as
bloint as a bat. Every time aw go in wi' mi cuts to owd Joe, He
gies me a cursin' an' bates me an' o; Aw've a warp i' one loom wi' boath
selvedges marred An' th'others as bad, for he's dressed it too hard.

227

Shurat East India Company's Depot, near Bombay.

bloint blind.

cuts lengths of cloth.

bates reduces price.

marred spoilt.

dressed sized.

stale steal.

'Merica war American Civil War, which began in 1861.

Yankees Northern Americans, usually; but possibly all Americans is to be understood here.

up the speawt into pawn.

lat lath.

feaw foul.

During the American Civil War, the Northerners blockaded the Southern ports, which prevented cotton from reaching Lancashire. In 1861, cotton was still the most important British industry, and most of the cotton spun in Lancashire came from America. A devastating cotton famine ensued in Lancashire, which was only partially offset by imports from India and Egypt. The Shurat cotton was inferior (indeed, for generations after this time, the word Shurat was used in Lancashire as a synonym for rubbish), which made work harder. At the same time the employers took advantage of the famine to force down wages to as little as 4s. and 5s. a week. The cotton spinners and weavers were very loyal in their support of the Northern side in America, but in the present ballad, which was written by Samuel Laycock of Stalybridge, a power loom weaver, a certain weariness finds expression.

Poor Frozen-Out Gardeners

We're broken-hearted gardeners, scarce got a bit of shoe;
Like pilgrims we are wandering and we don't know what to
    do.
Our furniture is seized upon, our togs are up the spout;
Cold winter it is come at last and we are all froze out.

Long time have we been seeking employment for to gain,
And we have suffered sorely, all through the heavy rain;
These times they are so very hard and the winter winds do
    blow:
Oh, think upon the poor folk in the bitter frost and snow.

Behold the wealthy squire, in his carriage he can ride,
Or, bless'd with all the comforts, sit down by a good
    fireside,
While with our aching hearts we are compelled to walk
    about
With a cabbage on a pole, and a-bawling 'All froze out.'

How pleasant for to rise up in the merry month of spring,
To hear the blackbird whistle and the nightingale to sing;
The gardener being so cheerful and early in the morn
Is busily engagèd in a-mowing of the lawn.

Sometimes so busily employed in trimming of the vine,
Or sowing little cabbages with a dibble and a line;
Laying out the beds and borders or stringing of the peas,
A-budding or a-grafting or pruning of the trees.

To gather from the honey-suckle, how busy are the bees,
To what they are in winter time when it begins to freeze;
The pretty maid a-milking do trip along so gay,
Or else across the meadows they're a-making of the hay.

In summer time the leaves upon the trees appear so green;
In autumn they do fade and fall and none are to be seen.
The hollyhock, the dahlia, the lily, pink and rose,
The turnips and the cabbages are all together froze.

Oh listen with attention before you close your doors,
And think upon the dreadful state all of the languishing
    poor;
Our families are starving, we can no longer stay,
So think upon the poor folk all on a winter's day.

We're broken-heart-ed gard-'ners, scarce got a bit of shoe;—— Like pilgrims we are wand-'ring, and we don't know what to do. Our fur-ni-ture is seized up-on, our togs are up the spout, Cold win-ter it— is—come at last and we are all froze out.

togs clothes.
up the spout in pawn.
a cabbage on a pole see below.
dibble pointed stick with which to make holes for planting seeds.

A rather unsympathetic account (and picture) of the frozen-out gardeners is given in *Chambers Book of Days*, which was published in 1863:

A protracted frost necessarily deranges the lower class of employments in such a city as London, and throws many poor persons into destitution. Just as sure as this is the fact, so sure is it that a vast horde of the class who systematically avoid regular work, preferring to live by their wits, simulate the characteristic appearances of distressed labourers, and try to excite the charity of the better class of citizens. Investing themselves in aprons, clutching an old spade, and hoisting as their signal of distress a turnip on the top of a pole or rake, they will wend their way through the West End streets, proclaiming themselves in sepulchral tones as *Frozen-Out Gardeners*, or simply calling, 'Hall frozen hout!' or chanting, 'We've got no work to do!' The faces of the corps are duly dolorous; but one can nevertheless observe a sharp eye kept on the doors and windows they are passing, in order that if possible they may arrest some female gaze on which to practise their spell of pity. It is alleged on good

grounds that the generality of these victims of the frost are impostors, and that their daily gatherings will often amount to double a skilled workman's wages. Nor do they usually discontinue the trade till long after the return of milder airs has liquidated even real claims upon the public sympathy (pp.110–111).

There is a further account in Mayhew, *London's Underworld*.

Cowd Stringy Pie

Over in Yorkshire a farmer did dwell,
And they called 'im Yaddy 'Ughes, and you all know 'im
   well;
He keeps four servants, it i'n't any lie,
And 'e feeds 'em all up on 'is cowd stringy pie,
And 'e feeds 'em all up on 'is cowd stringy pie.

And 'e's got nine 'osses and they're that thin,
You can count every bone as it ligs in the skin;
There's four bent in t' leg and there's four swung in t'back,
And he drives one along with his 'Ah gee woa back.'

He gets 'is lads up at a quarter past five
To gan off t' stables to see if they're still alive;
He feeds 'em on oats and 'e feeds 'em on bran,
And it rattles in their guts like a rusty owd can.

If any o' you lads wants to learn 'ow to plough,
Gan to owd Yaddy's, 'e'll soon learn you 'ow;
He'll keep you working without any pay
And expect you to plough four yakker a day.

And if any o' you lasses wants to learn to scour pans,
Well, gan to Mrs Yaddy's, you'll get mucky 'ands;
She'll keep you workin' the livelong day:
'Can I set you on, lass, next Martinmas Day?'

One day Yaddy to his shepherd did say,
'We 'ad an owd sheep died just three weeks today'.
'Fetch 'er up, bullocky, fetch 'er up on the sly,
And we'll give these young laddies some rare mutton pie.'

They fetched the sheep up, boiled 'er in a pot,
And they served 'er on t' table, she were reekin' 'ot;
And t' maggots crawled over 'er four inches thick,
But owd Yaddy 'ad a lad knockin, 'em off wi' a stick.

Well, over in Yorkshire, *etc.* (*repeat first verse*).

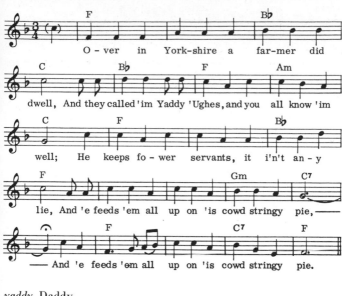

O-ver in York-shire a far-mer did dwell, And they called 'im Yaddy 'Ughes, and you all know 'im well; He keeps fo-wer servants, it i'n't an-y lie, And 'e feeds 'em all up on 'is cowd stringy pie, —— —— And 'e feeds 'em all up on 'is cowd stringy pie.

yaddy Daddy.
stringy pie rhubarb pie.
ligs lies.
yakker acre.
Martinmas 11th November.

The old system, whose passing Cobbett was lamenting in the 1820s and 1830s, was that farm workers should live in with the farmer and his family. This Yorkshire song indicates that the system continued into the later nineteenth century in some parts of England. It also indicates the disadvantage that farm workers who lived in were even more at the mercy of their employers than their fellows in industry. Such songs would be likely to get a hearing on occasions like the hiring fairs (see song on p.105), when the labourers got together to discuss their masters.

In the North-East of Scotland, the old system continued to exist until the early years of the present century. The farm workers lived together in barn-like buildings, called bothies, whence emerged a very fine corpus of songs, called bothy songs.

The Rest of the Day's your Own

One day when I was out of work a job I went to seek,
To be a farmer's boy.
At last I found an easy job at half a crown a week,
To be a farmer's boy.
The farmer said, 'I think I've got the very job for you;
Your duties will be light, for this is all you've got to do:
Rise at three every morn, milk the cow with the crumpled
    horn,
Feed the pigs, clean the sty, teach the pigeons the way
    to fly,
Plough the fields, mow the hay, help the cocks and hens to
    lay,
Sow the seeds, tend the crops, chase the flies from the
    turnip tops,
Clean the knives, black the shoes, scrub the kitchen and
    sweep the flues,
Help the wife, wash the pots, grow the cabbages and
    carrots,
Make the beds, dust the coals, mend the gramophone,
And then if there's no more work to do, the rest of the
    day's your own.'

I scratched my head and thought it would be absolutely
    prime
To be a farmer's boy.
The farmer said, 'Of course you'll have to do some
    overtime,
When you're a farmer's boy.'
Said he, 'The duties that I've given you, you'll be quickly
    through,
So I've been thinking of a few more things that you can do:
Skim the milk, make the cheese, chop the meat for the
    sausagees,
Bath the kids, mend their clothes, use your dial to scare
    the crows,

In the milk, put the chalk, shave the knobs off the pickled
    pork,
Shoe the horse, break the coal, take the cat for his
    midnight stroll,
Cook the food, scrub the stairs, teach the parrot to say his
    prayers,
Roast the joint, bake the bread, shake the feathers up in
    the bed,
When the wife's got the gout, rub her funny bone,
And then if there's no more work to do, the rest of the
    day's your own.'

I thought it was a shame to take the money, you can bet,
To be a farmer's boy.
And so I wrote my duties down in case I should forget
I was a farmer's boy.
It took all night to write 'em down, I didn't go to bed,
But somehow I got all mixed up, and this is how they read:
Rise at three, every morn, milk the hen with the crumpled
    horn,
Scrub the wife every day, teach the nanny goat how to lay,
Shave the cat, mend the cheese, fit the tights on the
    sausagees,
Bath the pigs, break the pots, boil the kids with a few
    carrots,
Roast the horse, dust the bread, put the cocks and hens
    to bed,
Boots and shoes, black with chalk, shave the hair on the
    pickled pork,
All the rest I forgot, somehow it had flown,
But I got the sack this morning, so the rest of my life's
    my own.

dial face.

This is a rather more light-hearted look at the relationship between
farm workers and farmers. As the reference to the gramophone
indicates, the song dates from the early twentieth century.

One day when I was out of work a job I went to seek, To be a farm-er's boy.——— At last I found an ea-sy job at half-a-crown a week, To be a farm-er's boy. ——— The farmer said, "I think I've got the ve-ry job for you; Your duties will be light, for this is all you've got to do.

Rise at three ev - 'ry morn, Milk the cow with the
Plough the fields, mow the hay, Help the cocks and the

crum-pled horn, Feed the pigs, clean the sty,
hens to lay, Sow the seed, tend the crops,

Teach the pigeons the way to fly; Chase the flies from the

tur - nip tops, Clean the knives, black the shoes,
Help the wife, wash the pots,

Scrub the kitchen and sweep the flues, Grow the cabbages

and car-rots, Make the beds, dust the coals,

Mend the gram-o-phone,—— And then if there's no more

work to do The rest of the day's your own.——

The Buffalo

Come all you young fellows that have a mind to range
Into some foreign country, your station for to change;
Into some foreign country away from home to go,
We lay down on the banks of the pleasant Ohio,
We'll wander through the wild woods and we'll chase the
    buffalo.

There are fishes in the river that are fitting for our use,
And high and lofty sugar canes that yield us pleasant juice,
And all sorts of game, my boys, besides the buck and doe,
We lay down, *etc.*

Come all you young maidens, come spin us up some yarn,
To make us some new clothing to keep ourselves full warm;
For you can card and spin, my girls, and we can reap and
    mow,
We will lay down, *etc.*

Supposing these wild Indians by chance should come us
    near,
We will unite together our hearts all free from care;
We will march down into the town, my boys, and give the
    fatal blow,
We will lay down, *etc.*

This song probably dates from the early eighteenth century, but it
can stand for the enormous movement which emigration became
during the nineteenth century. The movement began after 1815:

> All the circumstances of post-war England helped the great
> movement of colonization. The over-population that terrified
> Malthus, the economic and social troubles, the resentment felt
> by the freer spirits against the rule of squire and farmer, were
> all factors that went to build up the second British Empire,
> filling Canada, Australia and New Zealand with men and women
> of British speech and tradition (G. M. Trevelyan, *English Social
> History*, Penguin edn, 1967, p.487).

Later in the century, peaks in emigration coincided with slumps or disillusionment. Between 1847 and 1849, for example, a quarter of a million people emigrated each year. During the 1870s, thousands of farm workers, sometimes assisted by their union, emigrated to Canada and the United States. The numbers of emigrants from the British Isles averaged 50,000 per year in the 1830s and 120,000 in the 1850s. From England alone in the 1870s, the average was 100,000 per year.

Emigrants often suffered cruel hardships, both in travelling to the promised land and in settling there. The song gives a Utopian view, which must often have been rudely challenged by colonial reality.

Botany Bay

Come all young men of learning and a warning take by me,
I would have you quit night walking and shun bad company;
I would have you quit night walking, or else you'll rue the day,
You'll rue your transportation, lads, when you're bound for
    Botany Bay.

I was brought up in London Town at a place I know full
    well,
Brought up by honest parents, for the truth to you I'll tell;
Brought up by honest parents and reared most tenderly,
Till I became a roving blade, which proved my destiny.

My character soon was taken and I was sent to jail;
My friends they tried to clear me but nothing could
    prevail.
At the Old Bailey Sessions the judge to me did say,
'The jury's found you guilty lad, you must go to Botany
    Bay.'

To see my agèd father dear as he stood at the bar,
Likewise my tender mother, her old grey locks to tear;
In tearing of her old grey locks, these words to me did say,
'Oh son, oh son, what have you done, that you're going to
    Botany Bay?'

It was on the twenty-eighth of May, from England we did
    steer;
And all things being made safe on board we sailed down the
    river clear;
And every ship that we passed by, we heard the sailors say,
'There goes a ship of clever hands, and they're bound for
    Botany Bay.'

There is a girl in Manchester, a girl I know full well;
And if ever I get my liberty, along with her I'll dwell.
Oh, then I mean to marry her and no more go astray;
I'll shun all evil company, bid adieu to Botany Bay.

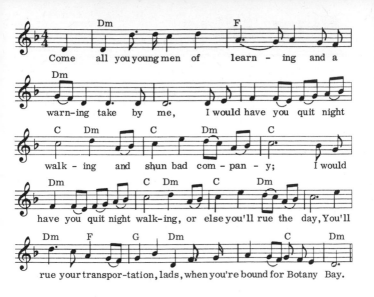

Come all you young men of learn-ing and a warn-ing take by me, I would have you quit night walk-ing and shun bad com-pan-y; I would have you quit night walk-ing, or else you'll rue the day, You'll rue your transpor-tation, lads, when you're bound for Botany Bay.

Other emigrants went unwillingly, as the guests of Her Majesty's Government: they were transported to the colonies. During the seventeenth and eighteenth centuries, Virginia and Maryland received convicts from England, but after America became independent, penal settlements were established in Australia and Tasmania (Van Dieman's Land). Botany Bay (near to what is now Sydney) received convicts between 1786 and 1853.

Rather a jolly song, beginning 'Farewell to old England for ever', is perhaps the best known, under the title of *Botany Bay*. It was written in 1885 for the music hall, and has none of the bitter heartbreak of the ballads contemporary with transportation. These made such a deep imprint on the popular imagination that they survived in the oral tradition for many generations; indeed, they are still to be found occasionally today.

Jim Jones

Oh listen for a moment, lads, and hear me tell my tale,
How o'er the sea from England's shore I was compelled to
  sail.
The jury says, 'He's guilty, sir', and says the judge, says he,
'For life, Jim Jones, I'm sending you across the stormy sea.

'And take a tip before you ship to join the iron gang,
Don't get too gay at Botany Bay or else you'll surely hang;
Or else you'll surely hang,' he says, says he, 'and after
  that, Jim Jones,
It's high upon the gallows tree the crows will pick your bones.

'You'll have no time for mischief, then, remember what I
  say;
They'll flog the poaching out of you when you get to
  Botany Bay.'
The waves were high upon the sea, the winds blew up in
  gales;
I'd rather be drowned in misery than go to New South
  Wales.

The winds blew high upon the sea and pirates came along,
But soldiers on our convict ship were full five hundred
  strong;
They opened fire and somehow drove that pirate ship away,
I'd rather have joined that pirate ship than come to
  Botany Bay.

For day and night the irons clang, and, like poor galley slaves,
We toil and moil and when we die must fill dishonoured
  graves;
But by and by I'll break my chains, into the bush I'll go,
And join the brave bushrangers there, Jack Donahue and Co.

And some dark night when everything is silent in the town,
I'll kill the tyrants one and all and shoot the floggers down;
I'll give the law a little shock – remember what I say;
They'll yet regret they sent Jim Jones in chains to Botany
  Bay.

iron gang gang of convicts, who worked chained together.
Jack Donahue ex-convict who escaped the gallows in 1828, and
    took to the bush. He was shot and killed by mounted police in
    New South Wales in 1830.

This ballad recounts some of the horrors of life in the convict
settlements of Australia and reveals some of the bitter defiance
which was engendered in the convicts. Many men took to the bush,
and took arms against their oppressors. The bushrangers are still
celebrated in song in the Australia of today.

It is significant that this ballad mentions poaching as a trans-
portable offence. Many English and Irish poachers were transported,
as were other types of criminals and political offenders, including
trade unionists. The Tolpuddle martyrs are a famous example from
the last category.

Curly Williams

Now there is a bloke whose name is Curly Williams,
Who never had a penny in his time;
He wasn't fond of work because it hurt him;
If you spoke about a job he used to sigh.
He used to loaf about outside the public houses,
And each day he'd scarcely anything to eat;
His clothes were always nicely ventilated,
And he lived in a little hovel up the street.
But he's moved to a bigger house now,
Living like a great big don,
In a great big, large, five-storey house
With a real bathroom and the gas laid on;
Lovely grounds all around it,
No longer will he mooch around the pubs,
For it ain't a villa or a mansion where he's living in,
They call it Wormwood Scrubs.

Now a gentleman that Curly owed a quid to
Was knocking where he used to live this morn;
He said that he would give me two and sixpence
If I could tell him where he'd gone;
Said I, 'Now why do you want to find him?'
'To summons him,' he murmured with a frown,
So I thought there's be no harm to tell him,
Before I pocketed his half a crown,
Why he's moved, *etc.*

On Monday last his landlord came to see him
And he said for rent he owed a lot of tin;
He said if he could find out where he'd moved to,
He would follow him and put the brokers in.
I said, 'The way he's treated you is shameful;
It's certainly a dirty bit of bizz;
And if you want to find out where he's moved to,
Well, if you listen I will tell you where he is:
Why he's moved,' *etc.*

quid pound.   *tin* money.

After 1853, transportation was largely replaced by penal servitude in British prisons.

Now there is a bloke whose name is Curly Williams, who never had a penny in his time; He wasn't fond of work because it hurt him; If you spoke about a job he used to sigh. He used to loaf a-bout out-side the pub-lic hous-es, And each day he'd scarcely an-y-thing to eat; His clothes were always nice-ly ven-ti-la-ted, And he lived in a little hovel up the street. But he's moved to a bigger house now, Living like a great big don, In a great big, large, five-stor-ey house With a real bathroom and the gas laid on; Lovely grounds all a-round it, No

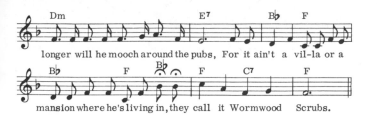

longer will he mooch around the pubs, For it ain't a vil-la or a

mansion where he's living in, they call it Wormwood Scrubs.

Wakefield Gaol

Good people all, give ear I pray,
And mark you well what I do say;
To my misfortunes great and small,
Oh list and I will tell you all.
I used to lead a joyous life,
Devoid of care, devoid of strife,
Could go to bed and fall asleep,
No ugly sprites did round me creep;
But oh, the touts and Cupid – 'gad,
They nearly drove me romping mad,
And from the Town Hall they did me trail
And whipped me into Wakefield Gaol.

Now when we got to the end of the route
The turnkey turned my pockets out,
To see if I had got such stuff
As blunt or grub, tobacco, snuff.
They took me then to try my size,
Colour of hair, colour of eyes,
The length of my nose from root to tip,
Or if I'd more than one top lip.
Then straight with me in a yard they goes
And offered me a suit of clothes.
The kids came out and did me hail:
Another new cock for Wakefield Gaol.

Then one of them said with a roguish leer,
'My fakin' kid, what brought you here?'
Says I, 'Now who d' you think, you lout,
Would bring me here that wasn't a tout?'
Then all came round like so many fools
And one of them spoke about the rules:
That each new cock must sing a song,
Or tell them a tale Bob knows how long,
Or break his wind, or give them a whack,
Or else be tied up to Black Jack;
And there they'd wallop him tooth and nail
With a large wet towel in Wakefield Goal.

I trotted and walked about the yard,
Thinks I, my case is wondrous hard,
When all at once I heard a din:
The deputy yardsman shouts 'Fall in.'
Then blowing down the yard they go
Like brutes turned out of a wild beast show,
Some cracked in skin and some in mind,
And some through cracks showed their behind.
Then one by one went round the tub
To get the county 'lowance of grub,
And blowed our ribs out like a sail
With skilly and whack in Wakefield Gaol.

At half past four, one of them said,
It was nearly time to go to bed,
And truth I found from him to creep,
For soon we all fell in two deep.
The turnkey shouts, as stiff as starch,
First 'Right face,' and then 'Quick march.'
We did, and caused a curious rush,
Like monkeys marching round a brush.
Such clinking of clogs and shaking of keys,
Croaking of bellies and shaking of knees,
Cursing of beds as hard as a nail,
It would starve the devil in Wakefield Gaol.

At seven next morning, up we got;
Each stoned his cell and cleaned his pot,
And then about the yard did lurch
Till all fell in to go to church.
There such dress did meet the view:
One arm was red, the other blue,
One leg was yellow, the other was grey;
Then the parson came to preach and pray.
He said Elijah went up in a cloud,
And Lazarus walked about in a shroud,
And Jonah lived inside of a whale:
It was better than living in Wakefield Gaol.

When service was over, all came back;
At eight fell in for skilly and whack,
Like pigs were crouched all as a lump;

At nine each took a turn at bump;
At ten we raised a glorious mill,
They fibbed each other with right good will;
At twelve we got a quiet house,
Then all fell in for cans of scouse.
But if there's a row, no matter how droll,
They pop the kids in Pompey's hole,
Where whack and water cocks their tail:
Oh, there's glorious doings in Wakefield Gaol.

But all young men be ruled by me,
Don't let your passions act too free,
And keep from each blue lobster's claw,
And run from each thief-taker's paw.
But if the fates should me increase
And make me deputy of police,
And this blue bottle turned about,
Oh, wouldn't I nicely serve him out:
I'd bone the tout in half a crack
And feed him well on skilly and whack;
Oh, wouldn't I make him droop his tail:
He should hunt for his dinner in Wakefield Gaol.

tout person who supplied information about racing form; in this
    case, presumably, incorrect information. Alternatively, a police-
    man(?).
turnkey warder.
blunt money.
cock fellow.
faking swindling.
whack bread.
stoned holystoned.
bump coarse cloth, which was sewed in prison.
mill fight.
fibbed struck.
scouse sort of meat and vegetable stew.
Pompey's hole punishment cell.
blue lobster policeman.
blue bottle policeman.
bone hit.
skilly gruel.

Good peo-ple all, give ear I pray, And mark you well what
I do say; To my mis-for-tunes great and small, oh
list and I will tell you all. I used to lead a
joy-ous life, De-void of care, de-void of strife, Could
go to bed and fall a-sleep, No ug-ly sprites did
round me creep, But oh, the touts and Cu-pid-'gad, They
near-ly drove me ramp-ing mad, And from the Town Hall they
did me trail And whipped me in-to Wake-field Gaol.

This ballad was very popular about the middle of the century.
Other versions, identical but for the name, mention Preston,
Kirkdale and Belle Vue Gaols as well as merely 'the County Gaol'.

New Bailey Tread-mill

In Manchester New Bailey we've got a new corn mill,
And those whose actions send them here of it will have
  their fill.
So prisoners now a caution take, obey me in a crack,
Or I will take my whip and flog you right well o'er your
  back.

Chorus
So it's work, work, mind, mind, work with free goodwill,
In Manchester New Bailey we've got a treading mill.

At six o'clock the bell does ring, to work we must proceed,
To turn this plaguey treading mill would kill a horse
  indeed;
If you should give him one black look, or offer to rebel,
He'd keep a Tommy every day and march you in the cell.

Now those may call this a cruel plan who are not fond of
  work,
But while you're here you must become as nimble as a cork.
Pull off your coat and try your strength, what you can
  undergo;
Oh dear, this cursèd treading mill, it makes me puff and
  blow,

If I work three months at this mill I fear I shall be dead;
I feel the flesh desert my bones, I wish I had been wed.
Had I a wife, a very good wife, she'd pity my sad case,
And by some means she'd teach me how to keep from such
  a place.

We prisoners here are bound and cannot once say nay;
This is a place of exercise, therefore we must obey.
If you attempt for to neglect, the consequence we tell:
You'll get the whip across your back and lodge in the
  back cell.

Your conversation makes me quake and tremble with great
  fear;

My collar bone will surely break, I wish I'd not come here.
The devil take your collar bone, your idle bones beside,
And mind your work or you will get the lash across your
   hide.

Now when these treadles you do tread, mind how you take
   your steps,
For if your foot should chance to slip, you'd get a smack i'
   th' chops;
Besides, your skilly they will stop and nothing you must
   fetch,
You'll ramble about all in your clogs, just like a forlorn
   wretch.

So recollect I caution you, beware of our strong nets;
For dainties we do not preserve to stuff a prisoner's guts.
If ever I get my discharge I'll labour with good will,
And no more taste of Manchester New Bailey's treading
   mill.

Manchester New Bailey this was in fact in Salford, though very near
   to Deansgate, Manchester. It existed from 1792 until 1871. Elizabeth Fry visited it in 1818.
corn mill in fact, the treadmill (see below).
skilly gruel.

Mr Cubitt designed the first prison tread-wheel. William (later
Sir William) Cubitt was a Lowestoft engineer. In 1818 he had had
occasion to visit the Suffolk County Gaol in Bury St Edmunds
and he had noticed a crowd of prisoners lounging about just
inside. . . . Cubitt had promised that he would try to devise a
simple means to keep the prisoners occupied, and a short while
later he had developed his human tread-wheel, which was to
form one of the central features of the British prison system for
the remainder of the century. The tread-wheel fulfilled a dual
function; it could be used for a practical purpose such as operating a mill, grinding corn or raising water: on the other hand, it
was a tiring, monotonous and degrading form of labour (A.
Babington, *English Bastille*, p.175).
Even a comparatively short spell in a House of Correction like
the dreaded 'Steel' (Bastille) in Coldbath Fields could be a highly
damaging experience. Here the treadmills were close compartments in which a prisoner remained for a quarter of an hour at a

time, vigorously treading down a wheel of twenty-four steps at a fixed rate. They were arranged in rows which 'gave them somewhat of the appearance of the stalls in a public urinal', the wheels turning a long axle attached to an ingenious apparatus of air-vanes that allowed it to revolve at exactly the right, agonizing speed. As a warder explained to the ever curious and compassionate Henry Mayhew, who visited the place in the 1850s – 'You see the men can get no firm tread like, from the steps always sinking away from under their feet and *that* makes it very tiring. Again the compartments are small, and the air becomes very hot, so that the heat at the end of a quarter of an hour renders it difficult to breathe' (K. Chesney, *The Victorian Underworld*, pp. 29–30).

Durham Gaol

You'll all have heard of Durham Gaol,
But it would you much surprise
To see the prisoners in the yard
When they're on exercise;
This yard is built around wi' walls
So noble and so strong:
Whoever goes there has to bide
His time, be it short or long.

Chorus
There's no good luck in Durham Gaol,
There's no good luck at all;
What is bread and skilly for,
But just to make you small?

When you go to Durham Gaol,
They'll find you with employ;
They'll dress you up so dandy
In a suit o' corduroy.
They'll fetch a cap without a peak,
And never ask your size;
And like your suit it's corduroy
And comes down over your eyes.

The first month is the worst of all,
Your feelings they will try;
There's nowt but two great lumps o' wood
On which you have to lie.
Then after that you get to bed,
Well it's as hard as stones;
At night you dursn't make a turn,
For fear you break some bones.

All kinds o' work there going on
Upon these noble flats:
Teasin' oakum, makin' balls,
And weavin' coco mats.
When you go in you may be thin,
But they can make you thinner;

If your oakum is not teased,
They're sure to stop your dinner.

The shoes you get is often tens,
The smallest size is nine;
They're big enough to make a skiff
For Boyd upon the Tyne.
And if you should be cold at nights,
Just make yourself at home:
Wrap your clothes around your shoes
And get inside o' them.

You'll get your meat and clothes for nowt,
Your house and firin' free;
All your meat's brought to the door –
How happy you should be.
There's soap and towel, and wooden spoon,
And a little baby's pot;
They bring you papers every week
For you to clean your bot.

Durham Gaol was completed in 1852.

oakum picking oakum was unravelling lengths of rope, and separating all the fibres.

makin' balls presumably a jocular reference to shot-drill, which was passing iron balls down a line of prisoners. During a quarter-hour stint at this punishment, a man would walk almost two miles, sideways, while picking up and putting down a twenty-four pound weight every three yards; alternatively, the balls referred to may have been wound from the hemp.

Boyd champion oarsman, at a time when sculling on the Tyne was a very popular sport.

Like *The Skeul-Board Man* (p.150), this ballad was written by Tommy Armstrong (1848–1919). It was based on his own experience, when he served a sentence in Durham Gaol for stealing a pair of stockings from the Co-op at West Stanley. He was drunk at the time and, from the way they were displayed, the stockings appeared to be bowlegged. Tommy was small and bow-legged and they seemed ideal for him.

A Dialogue and Song on the Starvation Poor Law Bill, between Tom and Ben

TOM Well, Ben, you are the very man I want to see.

BEN Well, what is the matter now?

TOM Why, I wanted to know if thee'st made any rhymes about this starvation Bill, as I have heard some call it.

BEN Why, the thought of living upon fifteen pence halfpenny per week has put me in such a fright that, though I tried, I could not please myself with it. To think that they should unite six or seven parishes together and victual the paupers at so much a head, as poor farmers take cattle to straw; to part a man from his wife, and the children from both; and not so much ground as a jail yard to walk in, which shocks me to the soul. Who knows what his latter end may be? They had better be as Lord Delamere said:

I would take them into Cheshire and there they would sow
Both flax and strong hemp for to hang them in a row;
You'd better to hang them and stop soon their breath,
If your Majesty please, than to starve them to death.

Success to old England, with peace, trade and plenty;
Of good meat abundance, and all kinds of dainty.
The grain is well housèd, with plenty in store,
Yet villains are griping and grinding the poor.

Poor widows may have I may say children three,
To be ta'en from their parents, no day-light to see;
Still more than all this, which will cause grief and strife,
A poor man must be parted from his own loving wife.

This puts me in mind of cruel Herod the King,
When Messiah was born, quite evil his sting;
All sweet little infants he did them disdain:
All babes two years old and under were slain.

O wretched of mortals where this Poor Bill takes place,
Some thousands I fear will soon end your race,
Be put in the grave for to mould and decay,
To rise up in triumph at the last Judgement Day.

There's Campbell and Lord John have plenty of store,
The blood of poor creatures will be placed at their door;
Must be all called aside, no matter how soon,
And swept off the earth with that cursèd old Brougham.

Now cometh sharp winter when the weather is cold,
How piercing it proves to the infirm and old;
All those who have thousands, they still crave for more,
All you that have plenty, pray think on the poor.

Now for to conclude these few lines which I've penned,
May the rich to the poor man still yet prove a friend;
The new Poor Law Bill, let it be cast away,
Abolished from England for ever I say.

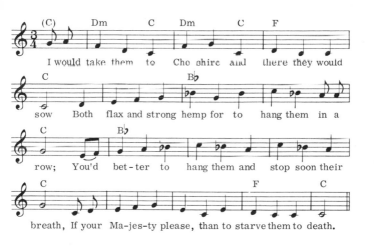

I would take them to Cheshire and there they would
sow Both flax and strong hemp for to hang them in a
row; You'd bet-ter to hang them and stop soon their
breath, If your Ma-jes-ty please, than to starve them to death.

Lord Delamere Tory peer (1767–1855) with estates in Cheshire.
Campbell Home Secretary.
Lord John Lord John Russell (1792–1878).
Brougham Lord Chancellor; responsible for piloting the bill through
the House of Lords. His name was pronounced 'Broom'.

The old system of parish relief for the poor went back to Elizabethan times. The Poor Law Amendment Act of 1834 brought in a new regime, administered by three commissioners, who rapidly became known as 'the three bashaws (pashas) of Somerset House'. The commissioners were empowered to group parishes into unions, where workhouses (which became known as 'unions') would be established. The able-bodied might receive no relief except within the workhouse, where conditions were deliberately made harsh. Married paupers were to be kept separate, in order to prevent child-bearing.

The new act was quickly implemented in the South of England, but it was resolutely – and, at times, violently – opposed in the

East and North. The new Bastilles, as they came to be called, were set on fire or pulled down. In many of the northern towns it was ten years or more before the act could be enforced. 'It created more embittered unhappiness than any other statute of modern British history' (E. J. Hobsbawm, *Industry*, p.229). It also created – or, at least, exacerbated – that fear and detestation of the workhouse which are reflected in Victorian literature. This trauma remained in the minds of ordinary people perhaps until 1945.

The present ballad is one of many which deal with the act of 1834. The ballad seems to have been part of the agitation against the legislation. Another ballad deals with the riots in East Anglia which followed the passing of the act.

The New Gruel Shops

Good people all I pray draw near that in this country
    dwell;
Concerning these new workhouses the truth to you I'll tell.
Now no relief they give the poor if out of work they drop,
For by this Act, off they are packed to those new gruel shops.

Chorus
May Providence protect the poor while on the earth they
    stop,
That none of them may have to go to these new gruel shops.

In England now like mushrooms they spring up from the
    ground,
And they will cost poor Johnny Bull full many a thousand
    pound;
He'll find this bill a bitter pill – it'll punch his belly
    through –
It'll cost him many a thousand pound for making water
    gruel.

The bedsteads there I do declare are made of iron strong;
The beds are filled with feathers fine, they're nearly two
    yards long.
No grates are there I do declare or smoke your eyes to
    torture:
For all the rooms are to be warmed by a pot of boiling water.

Each morning for their breakfast they're to have skilly
    gruel;
Poor women will not be allowed to have a cup of tea.
Men from their wives will parted be, indeed it is no joke;
And no snuff must the women take, men neither chew nor
    smoke.

For building these new workhouses some people did agree
Because they thought from poor rates the law would set
    them free;
But now they find out their mistake they scratch their
    wooden blocks

They do repent they did consent to build these new gruel
   shops.

Now to conclude and likewise end these lines which I have
   penned,
I hope there's no one present here my song it might offend.
Be kind unto the labouring poor who for your wealth do toil:
The Lord will surely bless you with the widow's cruse of oil.

feathers nearly two yards long horse hair.
skilly gruel prison gruel.

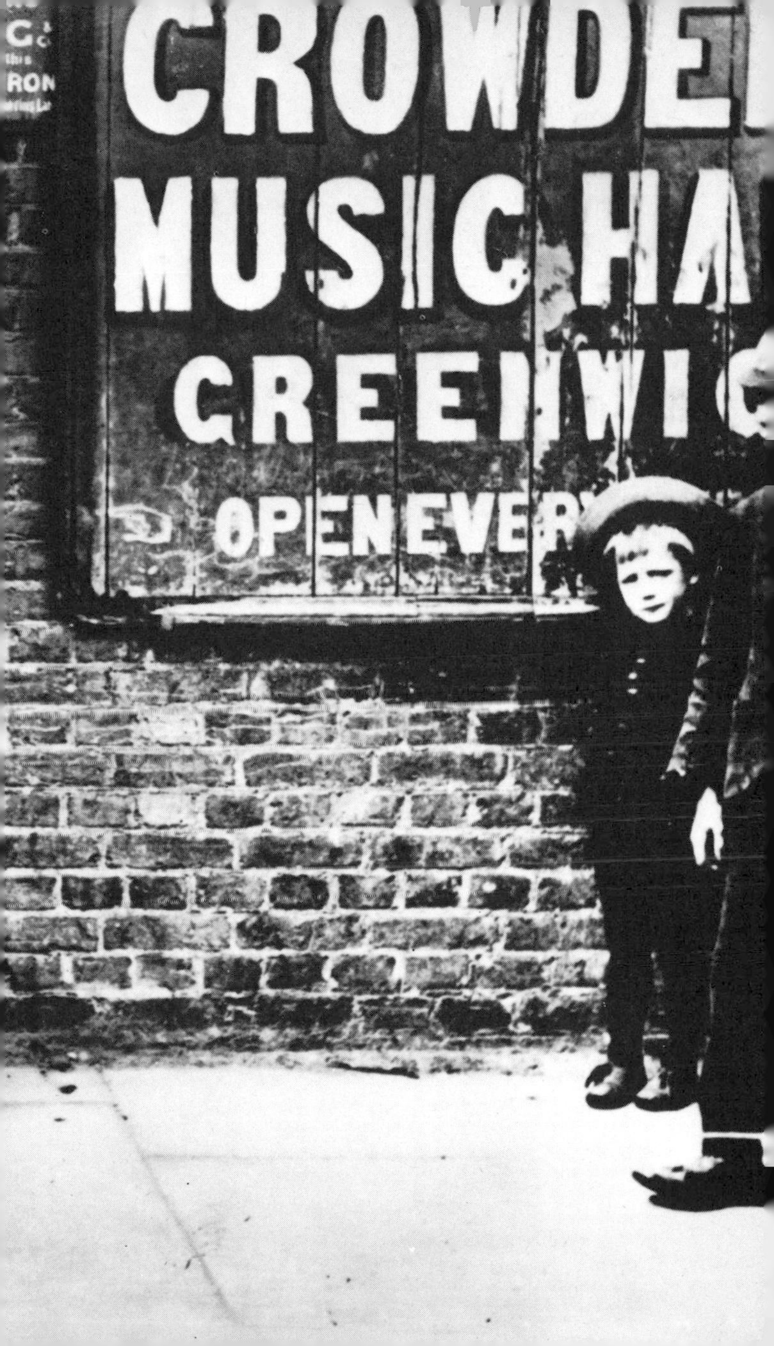
CROWDE
MUSIC HA
GREENWIC
OPEN EVE

New Song: 'To Hereford Old Town'

To Hereford Old Town a new hero is come down,
Oh, pray tell me where he does lie, lie, lie.
At the tradesman's next door, where he never was before,
He is gone for to talk, not to buy, buy, buy.

He says that it is clear free sugar brews good beer,
And so the malt tax it may stand, stand, stand.
Our ships that plough the main may bring us foreign grain,
So he cares not for farmer or for land, land, land.

The black men of Brazil, he would flay them to the heel,
So a farthing in sugar he saves, saves, saves.
Though millions it would cost that such trade should be lost,
And Britons no longer use slaves, slaves, slaves.

The Ballot and Free Trade and the gammon that is made
The subject of his jaw, jaw, jaw;
But the workhouse, like a prison, and policemen by the
dozen
They are the fruits of their law, law, law.

To separate in life the husband and the wife,
It is a part of their plan, plan, plan.
Of freedom though they prate, yet all freedom they hate,
And the rights both of woman and of man, man, man.

The Whig Commissioner Drone starves the poor unto the
bone,
And then kills them with steam and with stench, stench,
stench;
And for those that are dying wholesale coffins he is buying,
And in them soon their fate he will clench, clench, clench.

The Treasury at will may our hero's pocket fill,
But what can be done for his head, head, head?
I fear his lack of brains will frustrate all their pains,
For his noddle, sir, is filled up with lead, lead, lead.

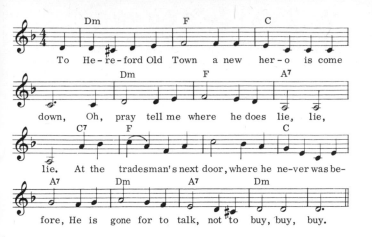

To He-re-ford Old Town a new her-o is come down, Oh, pray tell me where he does lie, lie, lie. At the tradesman's next door, where he ne-ver was be-fore, He is gone for to talk, not to buy, buy, buy.

This is rather a curious song attacking the Whig politicians who supported Reform ('the Ballot') and Free Trade, but also brought in the Poor Law Amendment Act and expanded the police force. Perhaps the 'new hero' was a parliamentary candidate at Hereford, or a supporter of Free Trade who was visiting the town. The song has a hardness and bitterness which characterized many of the popular social movements in the nineteenth century (see Part Five).

The People's Comic Alphabet

A stands for alphabet, I've turned it to rhyme,
And it is written about these times;
B stands for Bruce, who this session, we hear,
Has got a new dodge to stop our Sunday beer.

C stands for country, where the nobs have the sway,
If you ask for your rights, to prison straightway;
D stands for Dilke, he's the people's best friend,
He shows us the money paid for royalty to spend.

E stands for England, that place of great fame,
The workers make wealth for the masters to gain;
F stands for freedom, which we boast about,
If you've got no dinner, y' can freely go without.

G stands for Game Laws in this land so fair,
Where a man goes to prison for killing a hare;
H stands for House where the Lords they do sit,
It's time we gave peers all their notice to quit.

I stands for Ireland that's badly used been,
Soon they'll have their Parliament on College Green;
J stands for John Bull, who's taxed every way,
So a lot of fat Germans can all sport and play.

K stands for kingdom, Great Britain I mean, sir,
Heavily taxed for the fat lady at Windsor;
L stands for Lorne and also for Louise,
They'd thirty thousand pounds all in bright Scotch
    bawbees.

M stands for money, where's the poor man's share?
With rent and with taxes, his pocket's soon bare;
N for next election, we'll see soon no doubt,
MPs voting dowry will all get kicked out.

O stands for Odger, he'll abolish each tax,
The people cry, 'Go it, there's a bonny cock o' wax';
P stands for Parliament where tories whigs meet,

Where they have forty winks and rest their gouty feet.

Q stands for queen, who for nothing gets paid,
Though she can't keep her children on a thousand a day;
R stands for riches which the swells they all keep,
While, starving, the poor they can die in the street.

S for Scotch oatmeal, also for Scotch porridge,
Princess Louise likes it better than sausage;
T stands for tally man, when the husband's out,
Sells second-hand clothes that's been put up the spout.

U for useless palaces, cost ten thousand or more,
They'll turn Buckingham Palace into a soup kitchen for the
    poor;
V for Victoria, a large family she's got,
They all dip their hands in the poor man's pot.

W stands for workhouse, at the end of a hard life,
In these English bastilles they part man and wife;
X stands for ten, add five: fifteen, we hear,
The number of thousands Prince Arthur gets each year.

Y for young Brigham with his forty wives tight,
Five for each weekday, ten for Sunday night;
Z for zoological, all others surpasses,
Darwin says we're descended from gorillas and jackasses.

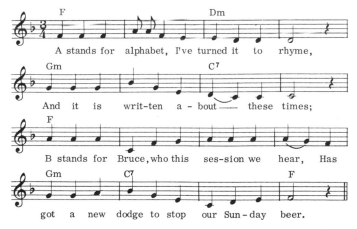

A stands for alphabet, I've turned it to rhyme,
And it is written about these times;
B stands for Bruce, who this session we hear, Has
got a new dodge to stop our Sunday beer.

Bruce Henry Bruce (1815–95) piloted a Licensing Bill through the House of Commons in 1872, which began to bring the drink trade under control (See Turner, *Roads to Ruin*).

Dilke C. W. Dilke (1843–1911) was an MP who campaigned for better conditions for the workers and who, in 1871–2 attacked in Parliament the expense to the country of the royal family, including, for example, the dowries voted for the queen's children.

Game Laws though far less severe than half a century earlier, the Game Laws were still irksome, to say the least. A Select Committee of the House of Commons was inquiring into the subject in 1873.

fat lady at Windsor Queen Victoria.

Lorne . . . Louise Louise (1848–1939) was one of Victoria's nine children. She received a dowry of £30,000 on her marriage to the Marquis of Lorne.

bawbee halfpenny.

Odger George Odger (1820–77) was a London trade unionist who made five unsuccessful attempts to enter Parliament.

cock o' wax fellow (a familiar form of address).

tally man see song on p.190.

spout pawn.

English bastilles workhouses (see songs on p.260ff.).

Prince Arthur another of Victoria's children (1850–1942).

young Brigham Brigham Young, a Mormon leader.

Darwin Charles Darwin (1809–82), the author of *The Origin of Species*.

These political alphabets were not uncommon in the nineteenth century. They were ephemeral, because the events they dealt with were quickly out of date. This one provides an interesting picture of radical, working-class opinion in 1873 or 1874.

5

The World Turned Upside Down

The Colliers' March

The summer was over, the season unkind,
In harvest a snow how uncommon to find;
The times were oppressive and, well be it known,
That hunger will strongest of fences break down.

'Twas then from their cells the black gentry stepped out
With bludgeons, determined to stir up a rout;
The prince of the party, who revelled from home,
Was a terrible fellow, and called Irish Tom.

He brandished his bludgeon with dexterous skill
And close to his elbow was placed Barley Will.
Instantly followed a numerous train,
Cheerful as bold Robin Hood's merry men.

Sworn to remedy a capital fault
And bring down the exorbitant price of the malt,
From Dudley to Walsall they trip it along
And Hampton was truly alarmed at the throng.

Women and children, wherever they go,
Shouting out, 'Oh the brave Dudley boys, O';
Nailers and spinners the cavalcade join,
The markets to lower their flattering design.

Six days out of seven poor nailing boys get
Little else at their meals but potatoes to eat;
For bread hard they labour, good things never carve,
And swore 'twere as well to be hanged as to starve.

Such are the feelings in every land,
Nothing Necessity's call can withstand;
And riots are certain to sadden the year
When sixpenny loaves but three-pounders appear.

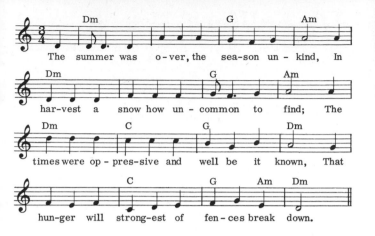

The summer was o-ver, the sea-son un-kind, In
har-vest a snow how un-common to find; The
times were op-pres-sive and well be it known, That
hun-ger will strong-est of fen-ces break down.

black gentry colliers.

Hampton Wolverhampton.

Oh the brave Dudley boys refrain of a contemporary song about a food riot (see R. Palmer, *Songs of the Midlands*, 1972).

nailing boys boys working in the nail trade.

This song was written by the Birmingham balladeer, John Freeth. It may have been inspired by the events of 21 October 1782, when there was a march from the Black Country into Birmingham:

> On Thursday a Party of Colliers . . . arrived here about four o' clock in the afternoon, and were met in the Bull-Ring by one of the Officers of the Town, who desired to speak with their Leader, who immediately appeared. He demanded of him, what he and his Party meant, in coming into the Town in that hostile manner? and was answered, They did not come with the intention of committing any Depredations, but to Regulate the Prices of Malt, Flour, Butter, Cheese etc. . . . The Gentleman promised them, if they would immediately go out of the Town peaceably, and commit no Outrage, that he would do everything in his power to have the Prices of the different articles they complained of properly regulated. . . . In the meantime . . . the Military were drawn up in the Square . . . and . . . they paraded in different Streets, with Drums beating, etc. (*Aris's Gazette*).

Such price-regulating protests, and indeed, riots, were endemic in the latter part of the eighteenth century.

NEW HA

MINERS 1877 1 AUGUST

The Rights of Mankind

To mortals who genuine liberty prize
And extension disdain on the laws of excise,
How glorious to see – can the heart wish for more? –
The Rights of Mankind spreading all the world o'er.

Chorus
Down a down down, down a down down,
Down a down down derry, down a down down.

The blaze in America first that began
O'er Europe is rapidly taking a run;
And France wrongs to crush in one year has done more
Than a century ever accomplished before.

Revolutions in states set the world on a roar,
The flame on the continent spreads more and more;
Madrid is alarmed and much startled is Rome,
For the people when roused will be sure to strike home.

To the heart not a conquest more pleasure bespeaks
Than that which the fetters of tyranny breaks;
May life's noblest nerves in the cause still be strained,
And the Rights of Mankind be for ever maintained.

Commercial concerns in all kingdoms we know,
Like the tide of the ocean will ebb and will flow;
But state-craft and priest-craft, if people are wise,
When brought to a level will never more rise.

Abolished by every despotic decree,
May the Turk live in peace and the Negro be free;
And Britons be all of one heart and one mind
In promoting the general good of mankind.

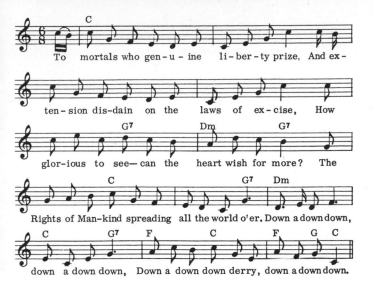

To mortals who gen-u-ine li-ber-ty prize, And ex-
ten-sion dis-dain on the laws of ex-cise, How
glor-ious to see— can the heart wish for more? The
Rights of Man-kind spreading all the world o'er. Down a down down,
down a down down, Down a down down derry, down a down down.

The blaze in America the American War of Independence lasted
    from 1775 until 1783, but America declared itself independent in
    1776.
France . . . in one year that is, presumably, since the revolution in
    1789.
the Turk a byword throughout the eighteenth century for illiberal-
    ism and backwardness.
the Negro be free slavery was not abolished by the British Parlia-
    ment until 1833, though the carrying of slaves in British ships was
    outlawed in 1806.

This ballad was written by John Freeth (cf. p.275) in 1790, the date
being provided by the reference to one year of the revolutionary
regime in France. 1790 was the year of Burke's impassioned attack
on the French Revolution, which inspired Tom Paine's book, *The
Rights of Man*. It is interesting to see John Freeth taking up an
extreme radical position. His attitude is, however, one of typically
eighteenth-century rationalism: all will be well, provided that we
are reasonable enough.

Watkinson and his Thirteens

That monster oppression, behold how he stalks,
Keeps picking the bones of the poor as he walks,
There's not a mechanic throughout this whole land
But more or less feels the weight of his hand;
That offspring of tyranny, baseness and pride,
Our rights hath invaded and almost destroyed.
May that man be banished who villainy screens,
Or sides with big Watkinson and his thirteens.

Chorus
And may the odd knife his great carcase dissect,
Lay open his vitals for men to inspect,
A heart full as black as the infernal gulf,
In that greedy, blood-sucking and bone-scraping wolf.

This wicked dissenter, expelled his own church,
Is rendered the subject of public reproach;
Since reprobate marks on his forehead appeared,
We all have concluded his conscience is seared.
See mammon his God and oppression his aim,
Hark! how the streets ring with his infamous name.
The boys at the playhouse exhibit strange scenes
Respecting big Watkinson and his thirteens.

Like Pharoah for baseness, that type of the devil,
He wants to flog journeymen with rods of steel,
And certainly would, had he got Pharoah's power:
His heart is as hard and his temper as sour.
But justice repulsed him and set us all free
Like bond-slaves of old in the year jubilee.
May those be transported or sent for marines
That works for big Watkinson at his thirteens.

We claim as true Yorkshiremen leave to speak twice,
That no man should work for him at any price,
Since he has attempted our lives to enthral,
And mingle our liquor with wormwood and gall.

Beelzebub, take him with his ill-got pelf,
He's equally bad, if not worse than thyself.
So shall every cutler that honestly means
Cry 'Take away Watkinson with his thirteens.'

But see, foolish mortals! far worse than insane,
Three-fourths are returned into Egypt again.
Although Pharoah's hands they had fairly escaped,
Now they must submit for their bones to be scraped.
Whilst they give themselves and their all for a prey,
Let us be unanimous and jointly say:
Success to our sovereign who peaceably reigns,
But down with both Watkinson's twelves and thirteens.

mechanic workman.

Joseph Mather wrote this song. He was born at Chelmorton, near
Buxton, Derbyshire, in 1737. In 1751 he started an eight-year

apprenticeship in Sheffield, to learn the file trade. He soon became well-known as a writer of satirical songs, which he was not above selling in the streets, sometimes while seated on a donkey or a bull, facing the tail. He also sang in public houses and at fairs and race meetings.

He was a strong supporter of the Radical cause in the 1790s. One of his songs, a parody of the national anthem, begins:

God save great Thomas Paine,
His 'Rights of Man' to explain
To ev'ry soul.
He makes the blind to see
What dupes and slaves they be,
And points out liberty,
From pole to pole.

His attacks on local dignitaries and employers were as fearless as they were virulent, and he became the acknowledged champion of the working people of Sheffield. They held him in enormous affection,

that man be ban-ished who vil-lain-y screens, Or

sides with big Wat-kin-son and his thir-teens. And

may the odd knife his great car-case dis-sect, Lay

o-pen his vi-tals for men to in-spect, A

heart full as black as the in-fern-al gulf, In that

greed-y, blood-suck-ing and bone-scrap-ing wolf.

and great numbers of them followed his funeral cortege, in 1804. Sixty years later, some of his songs were still remembered.

Watkinson and his Thirteens was 'perhaps the most popular of Mather's songs'.

I can never forget the impression made on my mind when a boy on hearing it sung by an old cutler. This event happened on a 'good saint Monday', during a 'foot ale' which was drank in the workshop. After the singer had 'wet his whistle' he requested his shopmates to assist in chorus, and then struck off in a manly voice, laying strong emphasis on the last two lines in each stanza, at the conclusion of which he struck his stithy with a hammer for a signal, when all present joined in chorus with such a hearty good will that would have convinced any person that *they felt* the 'odd knife' would have been well employed in dissecting Watkinson's 'vile carcase'. The *popular* opinion is that Watkinson

was a 'screw', and the *first* master who compelled his men to make thirteen for a dozen. It is further alleged that the song heart-broke him. This appears to have some support from the song *Watkinson's Repentance*, one verse of which shows that the 'gods of the gallery' sang him out of the theatre. Jonathan Watkinson resided in Silver Street, and was one of the principal manufacturers of the day. He was master cutler in 1787. . . . How far the conduct of Mr Watkinson merited Mather's denunciations cannot now be satisfactorily established. I have heard several old workmen say that he was a master who paid a *good price* for his labour, and was a kind-hearted man. If money had been his god I scarcely think he would have died broken-hearted. . . . I cannot ascertain when Watkinson died. He was living in 1790 . . . He was dead, however, in December, 1791 (John Wilson (ed.), *The Songs of Joseph Mather*, Sheffield, 1862, pp.63–4).

General Ludd's Triumph

No more chant your old rhymes about bold Robin Hood
His feats I do little admire.
I'll sing the achievements of General Ludd,
Now the hero of Nottinghamshire.
Brave Ludd was to measures of violence unused
Till his sufferings became so severe,
That at last to defend his own interests he roused,
And for the great fight did prepare.

The guilty may fear but no vengeance he aims
At the honest man's life or estate;
His wrath is entirely confined to wide frames
And to those that old prices abate.
Those engines of mischief were sentenced to die
By unanimous vote of the trade,
And Ludd who can all opposition defy
Was the grand executioner made.

And when in the work he destruction employs,
Himself to no method confines;
By fire and by water he gets them destroyed,
For the elements aid his designs.
Whether guarded by soldiers along the highway,
Or closely secured in a room,
He shivers them up by night and by day
And nothing can soften their doom.

He may censure great Ludd's disrespect for the laws,
Who ne'er for a moment reflects
That foul imposition alone was the cause
Which produced these unhappy effects.
Let the haughty the humble no longer oppress,
Then shall Ludd sheathe his conquering sword;
His grievances instantly meet with redress,
Then peace shall be quickly restored.

Let the wise and the great lend their aid and advice
Nor e'er their assistance withdraw,
Till full-fashioned work at the old-fashioned price

Is established by custom and law.
Then the trade when this arduous contest is o'er
Shall raise in full splendour its head;
And colting and cutting and squaring no more
Shall deprive honest workmen of bread.

No more chant your old rhymes about bold Rob-in Hood, His feats I do lit-tle ad-mire. I'll sing the achievements of Gen-er-al Ludd, Now the her-o of Nottingham-shire. Brave Ludd was to measures of vio-lence un-used Till his sufferings became so se-vere, That at last to de-fend his own interests he roused, And for the great fight did pre-pare. That at last to defend his own interests he roused, And for the great fight did pre-pare.

Ludd mythical leader of the Luddites.
abate reduce.
wide frames see below.
colting a 'colt' was one who had not served a proper apprenticeship;

colting therefore was the practice of employing workers who were
not properly trained.

cutting . . . squaring see below.

Luddism was essentially a conservative movement intended to
defend the existing situation against change, which represented a
lowering of standards, not only of wages but of workmanship.
In Nottinghamshire the Luddite campaign started in 1811 and went
on into the following year. The grievances of the framework knitters
(cf. song on p.204) were that they

> had found their livelihood half-ruined by the war, and on top
> of this their condition was sharply worsened by the selling on a
> large scale of 'cut-ups' made on 'wide frames'. A stocking frame
> is narrow, but there were in existence a large number of wide
> frames for knitting pantaloons and fancy stockings called 'twills'.
> Twills had gone out of fashion; pantaloons, whose chief market
> was the Continent, could not be sold because of the war. Un-
> scrupulous owners had their weavers weave large pieces of cloth
> on the now idle wide frames and then cut the pieces by scissors
> into the shape of stockings, gloves, or whatever else it might be.
> These 'cut-ups' were then stitched up: having no selvedges like
> the true stockings they rapidly fell to pieces. But the shoddy was
> ruining the market. The Luddites appeared in village after village
> and smashed the wide frames, and any other frames worked by
> un-apprenticed labour. A good many masters, though they did
> not approve of the methods, approved of the results (G. D. H.
> Cole and R. Postgate, *The Common People 1746–1846*, p.185).

The ballad has been preserved in manuscript in the Home Office
papers, presumably thanks to a magistrate or an informer who sent
it up as evidence. The tune used was that of a popular song of the day,
Poor Jack, by Charles Dibdin, the patriotic song-writer.

Hunting a Loaf

Good people I pray, now hear what I say,
And pray do not call it sedition;
For these great men of late they have cracked my poor
    pate:
I'm wounded, in a woeful condition.

Chorus
And sing fal lal the diddle i do,
Sing fal the diddle i do,
Sing fal the lal day.

For in Derby it's true and in Nottingham too,
Poor men to the jail they've been taking;
They say that Ned Ludd, as I understood,
A thousand wide frames has been breaking.

Now it is not bad there's no work to be had,
The poor to be starved in their station;
And if they do steal they're straight sent to jail,
And they're hanged by the laws of the nation.

Since this time last year I've been very queer,
And I've had a sad national cross;
I've been up and down from town to town,
With a shilling to buy a big loaf.

The first that I met was Sir Francis Burdett,
He told me he'd been in the Tower;
I told him my mind a big loaf was to find,
He said, 'You must ask them in power.'

Then I thought it was time to speak to the Prime,
For Perceval would take my part;
But a Liverpool man soon ended the plan:
With a pistol he shot through his heart.

Then I thought he'd a chance on a rope for to dance,
Some people would think very pretty;
But he lost all his fun, through the country he'd run,
And he found it in fair London city.

Now ending my song I'll sit down with my ale,
And I'll drink a good health to the poor;
With a glass of good ale I have told you my tale,
And I'll look for a big loaf no more.

Good peo-ple I pray,— now hear what I
say, And pray do not call it se - di-tion;—
— For these great men of late they have cracked my poor
pate: I'm wounded, in a woe-ful con - di - tion.
And sing fal lal the did-dle i do, Sing
fal the did-dle i do, Sing fal the lal day.

wide frames see note on previous song.

hanged it is said that in 1800 the death penalty existed for 200 offences.

a big loaf the wars with France from 1793–1815 were accompanied by rising prices, a particularly high level being reached in 1813, when prices were twice as high as in 1790. The price of wheat rose from 95s. 3d. a quarter in 1811 to 126s. 6d. in 1812.

Sir Francis Burdett radical MP.

Perceval Prime Minister (see below).

On the 11 May (1812) the Prime Minister, Perceval, was assassinated in the House of Commons. For a day the country was in turmoil. Popular elation was undisguised. . . . The crowd in

Nottingham celebrated, and 'paraded the town with drums beating and flags flying in triumph'. In London itself crowds gathered outside the House of Commons as the news seeped out, and as the assassin, John Bellingham, was taken away there were 'repeated shouts of applause from the ignorant or depraved part of the crowd'. The news that Bellingham was probably deranged, and had acted from motives of private grievance, was received almost with disappointment. . . . When Bellingham went to the scaffold, people cried out 'God bless him', and Coleridge heard them add: 'This is but the beginning' (E. P. Thompson, *The Making of the English Working Class*, p.570).

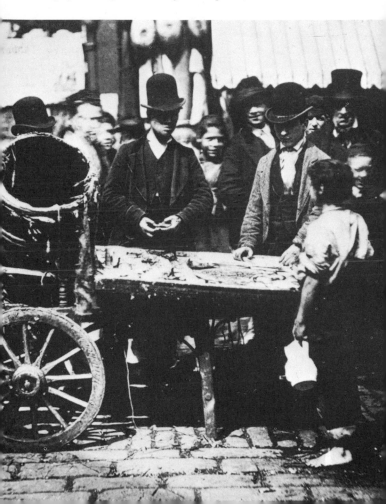

A Radical Song

Ye friends to Reform, prepare for good fun,
Under your feet your enemies tread;
The grand revolution's nearly begun,
Now is the time for blood to be shed.

Chorus
Freedom, freedom, plunder and freedom,
We will have freedom and blood on our bread.
Freedom, freedom, shoot 'em and bleed 'em;
All that won't join we'll knock on the head.

The prince our petitions refuses, of course,
Under your feet, etc.
So now is the time to try physical force,
Now is the time, etc.

The old constitution we'll quickly pull down,
A fig for the Lords, the Commons and Crown.

In Liberty's cause, we'll volunteer all,
And those that won't help, by force we must haul.

No labour! no taxes! no prisons! no laws!
Take what you want, to aid the good cause.

All soldiers we'll kill in this grand reformation,
Then bloodshed we'll stop, and bring peace to the nation.

The priest must be hanged, and the Bibles all burnt,
For fear qualms of conscience from them should be learnt.

Would the Radical Frenchmen ever have braved
All laws, had they thought they had souls to be saved?

Blaspheme and the Devil may come if he will;
He's of old a reformer, he'll favour us still.

And should he prepare us in hell a warm berth,
We'll forestall him by making a hell upon earth.

Then down with religion and laws at a blow!
Huzza for Hunt, Wooler, Paine, Satan and Co.

Hunt Henry, Radical politician (see p.297).
Wooler T. J. Wooler (1786–1853), editor of the Radical weekly newspaper, *The Black Dwarf*.
Paine Thomas (see notes on pp.279 and 283).

This street ballad probably dates from the post-war years of 1816 or 1817, which saw a resurgence of Radical activity, and of reaction to it. The association of the Radicals in the ballad with infernal forces (last three verses) is pursued further in another sheet from the same printers (Munday and Slatter, of Oxford), entitled *The Devil and the Radicals*:

From his brimstone bed at the break of day
A mobbing the Devil is gone,
To visit his Radical Friends in Town,
And to see how Reform goes on.

A New Song on the Peterloo Meeting

Rise, Britons, rise now from your slumber,
Rise and hail the glorious day.
Come and be ranked with the number.
With true friends of liberty.
Don't you see those heroes bleeding,
Lying in their crimson gore,
Britain's sons who died for freedom,
And who fell to rise no more.

It was the sixteenth day of August,
Thousands met on Peterloo plain,
Where we arrived, of fear regardless,
Little we knew of their dreadful schemes;
When, lo, we spied them near advancing,
With swords drawn, on mischief bent,
Rushed through the crowd with horses prancing,
'Twoud make a heart of stone relent.

But matchless Hunt, that valiant hero,
His name it shall recorded be;
Says he, 'My friends, I'll never leave you,
Though death be my destiny.'
Straight to New Bailey then they brought him,
In a dungeon close confined;
Then to Lancaster they did send him,
For conspiracy as I've been told.

Britannia's sons so famed for bravery,
Who fought so bold for freedom's cause,
Now you're doomed to cruel slavery,
And oppressed by so many laws.
So Britons, let's no longer greet them,
But endeavour to be free,
Let the air resound and echo
Shouts of Hunt likewise Wolseley.

Rise, Bri - tons, rise now from your slum - ber,
Rise and hail the glor-ious day. Come and be ranked
with the num - ber, With true friends of li-ber-ty. Don't you
see those her - oes bleed - ing, Ly - ing
in their crim-son gore, Bri-tain's sons who
died for free - dom, And who fell to rise no more.

Peterloo plain an area of open land near the centre of Manchester, called St Peter's Field (partly coextensive with what is now St Peter's Square).

Hunt Henry Hunt, radical MP, who was to have addressed the meeting, but was arrested and imprisoned.

New Bailey see p.254.

Wolseley Sir Charles Wolseley, supporter of the radicals.

The story of Peterloo is well known. On 16 August 1819 a large crowd assembled on St Peter's Field to hear 'Orator' Hunt speak on the subject of Parliamentary reform. The crowd was dispersed by a cavalry charge. Eleven people were killed and some 400 injured. The shock and outrage which resulted ensured that Peterloo would never be forgotten.

The events were commemorated in a number of ballads, the best of which has survived only in incomplete form:

'Twas on the sixteenth day of August,
Eighteen hundred and nineteen,

A meeting held in Peter Street
Was glorious to be seen;
Joe Nadin* and his big bull-dogs,
Which you might plainly see,
And on the other side
Stood the bloody cavalry.

Chorus
With Henry Hunt we'll go, my boys,
With Henry Hunt we'll go;
We'll mount the cap of liberty
In spite of Nadin Joe.

It is of interest that the tune specified for our ballad was that for
Parker's Widow, a lament for Richard Parker, who was executed in
1797 for his part in the naval mutiny at the Nore.

*Deputy Constable of Manchester, 1801–21 who organized a system of
  spies and informers in order to combat the radical movement.

New Hunting Song

All you that are low-spirited, I think it won't be wrong
To sing to you a verse or two of my new hunting song;
For hunting is in season, the sport has just begun,
And heroes they will have their fun with their fine dog
    and gun.

Chorus
Oh, a-hunting we will go, my boys, a-hunting we will go,
We'll lay out schemes and try all means to keep the poor
    man low.

It's one of our brave huntsmen, my song I will commence,
Brave Bonaparte I will begin, he was a man of sense;
From Corsica he did set off to hunt upon a chance,
He hunted until he became the Emperor of France.

And Nelson for his hunting he got the nation's praise,
He was the greatest huntsman that hunted on the seas;
He and his war-like terror, a-hunting bore away,
A musket ball proved his downfall in Trafalgar Bay.

Now Wellington at Waterloo, he had the best of luck,
He hunted from a lieutenant till he became a duke;
But men that did fight well for him, and did him honours
    gain,
He tried the very best he could to have their pensions ta'en.

O'Connor round the country, a-hunting he did go,
With meetings called in every town to tell the truth, you
    know;
The tyrants tried to keep him down but that was all in
    vain:
The people swear they'll back him up and have their rights
    again.

Prince Albert to this country came a-hunting for a wife,
He got one that he said he loved far dearer than his life;
Oh, yes, he got the blooming queen to dandle on his knee,
With thirty thousand pounds a year paid from this
    country.

They're hunting up the beggars through the country every
    day,
And hawkers if they do not all a heavy licence pay;
They won't allow the poor to beg, it's against the law to
    steal,
For the beggars there's the bastille and the others go to
    jail.

Now to conclude my hunting song, I hope you will agree,
The poor men they are starving while the rich will have
    their spree;
And to complain it is a crime, so poor you must remain,
The parson says, 'Contented be, and you will heaven gain.'

O'Connor Feargus O'Connor (1794–1855), journalist, orator, MP,
    Chartist leader.
Prince Albert married Queen Victoria in 1840.
bastille workhouse.

This ballad seems to have been popular for a number of years
during the early 1840s. The verses about Napoleon, Nelson, Wellington and Prince Albert are common to all versions, but the
others change. A verse about O'Connell is sometimes substituted
for the one about O'Connor, and John Frost, who led the abortive
Chartist attack on Monmouth in 1839 (being transported for his
pains), has a verse in some versions:

John Frost in Wales a hunting went, and well knew how to ride,
He had a fine bred Chartist horse, but got on the wrong side,
If he had held the reins quite firm in his own hand,
They'd ne'er have hunted him into Van Dieman's Land.

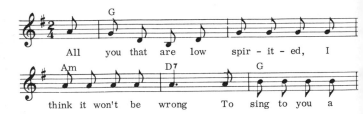

verse or two of my new hunt-ing song; For hunt-ing is in sea-son, the sport has just be-gun, And her-oes they will have their fun with their fine dog and gun. And a-hunt-ing we will go, my boys, a - hunt-ing we will go, We'll lay out schemes and try all means to keep the poor man low.

The Chartists are Coming

What a row and a rumpus there is I declare,
Tens of thousands are flocking everywhere;
To petition the Parliament, onward they steer,
The Chartists are coming, oh dear, oh dear.
To demand equal justice, their freedom and rights,
Pump-handles and broomsticks, lawk, how they can fight;
The nation, they say, is o'erwhelmèd with grief,
A peck loaf for two pence and four pounds of beef.

Chorus
Hurrah for old England and liberty sweet,
The land that we live in and plenty to eat;
We shall ever remember this wonderful day,
The Chartists are coming, get out of the way.

Such a number together was never yet seen,
Hurrah for the Charter and God save the Queen;
And when that the Charter old England has got,
We'll have stunning good beer at three halfpence a pot.
A loaf for a penny, a pig for a crown,
And gunpowder tea at five farthings a pound;
Instead of red herrings we'll live on fat geese,
And get lots of young women at two pence apiece.

The bakers and grocers, look how they do laugh,
With dustmen and coalheavers, armed with a staff;
Five thousand old women, oh, how they do sing,
With frying pans, fenders, and big rolling pins.
There's Russell and Bobby, old Nosey and Hume,
With pistols and bayonets, big muskets and brooms;
Load away, fire away, and chatter and jaw,
Shoot at a donkey and knock down a crow.

See the lads of old Erin for liberty crow,
Smith O'Brien for ever and Erin-go-bragh;
Peace and contentment, then none can we blame,
Plenty of labour and paid for the same.
Some are rolling in riches and luxury too,

302

While millions are starving, with nothing to do;
Through the nation prosperity soon will be seen,
Hurrah for Great Britain and God save the Queen.

To Kennington Common in droves they repair,
'Cause Smith O'Brien and Feargus are there;
A-telling the story would reach, sir, indeed,
From the Land's End of England to Berwick on Tweed.
The Charter, the Charter, or England shall quake,
I wish they may get it, and no grand mistake,
Then Feargus shall be a prime minister keen,
And Smith O'Brien a page to the Queen.

Such constables there is in London, now mark,
There's tailors and shoemakers, labourers and clerks,
Gaslightmen, pickpockets, and firemen, too,
Greengrocers and hatters, pork butchers and Jews,
Lollypop merchants and masons a lot,
And the covey that hollers 'Baked taters all hot.'
They're sworn to protect us and keep well the peace,
To frighten the Chartists and help the police.

fenders metal surrounds for fires.
Russell Lord John Russell.
Bobby Sir Robert Peel.
old Nosey Wellington.
Hume Joseph Hume.
Erin-go-bragh Ireland for ever.
Feargus Feargus O'Connor (see previous song).
Kennington Common site of big Chartist demonstration in 1848.
Smith O'Brien Irish nationalist and Chartist (1803–64).
help the police a large number of special constables was sworn in
   to help control the Kennington demonstration.

The Charter called for universal suffrage (for men), the abolition
of property qualifications for holding a seat in Parliament, annual
Parliaments, equal representation, the payment of MPs, and vote
by ballot. In 1848 a great petition was organized in support of the
Charter. The petition secured, it was said, five or six million signatures, and it was decided to hold a mammoth demonstration at
Kennington Common on 10 April, followed by a march to the House
of Commons, where the petition would be presented. Wellington
forbade the demonstration, which took place nevertheless, with an

attendance variously estimated between 25,000 and 125,000. London was packed with troops and special constables. O'Connor agreed not to attempt to march on the House of Commons; the petition was taken there in a cab and found to have rather less than two million signatures, including forgeries in the names of Queen Victoria and the Duke of Wellington. Chartism went into a decline from which it did not recover.

The ballad reflects the exuberance of the days leading up to 10 April, and may well have been on sale in the streets on that occasion. It is an interesting expression of revolutionary enthusiasm and high good humour. Its desire for the good life perhaps underlies the decline of Chartist support in the 1850s, when some of the hardship and want of the 1840s was disappearing.

What a row and a rum-pus there is I de-clare, Tens of thou-sands are flock - ing ever - y-where; To pe-ti-tion the Par - lia-ment, on-ward they steer, The Chartists are com-ing, oh dear, oh dear, To de-mand e-qual jus - tice, their free-dom and rights, Pump-han-dles and broomsticks, lawk, how they can fight; The na-tion, they say, is o'er - whel - med with grief, A

peck loaf for two pence and four pounds of beef. Hur-
-rah for our Eng-land and li - ber-ty sweet, The
land that we live in and plen - ty to eat; We shall
e - ver re-mem-ber this won - der-ful day, The
Chartists are com-ing, get out of the way.

The Best-Dressed Man of Seghill
or The Pitman's Reward for Betraying his Brethren

It was on March the nineteenth day,
Eighteen hundred and thirty one O,
A man from Earsdon Colliery
His brethren did abscond O;
As other men were standing off,
He would not do the same O;
For idle work would never do,
He'd rather bear the shame O.

And to the Seghill binding he
Did come with all his might O;
For to deceive his brethren dear
He thought it was but right O;
And Black J. R. made him believe
That he was in no danger,
And to the office he might go,
Because he was a stranger.

But I will tell his troubles here;
As he came from the binding O,
They stripped him there of part of his clothes
And left his skin refining O.
Black J. R. was most to blame
He lost all but his lining O,
And when he came to Hallowell,
His skin so bright was shining O.

They left him nothing on to hide
That good old man the priest O,
But there they hung on him his hat,
He was so finely dressed O.
They set him off from there with speed
To an ale-house by the way O,

And there the Earsdon men did sit
A-drinking on that day O.

But of their minds I cannot tell
When they did see him coming O;
The priest he had within his hat
And he was hard a-running O.
The Earsdon men they set him off
From there to the machine O
That stands upon the allotment hill;
He there himself did screen O.

And there beneath a good whin bush
His priest and he sat lurking O.
'I'll never go back to Seghill,
But I will hide in Murton O.'
And so remember you that come
Unto Seghill to bind O;
You'd better think upon the man
That we have tret so kind O.

Earsdon and the other places named are in County Durham.
binding hiring or contracting of labour.

During a strike at Earsdon Colliery in 1831 one of the men attempted
to take work at a neighbouring mine, which his fellow workers felt
was a betrayal of the common cause. Their reprisals against him
illustrate a long history of struggle between striking miners and
blacklegs, in which the blacklegs are often treated a good deal less
'kindly'.

The strike resulted from the first attempt of the Durham and
Northumberland miners to form a union.

> The union, which included all the mineworkers in the two
> counties, was known as Hepburn's union after Thomas Hepburn
> the Hetton pitman, its founder and leader. In 1831 at a great
> meeting on the Black Fell near Chester-le-Street, followed a
> few days later by another on the Town Moor at Newcastle, the
> pitmen decided to strike for better conditions. Their struggle
> with the employers lasted nearly ten weeks. The authorities
> concentrated troops in the district, called out the local yeomanry
> and even brought a detachment of eighty marines from Ports-
> mouth to the Tyne by sea. These precautions excited a violent

temper in the men who threw corves and winding machinery down the pit shafts at Blyth, Bedlington, Hebburn, Jesmond and other places. In June the employers conceded the miners' main demands, including a maximum working day of twelve hours for boys (S. Middlebrook, *Newcastle Upon Tyne*, pp.176–7).

The following year, despite a four-month strike, the union was broken by the employers.

The ballad dates from April 1831.

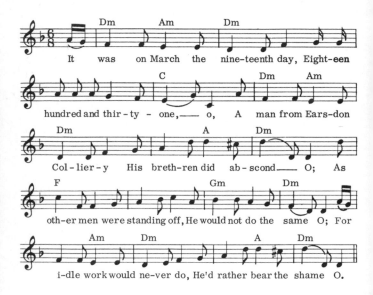

It was on March the nine-teen day, Eight-een
hundred and thir-ty - one,— o, A man from Ears-don
Col - lier - y His breth-ren did ab - scond— O; As
oth-er men were standing off, He would not do the same O; For
i-dle work would ne-ver do, He'd rather bear the shame O.

Striking Times

Cheer up, cheer up, you sons of toil and listen to my song,
While I try to amuse you all – it will not take me long.
The working men of England at length begin to see,
They've made a bold strike for their rights in 1853.

Chorus
And it's high time that working men should have it their
    own way,
And for a fair day's labour receive a fair day's pay.

This is the time for striking, at least it strikes me so,
Monopoly has had some knocks, but this must be the blow;
The working men by thousands complain their lot is hard,
May order mark their conduct and success be their reward.

Some of our London printers this glorious work begun,
And surely they've done something, for they've upset the
    Sun.
Employers must be made to see they can't do what they
    like;
It is the masters' greediness that causes men to strike.

The labouring men of London on both sides of the Thames,
They made a strike last Monday, which adds much to their
    names.
Their masters did not relish it, but made them understand;
Before the next day's sun had set, they gave them their
    demand.

The unflinching men of Stockport, Kidderminster in their
    train,
Three hundred honest weavers struck, their ends all for to
    gain.
Though masters find they lose a deal the tide must soon be
    turning;
They find the men won't quietly be robbed of half their
    earning.

Our London weavers mean to show their masters and the
  trade
That they will either cease to work or else be better paid.
In Spitalfields the weavers worked with joy in former ages,
But they're tired out of asking for a better scale of wages.

The monied men have had their way, large fortunes they
  have made,
For things could not be otherwise, with labour badly paid;
They roll along in splendour and with a saucy tone,
As Cobbett says, they eat the meat, the workman gnaws
  the bone.

In Liverpool the postmen struck and sent word to their
  betters,
Begging them to recollect that they were men of letters;
They asked for three bob more a week and got it in a crack,
And though each man has got his bag they have not got
  the sack.

The coopers and the dockyard men are all a-going to strike,
And soon there'll be the devil to pay without a little mike.
The farming men of Suffolk have lately called a go,
And swear they'll have their wages rose before they reap or
  sow.

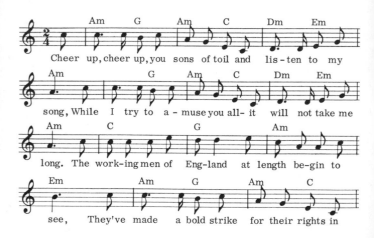

Cheer up, cheer up, you sons of toil and lis-ten to my
song, While I try to a-muse you all- it will not take me
long. The work-ing men of Eng-land at length be-gin to
see, They've made a bold strike for their rights in

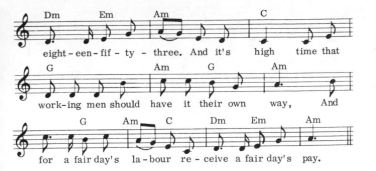

eight-een-fif-ty-three. And it's high time that work-ing men should have it their own way, And for a fair day's la-bour re-ceive a fair day's pay.

mike leisure.

Cobbett William (1763–1835). Some twenty years after his death, his name and his words were still sufficiently well-known to be quoted here.

The London Trades Council was not formed until 1862, nor the Trades Union Congress until 1868, but there was a good deal of trade union activity in the early 1850s which anticipated later developments. The tone of this song is confident, jaunty, and rather ruthless.

The Cotton Lords of Preston

Have you not heard the news of late
About some mighty men so great?
I mean the swells of Fishergate,
The Cotton Lords of Preston.
They are a set of stingy blades,
They've locked up all their mills and shades,
So now we've nothing else to do
But come a-singing songs to you.
So with our ballads we've come out
To tramp the country round about,
And try if we cannot live without
The Cotton Lords of Preston.

Chorus
Everybody's crying shame
On these gentlemen by name.
Don't you think they're much to blame,
The Cotton Lords of Preston?

The working people such as we
Pass their time in misery,
While they live in luxury,
The Cotton Lords of Preston.
They're making money every way
And building factories every day,
Yet when we ask them for more pay,
They had the impudence to say:
'To your demands we'll not consent;
You get enough, so be content' —
But we will have the ten per cent
From the Cotton Lords of Preston.

Our masters say they're very sure
That a strike we can't endure;
They all assert we're very poor,
The Cotton Lords of Preston.

But we've determined every one
With them we will not be done,
And we will not be content
Until we get the ten per cent.
The Cotton Lords are sure to fall,
Both ugly, handsome, short and tall;
For we intend to conquer all
The Cotton Lords of Preston.

So men and women, all of you,
Come and buy a song or two,
And assist us to subdue
The Cotton Lords of Preston.
We'll conquer them and no mistake,
Whatever laws they seem to make,
And when we get the ten per cent
Then we'll live happy and content.
Oh then we'll dance and sing with glee
And thank you all right heartily,
When we gain the victory
And beat the Lords of Preston.

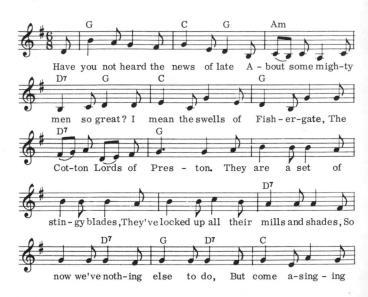

Have you not heard the news of late A - bout some might-y
men so great? I mean the swells of Fish - er-gate, The
Cot-ton Lords of Pres - ton. They are a set of
stin - gy blades, They've locked up all their mills and shades, So
now we've noth-ing else to do, But come a-sing - ing

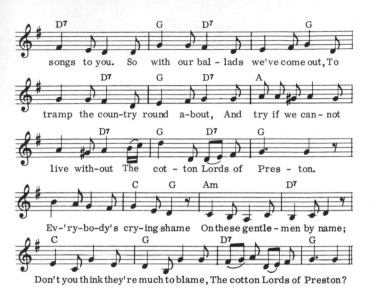

songs to you. So with our bal - lads we've come out, To
tramp the coun-try round a-bout, And try if we can - not
live with-out The cot - ton Lords of Pres - ton.
Ev-'ry-bo-dy's cry-ing shame On these gentle - men by name;
Don't you think they're much to blame, The cotton Lords of Preston?

One of the strikes (which soon became a lock-out) taking place in 1853 was at Preston, where the cotton weavers were asking for a 10 per cent increase. Charles Dickens went to Preston in the following year when the dispute was still in progress, and wrote about what he saw, in the press and in his novel *Hard Times*.

The strike helped to develop collective bargaining and industrial conciliation and arbitration machinery. Professor Perkin comments:

> The Preston cotton stoppage of 1853 was probably a more important turning point than that of the engineers the previous year. It began as a selective or 'rolling' strike for higher pay (10 per cent) – not a promising basis for public sympathy in mid-Victorian England – but the action of the employers in turning it into a lock-out of over 20,000 workers, their stubbornness in refusing to negotiate, the manifest injustice of the magistrates in arresting the workers' leaders for peaceful dissuasion of Irish blacklegs while allowing the employers to organize a provocative triumphal procession of the latter, and the skill and patience of the strike leaders in presenting their case and discouraging all violence, all earned the union the sympathy of the national press. . . . It was the first major strike for increased pay which earned the strikers the sympathy and support, if not the approval, of the middle-class public (*Origins*, op.cit, pp.398–9).

The Lock-Out

I know a stingy fellow and his name is Farmer Grab
And he doesn't live so very far away;
He's more prickly than a thistle and much sourer than a
    crab
And he's duller than a lump of clay.

Chorus
And it's oh, oh, oh, oh, what a pretty go,
He's locked out his men you know;
But had he known before that he could get no more
He never would have served them so.

Now he swore just like a trooper before the week was out
That every man the union should drop;
But they told him in the north there was work enough, no
    doubt,
And they didn't very much care to stop.

He asked for their cards but he asked for them in vain,
And when in his rage he could speak,
He vowed that never should they work for him again
At the rate of twelve bob a week.

Now when he began for to give his men the sack,
They quickly found much better work to do.
He thinks about the harvest and he wishes they were back,
And his face is growing awfully blue.

The union in this song was the National Agricultural Labourers'
Union, which was formed in 1872 under the leadership of Joseph
Arch. Its back was broken in 1874 by a combination of recession in
agriculture and a prolonged lock-out by the farmers. The union
arranged for many farm workers to emigrate to Canada and the
USA. Despite defeat, Arch's union was an important forerunner of
today's National Agricultural and Allied Workers' Union.

In common with other disputes, the lock-out of 1873 produced
many songs. This one was sung to the tune of a popular song of the
day, *Old Uncle Ned*, by Stephen Foster.

I know a stingy fellow and his name is Farmer Grab And he
does-n't live so ve-ry far a - way; He's more
prickly than a thistle and much sourer than a crab And he's
dul-ler than a lump of clay. And it's
oh, oh, oh, oh, what a pret-ty go, He's locked out his men you
know; But had he known be-fore that
he could get no more He never would have served them so.

Happy Land

Happy land! happy land!
Is now the chaunt in every street.
Happy land! happy land!
Sings every one you meet.
The ballad-singer, minus clothes,
Shirtless, coatless, and
With buckets none to shield his toes,
He warbles 'Happy land!'

Happy land! happy land!
Exclaims the swell, reduced in pelf;
To the parish workhouse goes,
Where the official elf
Who no humanity e'er owns,
Commands him to depart,
Gives him a ticket to break stones
Or drag a water cart.

Happy land! happy land!
Cries, perhaps, a hungry group;
A cook shop view with longing eyes,
For a good blow-out of soup.
On each hot joint their eyes do dwell,
Bowels yearning, there they stand,
Then walk away – their share a smell –
And warble 'Happy land!'

Happy land! happy land!
Ne'er from thee I wish to stray,
The soldier cries, because, d'ye see,
He cannot get away.
For nothing flogged, with grief he sighs,
While probably the band
Strike up to drown the wretch's cries,
To the tune of 'Happy land!'

Happy land! happy land!
Thy fame resounds from shore to shore;

Happy land! where 'tis a crime,
They tell us, to be poor.
If you shelter cannot find,
Of you they'll soon take care:
Most likely send you to grind wind
For sleeping in the air.

Happy land! happy land!
To praise thee, who will cease?
To guard us, pray, now ain't we got
A precious New Police?
A passport we shall soon require,
Which by them must be scanned,
If we to take a walk desire –
Oh, ain't this happy land?

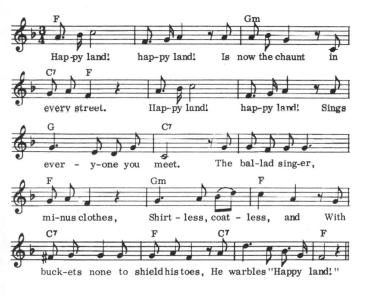

Hap-py land! hap-py land! Is now the chaunt in
every street. Hap-py land! hap-py land! Sings
ever-y-one you meet. The bal-lad sing-er,
mi-nus clothes, Shirt-less, coat-less, and With
buck-ets none to shield his toes, He warbles "Happy land!"

buckets shoes.
flogged flogging as a punishment in the British Army was not for-
mally abolished until 1881.
grind wind i.e. on the treadmill.
New Police dates from the act of 1829.

Happy land was rather a vapid, but successful song, which expressed what we have come to regard as a typically Victorian optimism:

Happy land! happy land! Whate'er my fate in life may be,
Still again! still again! My thoughts will cling to thee!
Land of love, and sunny skies, rich in joy and beauty,
Merry hearts, and laughing eyes still make affection's duty . . .

and so on. It was parodied by an entertainer called Prest, and sung 'at the London Concerts'. The parody is a bitter reminder of that part of society which benefited least from Victorian progress.

The World Turned Upside Down

Through eating too much supper
Before I went to bed,
Strange thoughts came o'er my slumber,
Strange thoughts came in my head.
This world seemed topsy-turvy,
And people of renown,
Were doing the most peculiar things,
As the world turned upside down.

Sims Reeves was dancing a hornpipe
And Santley doing a fling;
And Blondin came from the tight rope
A tenor song to sing.
Now Toole he was a-playing Hamlet
And Phelps he was a clown;
Buckstone he was an acrobat
As the world turned upside down.

Westminster Hall it was a chapel,
Hawkins began to preach;
Dr Kenealey nursed the baby,
While his wife she made a speech.
Dr Manning was Lord Chief Justice
And wore a splendid crown,
And Onslow sat all on the jury
As the world turned upside down.

Now Bismarck he was a pious quaker
And always prayed for peace;
John Bright he went for a soldier
And Ayrton joined the police.
Mr Lowe was grinding an organ
And touched his hat for a brown;
And Gladstone joined the Shakers
As the world turned upside down.

I dreamt there were no workhouses
And there were no starving poor;
And nations never did quarrel,
Nor never went to war.
I thought all men they were angels,
And women ne'er wore a frown;
Old maids they had large families
As the world turned upside down.

Through eat-ing too much sup-per Be-fore I went to bed, Strange thoughts came o'er my slum-ber, Strange thoughts came in my head. This world seemed top-sy-tur-vey, And peo-ple of re-nown, Were do-ing the most pe-cu-liar things, As the world turned up-side down.

Sims Reeves famous tenor singer (1818–1900).
Santley celebrated opera singer (1834–1922).
Blondin tight-rope walker (1824–97).
Toole actor-manager (1830–1906); 'the last low comedian of the old school' (*Dict. Nat. Biog.*).
Phelps an actor (1804–78).
Buckstone comedian and writer of farces (1802–79).
Hawkins presumably Francis (1794–1877), a doctor.
Dr Kenealey barrister, whose stormy career included disbarment and imprisonment (1819–1880); from 1875–80 was an MP.

Dr Manning murderer who was hanged in 1849.

Onslow humorous draughtsman and engraver (d.1886).

John Bright orator and statesman (1811–89); opposed war with Russia in 1853 and advocated neutrality in Turkish problem in 1876.

Ayrton criminal?

Mr Lowe possibly Robert (1811–92), who was Home Secretary from 1873–4.

brown halfpenny.

Shakers an American celibate and communistic religious sect which had some adherents in this country, and was in the news in the middle 1870s.

This broadside seems to date from the mid-1870s. The idea of turning the world upside down is centuries old. It led to customs like the Feast of Fools and the temporary reigns of Lords of Misrule and Boy Bishops in the Middle Ages and, indeed, up to the seventeenth century. It also inspired visions of Utopia, of the ideal land of Cockayne.

The present ballad is partly satirical in intent, but it also reveals a yearning for a better world.

Poor Man's Heaven

Kind friends, gather near, I want you to hear
A dream that I had last night;
There's a land o'er the sea for you and for me,
Where we won't have to struggle and fight.
There's real feather beds where we'll lay our heads
In a nice private room for each one;
There's shoes without holes and pants without holes
And no work up there to be done.
In Poor Man's Heaven we'll have our own way,
There's nothing up there but good luck,
There's strawberry pie that's twenty foot high
And whipped cream they bring in a truck.

We'll know how it feels in an automobile
With a footman to open the door;
And if someone gets smart, we'll take him apart,
And spread him all over the floor.
In Poor Man's Heaven we'll have our own way
And each man will help with his mate;
And if someone comes up to sell us a pup,
We'll soon chuck him over the gate.

We'll run all the banks and shoot all the cranks
And we won't give a darn who we hurt;
And the millionaire's son won't have so much fun
When we put him to shovelling dirt.
In Poor Man's Heaven we'll have our own way
And we won't have nothing to fear,
And we'll eat all we please from ham and egg trees
That grow by the fountains of beer.

We'll live on champagne and ride in a train
And sleep in a pullman at night;
And if someone should dare to ask for our fare
We'll haul off and put out his light.
In Poor Man's Heaven we'll live at our ease,
No skilly and beans over there;

But we'll be fed on breakfast in bed
And served by a fat millionaire.

We won't have to yearn for money to burn
Because we'll own a big money press
That we'll run at full speed and make all we need,
And we'll be the guards of the rest.
The landlords we'll take and tie to a stake
And make 'em give back all our dough;
Then we'll let 'em sweat and learn what they'll get
When they go to that hot place below.
In Poor Man's Heaven we'll own our own home
And we won't have to work like a slave;
But we'll be proud to sing right out loud
The land of the free and the brave.

This is another utopia, rather dream-like and even surrealistic.
It was taken down from the singing of an East Anglian farm labourer
in 1935, but it seems to have an American flavour. Perhaps it was
brought to England by a returning emigrant.

Kind friends, ga-ther near, I want you to hear a dream that I had last night. There's a land o'er the sea, for you and for me where we won't have to strug-gle and fight. There's real feather beds, where we'll lay our

heads, In a nice pri-vate room for each one.____

____ There's shoes with soles and pants with-out

holes And no work up there to be done.____

In Poor Man's Hea-ven we'll have our own

way, There's noth-ing up there but good luck,____

____ There's straw-ber-ry pie that's twen-ty foot

high And whipped cream they bring in a truck.____

Sources

Photographs Source List

Select Bibliography and Discography

Index of First Lines

Acknowledgements

Sources

page

22 Text: *The London Singer's Magazine*, n.d., p. 232. The song is described as 'a popular parody on *The Sea*', and this tune has been used.

28 Text: by John Freeth, in *A Warwickshire Medley, or, The Convivial Songster*, 1780. To the tune of: *The Warwickshire lad*, by Charles Dibdin (1745–1814).

31 Text: *Fairburn's New Dashing Songster for 1822*, p.8; abridged and adapted (Birmingham Reference Library, no. 401061). To the tune of: *An old woman clothed in grey* (W. Chappell, *Popular music of the olden time*, 1855–59, p. 456).

34 Text: broadside issued by a Manchester printer whose name is illegible (Madden Collection 18/485, Cambridge University Library). Tune (not indicated): *Rosetta* (Cecil Sharp MS Collection, Clare College, Cambridge).

40 Text: broadside printed by Harkness of Preston (Madden 18/1107). Tune (not indicated): *The piper's tunes* (C. O'Lochlainn, *Irish Street Ballads*, Dublin, 1939, p. 22).

42 Text: broadside printed by Kendrew of York (British Museum 1870 c 2), except for verse 6, which has been added from *The Bold Navigator*, another broadside version of the same ballad, printed by Bebbington of Manchester (Ballads Q 398.8 S9 vol. 1, Manchester Central Library). Tune (not indicated): *Gee ho dobbin* (J. Stokoe and S. Reay, *Songs and Ballads of Northern England*, n.d. (1899?), p. 84). Versions of this tune often used for songs of a social or political nature.

46 Text: broadside (abridged) printed by Russell of Birmingham (BM 1876 e 2). Tune (not indicated): *The bold trooper* (F. Kidson, *English Peasant Songs*, n.d. [1926], p. 84).

50 Text: broadside (abridged) printed by Russell of Birmingham (BM 1876 e 2). Tune (not indicated): *The sailor's frolic* (Hammond MS Collection, Vaughan Williams Memorial Library). The chorus has been added with the tune.

52 Text: broadside printed by Smith of Leicester (Madden 20/141). Tune (not indicated): *Villikins and his Dinah*. Alternatively, the tunes on pages 47 and 51 may be used.

56 Text: broadside printed by Pratt of Birmingham (s.n. *Warbling Waggoner*, Kidson Broadside Collection, vol. 2, p. 75, Mitchell Library, Glasgow). Tune: s.n. *The Waggoner* (Vaughan Williams MS Collection, BM).

59 Text: broadside (abridged) printed by Broadhurst of Norwich

(Norwich Public Library). Tune (not indicated): *The rakes of mallow.*

62 Text: *London Singer's Magazine*, pp. 12–13. Tune: *The good old days of Adam and Eve.* The piece is described as 'An original comic song, written by Mr S. Blackshaw, and sung at the theatres'.

65 Text: broadside (abridged) printed by Cadman of Manchester (Kidson Broadside Collection, vol. 9, p. 163). Tune: *The bold dragoon* (*Davidson's Universal Melodist*, n.d. [1854?], vol. 1, p. 403).

68 Test: (abridged): J. Harland, *Ballads and Songs of Lancashire*, 1875. Tune (not indicated): *Belfast town* (Sam Henry Collection).

71 Text: 'written (or collected) by Dr Moorman, President of the Yorkshire Dialect Society about 1900'. Tune: 'written by Dave Keddie of Bradford about 1960', English Folk Dance and Song Society.

73 Text: broadside printed by Harkness of Preston (Madden 18/475). Tune: *Bow, wow, wow* (*Davidson's Universal Melodist*, vol. II, p. 270).

78 Text: by James Dobbs (1781–1837); issued on a broadside printed by Jackson of Birmingham (BM 1876 e 2). Tune: *Duncan Grey.*

83 Text: broadside (abridged) printed by Russell of Birmingham (BM 1876 e 2). Tune (not indicated): *The besom maker* (Hammond MSS, D. 126).

88 Text: printed by Harkness of Preston (Madden 18/690). Tune: *Irish Molly O* (P. W. Joyce, *Old Irish Folk Music and Songs*, 1909).

92 Text: *Songs Relating to Sheffield*, pp. 86–8; abridged and adapted (J. Wilson, *The Songs of Joseph Mather . . . and Miscellaneous Songs Relating to Sheffield*, Sheffield, 1862). The chorus (with a change of name) has been added from a parallel broadside version, printed by Wrighton of Birmingham, under the title of *Saturday Night at Birmingham* (Houghton Library, Harvard University). This broadside also indicates the tune: *Nottingham ale*, also known as *Lillibulero* (Chappell, p. 573).

95 Text: C. F. Forshaw, *Holroyd's Collection of Yorkshire Ballads*, 1892, p. 19 (one verse omitted). Tune: *All among the leaves so green O.*

98 Text: broadside (abridged) printed by Thompson of Dudley (Kidson Broadsides, vol. 9, p. 210). Tune (not indicated): *The rigs of London Town* (Sharp MSS no. 1623).

102 Text: broadside (abridged) printed by Ordoyno of Nottingham (Madden 20/68). Tune (not indicated): *The wee article*, Sam Henry Collection.

105 Text: broadside (abridged) printed by Kendrew of York (BM 1870 c 2). Tune (not indicated): *A-nutting we will go* (Sam Henry Collection).

110 R. Dunstand, *Cornish Dialect and Folk Songs*, 1932, p. 22.

112 Text: *Chambers Book of Days*, vol. II, 1863, p. 566. Tune: Mrs Gutch and M. Peacock, *Country folk-lore: Lincolnshire*, 1908, 263–4.

120 *In Corvan's Song Book, No. 1*, printed by W. R. Walker of Newcastle (no. 79 in F. M. Thomson, *Newcastle Chapbooks in Newcastle upon Tyne University Library*, Newcastle, 1969). Tune: *Nae luck about the hoose* (see page 142).

123 Text: J. Harland, *Ballads and Songs of Lancashire*, 1875. Tune: *The Rolbeck Moor cock fight* (F. Kidson, *Traditional tunes*, Oxford, 1891, p. 136).

125 Text: A. Williams, *Folk Songs of the Upper Thames*, 1923, p. 223. Tune: (not indicated): *The jolly waggoner* (Kidson Manuscript Collection, Mitchell Library, Glasgow).

130 Text: broadside without imprint (Firth Collection, Sheffield University Library). Tune: *The rambling sailor* (Baring-Gould MS Collection, no. LXXXVII, Plymouth City Library).

133 *The Iron Muse*, Topic Record 12T86.

135 Text: broadside printed by Bebbington of Manchester (Ballads Q 398.8 s.9, vol. 2, p. 356, Manchester Central Library). Tune: *The wonderful crocodile* (Kidson MS Collection).

138 Text: broadside printed by Wood of Birmingham (Ballads, Birmingham Reference Library, no. 119932, p. 77). Tune: s.n. *The brisk young batchelor* (C. Sharp, *English Folk Songs*, selected edn, 1921, vol. 2, pp. 60–1). Chorus added with tune.

142 Text: broadside printed by Pitts of London (Douce Collection, IV 51, Bodleian Library). Text on page 144: broadside printed by Walker of Norwich (Douce IV 52). Tune for both: *Nae luck aboot the hoose*.

148 N. Buchan, *101 Scottish songs*, Collins, 1962, p. 138.

150 *Tommy Armstrong*, Topic Records, 12T122.

154 Text: verses 1–5, collected by H. E. D. Hammond from George House, Beaminster, Dorset, 1906; verse 6 and tune, collected by Hammond from Mrs Sartin, Corscombe, Dorset, 1906 (*Journal* of the Folk Songs Society (JFS), vol. VII, pp. 66–7).

156 Text: broadside (abridged) printed by Buick of London (from a collection of ballads in the BM; communicated by Norman Longmate). Tune (not indicated): *Brighton camp* (Chappell p. 710); otherwise known as *The girl I left behind me*.

160 From the singing of Roy Palmer, who learned the song while living in the Barnsley area, 1961–63. The tune is called *Ach du liebe Augustin*.

162 Text: broadside printed by Gilpin of Oldhall Street (the town unspecified). Tune (not indicated): *The valleys of Screen* (Sam Henry Collection). Alternatively, the tune on page 189 may be used.

166 Text: broadside printed by Wood of Birmingham (Ballads, no. 119932, p. 124, Birmingham Reference Library). Tune (not indicated): *The married man's lament* (adapted) (*Lyric Gems of Scotland*, 1856).

168 Text: broadside printed by Pratt of Birmingham (BM 1876 e 2). Tune: s.n. *I likes a drop of good beer* (Kidson MS Coll.).

172 Text: broadside (abridged) printed by Bonner and Henson of Bristol (Madden 23/170). Tune: *Derry down* (Chappell 677). The chorus has been partly added with the tune.

175 Text: in *Harvest Songster*, printed by Pitts of London (Birmingham Reference Library, no. 401061). Tune: *Sing tantararara, rogues all*.

179 Text: broadside printed by Ford of Chesterfield (Derby Public Library). Tune: s.n. *We're a' noddin'* (adapted) (*Davidson's Universal Melodist*, vol. 1, p. 192).

183 Text: broadside (abridged) printed by Pratt of Birmingham (Madden 21/148), collated with another, printed by Birt of London (Madden 12/73). Tune: *A-nutting we will go*.

188 Text: broadside printed by Swindells of Manchester (Oldham Collection, Oldham Study Centre, Werneth Park, Oldham). Tune (not indicated): *The rant* (Chappell 554). This tune was often used for satirical songs.

190 Text: broadside printed by Pratt of Birmingham (Kidson Broadsides, vol. 2, p. 46). Tune (not indicated): as for page 103, page 106 or page 185.

196 S.n. *The ship carpenter's wife*, in the Sam Henry Collection.

200 Collected by Hammond (in C. Sharp, *English County Folk Songs*, Novello, 1961, p. 26).

204 Text: broadside printed by Ordoyno of Nottingham (Madden 20/72). Tune: *Derry down* (Chappell 350). There is a considerable number of *Derry down* tunes, see pages 173 and 279.

207 Text: broadside printed by Harkness of Preston (Madden 18/689). Tune: Kidson, *Garland*, p. 94.

210 Text: broadside printed by Wright of Birmingham (Madden 21/743). Tune: *Dublin Jack of all trades* (O'Lochlainn, p. 80); slightly adapted.

214 Text: broadside printed by Plant of Nottingham (Madden 20/84). Tune: *Lisbon* (JFS II 22).

218 Text: broadside printed by Harkness of Preston (Madden 18/1042). Tune (not indicated): *Skewball*. Alternatively, the tunes on pages 103, 106, 185 and 310 may be used.

223 Text: broadside printed by Bebbington of Manchester (Kidson Broadsides, vol. 10, p. 90). Tune (not indicated): *The plains of Waterloo* (F. Kidson, *Traditional tunes*, p. 121).

226 Text: *The Collected Writings of Samuel Laycock, 1900*, pp. 15–17. Tune: *Rory O'More* (A. L. Lloyd, *Folk Song in England*, 1967, p. 405).

230 Text: broadside printed by Sharp of London (Nottingham University r PR1181 B2). Tune: *Dives and Lazarus* (Chappell 748).

234 Collected by Mr Dave Hillery from Mrs Ada Cave of York in 1965.

236 By J. P. Long and Worton David (*Old Time Comic Songs, no. 1*, Francis, Day and Hunter Ltd). Also printed in *English Dance and Song*, Winter 1967.

240 W. A. Barrett, *English Folk-Songs*, 1891, no. 10.

242 Ibid, no. 52.

244 C. Macalister, *Old Pioneering Days*, 1907 (published in Australia). To the tune of: *Irish Molly* (see page 89).

247 Collected by Mr George Ewart Evans from James Knights (born 1880), of Woodbridge, Suffolk, 28 March 1968.

250 Text: broadside printed by Harkness of Preston (Madden 18/1117). Tune: s.n. *Kirtle gaol* in W. R. Mackenzie, *Ballads and Sea Songs from Nova Scotia*, Harvard U.P. 1928.

254 Text: broadside printed by Swindells of Manchester (Oldham Collection). Tune: *Nae luck* (see pages 120 and 142).

257 Text: T. Armstrong, *Song Book*, 1909. To the tune of: *Nae luck aboot the hoose* (see pages 120, 142 and 253).

260 Text: broadside (abridged) printed by Taylor of Birmingham (Madden 21/578). Tune (not indicated): *The keepers and poachers* (JFS VIII 7).

264 Text: broadside printed by Willey of Cheltenham (Madden 23/497). Tune (not indicated): *The seven joys of Mary*. This traditional carol tune was used for a number of songs dealing with social grievances, during the nineteenth century.

268 Text: broadside printed by Weymss of Hereford (Hereford Public Library). Tune: *There was a little man, and he had a little gun*, which is otherwise known as *Dumb, dumb, dumb*.

270 Text: broadside without imprint (Nottingham University Library Album 89375). Tune (not indicated): based on *The sailor's alphabet* (I. Gundry, *Canow Kernow*, 1966, p. 52). Alternatively, the tune on page 53 may be used.

274 Text: John Freeth, *Political Songster*, 6th edn, 1790. Tune *The Staffordshire fox-chase*. This has not been traced, and a tune composed by Pamela Bishop has been used.

278 By John Freeth (ibid.). To the tune of: *Old Homer* (Chappell, p. 677).

281 J. Wilson (ed.), *The Songs of Joseph Mather*, Sheffield, 1862, pp. 63–5. Also on a broadside in Sheffield City Library, s.n. *W——'s thirteens, indicted by Five Penknife Cutlers*. Tune (not indicated): *Packington's Pound* (Chappell, p. 123).

286 Text: Public Record Office H. 42. 119, dated 27 January 1812; abridged. Tune: *Poor Jack*, by Charles Didbin; adapted.

289 Text: broadside without imprint (Derby Broadsides, Derby Public Library no. 8672). Tune (not indicated): Sweet Kitty (JFS II 48); adapted. Chorus partly added with tune.

294 Text: broadside (abridged) printed by Munday and Slatter, Oxford (London University Library Broadside Collection, 677[2].) To the tune of: *Lillibulero* (see page 93).

296 Text: broadside without imprint (Ballads BR F 824.04 BA1, p. 134, Manchester Central Library). Tune: *Parker's widow*, otherwise known as *The death of Parker* (JFS VIII 188). The Parker in question was executed in 1797 after the mutiny at the Nore.

299 Text: broadside printed by Pratt of Birmingham (Ballads by Catnach and others, Norwich Public Library Z821.024). Tune: *A-hunting we will go. A-nutting we will go* will also serve.

302 Text: broadside printed by Paul of London (Place Collection, set 47, part 1, f. 301; communicated by Mr David Woodway). Tune: *The bailiffs are coming*, which I presume to be the same as *The Campbells are coming*.

306 Text: abridged and adapted from that given in A. L. Lloyd, *Come all ye Bold Miners*, 1952, p. 91. Tune (not indicated): *The peelers and the goat* (JFS II 259).

309 Text: J. Ashton, *Modern Street Ballads*, 1888; abridged. Tune by Sandra Faulkner, based on a version of *The Dewy Rain*.

313 Text: broadside printed by Harkness of Preston (Madden 18/1312). Tune: *The king of the Cannibal Islands*.

316 By Howard Evans (*Songs for Singing at Agricultural Labourers' Meetings*, Leamington, n.d. 1874?). To the tune of *Old Uncle Ned*, by Stephen Foster.

318 Text: *London Singer's Magazine*, p. 118. Tune: *Happy land* by B. F. Rimbault (1816–76). The original words were by James Bruton (1806–67).

321 Text: broadside without imprint (Kidson Broadsides, vol. 10, p. 247). Tune: *Upside down* (Sam Henry Collection).

324 Collected by A. L. Lloyd from Mr Jumbo Brightwell of Eastbridge, Suffolk, in 1935.

Photographs Source List

page

1   *A Long-song Seller of the C.18.* The long-song seller sold several different ballads made into one continuous roll of paper, and priced them according to length. (John Foreman, *The Broadsheet King*)

2   *A Magazine Seller in Ludgate Circus, London, in the early 1890s.* The photographer was Paul Martin (1864–1942) who took photographs of London street scenes in the 1890s with a concealed camera. (Victoria & Albert Museum)

9   *A Token showing John Freeth, The Birmingham Poet.* (Roy Palmer)

    A Picture of Ned Corvan in one of his musical roles, 'Catgut Jim'. (North Magazine)

    Samuel Laycock. (Manchester Public Libraries)

    Tommy Armstrong. (North Magazine)

11   *A section from Plate 11 of Hogarth's engravings of 'The Idle Prentice' 1747.* (British Museum)

    The Industrious Prentice, an engraving by William Hogarth, a detail from Plate 6 of the series. (British Museum)

12   *'Old Sarah', the Blind Hurdy-Gurdy Player,* from a daguerrotype by Beard. She is portrayed and described in Henry Mayhew's *London Labour and the London Poor.*

13   *A Crippled Ballad Seller of the late C.18.* He is hawking his ballads in the worst weather conditions. (Radio Times Hulton Picture Library)

15   *An early C.18 Broadsheet* published by J. Catnach, one of the most prolific of the ballad publishers. (Mansell Collection)

16   *A Broadsheet written by Ben Boucher,* a famous Dudley balladeer. The song was written for the 1832 Parliamentary Elections. (Dudley Library)

17   *A Travelling Ballad-Seller of the 1890s.* (Hereford City Library)

23   *The Toll-Keeper at Putney Bridge Toll Gate taking money from a traveller in 1880.* Photograph by W. Field. (D. C. Harrod)

26–7   *A Bargee Family living and working on the Shropshire Union Canal.* Anonymous photograph.

30   *Coal-Barge and Horses.* Anonymous photograph. In the mid C.19 canals were an important form of individual transport.

33   *A Cast-Iron Gate at 11, Wellington Street, Leicester.* Anonymous photograph. This was built around 1866. (Leicester Museum)

38–9   *Navvies on the London to Leicester railroad.* Photograph by

S. W. A. Newton, *c.*1890s. This photographer completed the mammoth task of recording the building of this railway from start to finish. (Newton Collection, Leicester Museum)

44–5 *The Building of the Manchester Ship Canal.* Anonymous photograph. This was opened in 1894. Although the bulk of this work was done with manpower, steam engines were starting to be used. The bridge in the photograph is again made of cast-iron. (Manchester Central Reference Library)

48–9 *New Street Railway Station, c.1900.* Photograph by Thomas Lewis. This station was designed by William Livlock and built in 1845. The photograph is one of a series of Birmingham taken by the photographer between 1870 and 1913. (John Whybrow Collection)

49 *Early Steam Engine, c.1850.* Anonymous photograph. (Roy Palmer)

54 *A Coach leaving the Three Crowns Hotel, Horsefair Street, Leicester in 1866.* Anonymous photograph. (Leicester Museum)

58 *A Railway Ticket-Examiner setting the Train Indicator at Leicester Central Station.* Anonymous photograph. The photograph was taken on 18 October, 1870. (Newton Collection, Leicester Museum)

61 *Gang of Plate-Layers manhandling a trolley full of sleepers near Bulwell, Leicestershire.* Anonymous photograph. (Newton Collection, Leicester Museum)

64 *A View of Oldham Factories taken from the gasworks.* Anonymous photograph. (Manchester Public Library)

67 *Steel Works, Penistone.* Anonymous photograph.

70 *Dalesman Dipping Sheep on Fylingdale Moor in Yorkshire.* Photograph by Frank Meadow Sutcliffe. Several of the men are wearing the bowler hats of the region, called 'mullers'. (W. Eglon Shaw)

76–7 *Liverpool Docks.* Anonymous photograph. (Liverpool Public Library)

80–81 *Smithfield Market, Moat Row, c.1881.* Photograph by Thomas Lewis. This market was on the site of Peter de Birmingham's Manor House and at the time of the photograph had just changed from a cattle market to a vegetable market. (John Whybrow Collection)

82 *Two Old Tipplers enjoying the Festivities at Bidford Mop, in 1899.* Photograph by Sir Benjamin Stone (1838–1914). Birmingham Reference Library)

86–7 *The Transportation of the Anchor of the Great Titanic, 1912.* Anonymous photograph. This was towed by 20 horses from Neatherton to Dudley Port Station. The Titanic sank on its maiden voyage on April 14th of the same year. (Dudley Library)

94 *A Group of Men drinking, c.1860.* Anonymous photograph. At this period any person being photographed had to keep very still because of the long exposure needed. Similar groups can be seen in the early photographs of D. O. Hill and Adamson. (Radio Times Hulton Picture Library)

97 *A Select group of Actresses from Holloway's show.* Photograph by Sir Benjamin Stone. This was taken at Lichfield Greenhill Bower, in 1903. (Birmingham Reference Library)

99 *Farm Workers on Home Farm, Newcastle upon Tyne.* Anonymous photograph. (Museum of English Rural Life, Reading)

100–101 *The West Aspect of the Nottingham Goose Fair in 1914.* Anonymous photograph. At this time the fair had already become almost purely devoted to entertainment and the geese are nowhere to be seen. The Goose Fair still occurs, but its site has now been moved outside the town. (Nottingham Public Library)

104 *The East Aspect of Nottingham Goose Fair in 1908.* Anonymous photograph. (Nottingham Public Library)

107 *A Hiring Fair at Burford, Oxfordshire, c.1900.* Anonymous photograph. (Tosley Museum, Burford)

109 *Three Men at the Stratford-upon-Avon 'Mop' in 1899.* Photograph by Sir Benjamin Stone. They are dressed in their smartest clothes, and wear whipcords in their lapels to indicate that they seek situations as carters. (Birmingham Reference Library)

117 *A Notice issued on 6 November 1830.* This was a counter-attack to the attempts made to stop the custom of Bull Running. (Phillips Collection, Stamford Town Hall)

118–19 *Actors and Actresses of Holloway's Show.* Photograph by Sir Benjamin Stone. This was taken at Lichfield Green Bower, 1903. The players are in theatrical costumes. Their manager is in the centre of the picture wearing a bow-tie. (Birmingham Reference Library)

124 *Interior of a Liverpool Public House, c.1880.* Anonymous photograph. (Liverpool Public Library)

126 *The Hallaton Bottle-kicking and Hare-pie Festival in 1905.* Photograph by Sir Benjamin Stone. Men displaying casks of beer and the hare-pie to the crowd. (Birmingham Reference Library)

132 *Workers at a Woollen Mill in Llanidloes, Wales.* Anonymous photograph. (National Library of Wales)

137 *Yarmouth Sands, 1892.* Photograph by Paul Martin. (Victoria and Albert Museum)

140–41 *Women gathering Driftwood on Whitby Beach.* Photograph by Frank Meadow Sutcliffe (1853–1941), another notable

Victorian photographer who is especially famous for his photographs of Whitby in Yorkshire. (W. Eglon Shaw)

143 *Washerwomen, c.1904.* Anonymous photograph. (Kodak Museum)

146 *Washerwoman, c.1904.* Anonymous photograph. (Kodak Museum)

147 *A Sleeping Miner.* Anonymous photograph. Miners were permanently scarred by the coal dust which got into their cuts as they worked. (National Coal Board)

149 *Fancy Goods Stall in the 1870s.* Anonymous photograph. (from 'Past Positive' by Gordon Winter)

153 *Brick-building in a Leeds Primary School.* Anonymous photograph. From a collection of photographs of school activities made at the beginning of this century. (Leeds School Board)

155 *A Boy Apprentice on the Leicester–London Railroad.* Photograph by S. W. A. Newton. (Newton Collection, Leicester Library)

161 *Irish Immigrants in Kensington Market Court, c.1860.* Anonymous photograph. These conditions were fairly typical of those endured by the urban poor. (Kensington Library)

164–5 *Girls enjoying themselves at Hampstead Fair in 1898.* Photograph by Paul Martin. (Kodak Museum)

170–71 *Temperance Procession, c.1906.* Outside the Sir Richard Cobden Inn. (Kodak Museum)

174 *Lydiat's Butcher's Shop in June 1882.* Photograph by W. Field. This shop used to be in Putney High Street. (D. C. Harrod)

178 *A Barefoot Boy drinking Sherbert.* Anonymous photograph. The stall was outside Greenwich Park, c.1884. (Spurgeon Collection, Greenwich Library)

182 *Singing Ballads to a Banjo Accompaniment, c.1902.* Anonymous photograph. (Kodak Museum)

185 *Buying Vegetables in Whitby market place, 1884.* Photograph by Frank Meadow Sutcliffe. (W. Eglon Shaw)

186–7 *Shops at 5–6, Junction Place in Hackney, 1907.* (GLC Photo Library)

189 *An Assistant Demonstrating the Function of a Hearse.* Anonymous photograph. Photograph taken outside Merry, the undertakers, in Abbey Walk, Cambridge. (Cambridge Folk Museum)

193 *Women Picking Coal from the Ground.* Anonymous photograph. The trench was being cut in Holyhead Road, Wednesbury, Staffordshire 1887. (Dudley Public Library)

194–5 *Wedding Group, c.1900.* Anonymous photograph. (Kodak Museum)

202–203 *Yorkshire Tramps at Lealholm, Yorks.* Photograph by Frank Meadow Sutcliffe. Willie Wedgewood is wearing a postman's hat. (W. Eglon Shaw)

205 *Hand-Frame Knitters making Stockings at Leicester Hosiery Factory.* Anonymous photograph. (Leicester Museum)

206 *Weaving Operators at Work.* Anonymous photograph. A great Yorkshire factory (probably Bradford). A photograph taken from the book *Britain at Work,* 1905. (Mary Evans Picture Library)

210 *Gingerbread-Seller.* Anonymous photograph. Greenwich 1884. (Greenwich Library)

211 *Seller of second-hand Top Hats.* Anonymous photograph. This is taken from a collection of photographs of London street-life, taken for the Reverend Charles Spurgeon in the 1880s and 1890s. They were used to illustrate his lectures. (Spurgeon Collection, Greenwich Library)
Rabbit-Seller, 1884. Anonymous photograph. (Spurgeon Collection, Greenwich Library)

212 *A Muffin Man, 1885.* Anonymous photograph. (Spurgeon Collection, Greenwich Library)

213 *Porters at Billingsgate Fish Market.* Anonymous photograph. They are wearing headgear on which they balanced stacks of woven baskets. Photograph taken in the early 1890s. (Victoria & Albert Museum)

216–17 *Poverty-stricken Family at Xmas, c.1900.* Anonymous photograph. (Mansell Collection)

221 *Welsh Miners Queueing for their Wages.* Anonymous photograph, *c.*1900. (National Coal Board)

222 *Francis Payne, a 98-year-old Leicester Cobbler in 1924.* Anonymous photograph. (Leicester Museum)

228–9 *Church of England Temperance Society Tea Stall.* Anonymous photograph. This was taken outside St Alfege's Church, Greenwich. (Spurgeon Collection, Greenwich Museum)

232–3 *The Outdoor Staff of Hardingham Hall, Norfolk, c.1860.* Anonymous photograph. (Sir Bartle Edwards/Norwich Public Library)

239 *Lunch-Break in the Fields.* Photograph by Frank Meadow Sutcliffe. (W. Eglon Shaw)

245 *A Scene on board the Emigrant Ship 'Royal Edward', 1910.* Anonymous photograph. (Radio Times Hulton Picture Library)

246–7 *Wormwood Scrubs.* Anonymous photograph. (Hammersmith Public Library)

249 *An Ancient 'Lock-up' at Snareston, Nr Twycross, Leicestershire.* Photograph by Sir Benjamin Stone. These were formerly used as local prisons for Parish misdemeanours. (Birmingham Reference Library)

256 *A Treadmill at Old Boro' Jail in High Cross Street, Leicester in 1823.* A watercolour by H. Goddard. (Leicester Museum)

258–9 *The Leicester Borough Police force at the Guildhall, c.1855.* Anonymous photograph. (Leicester Museum)

262–3 *Men at Dinner in St Marylebone Workhouse, York Gate, Regents Park.* Anonymous photograph. The photograph is taken from 'Living London', 1900. (Mary Evans Picture Library)

266–7 *A Blind Fiddler in Greenwich, 1884.* Anonymous photograph. (Spurgeon Collection, Greenwich Library)

276–7 *A Group of Miners at the New British Iron Company at New Hawne, 1 August 1872.* Photograph by Arthur Clarke, Stourbridge. (National Coal Board)

280 *A Blacksmith at Mowmack Hill Depot, Leicester.* Anonymous photograph. The blacksmith did a variety of jobs from sharpening picks, to shoeing horses, to forging a new part for a machine. (Leicester Museum)

284 *Grinders at Work.* Anonymous photograph. The table cutlery department of George Butler's at the beginning of the century. (George Butler & Son)

285 *Women finishing Knives ready for Dispatching in the Pocket Knife Department.* Anonymous photograph. (George Butler & Son)

291 *Fish Vendor at St Giles in 1870s.* Anonymous photograph. Photograph taken from 'Street Incidents', 1881. (Trustees of British Museum)

292–3 *A Speaker addressing a Strike Meeting.* Anonymous photograph. (National Coal Board)

295 *A Meeting of the President and Committee on the Anniversary of the Eight Hours Day, 1858.* Photograph by C. Nettleton of Carlton. (Radio Times Hulton Picture Library)

298 *Mounted Police moving in to break up a Meeting during the 1912 Dock Strikes.* Anonymous photograph. (Radio Times Hulton Picture Library)

312 *Two Barefoot Workers at a Staffordshire Brickworks, c.1900.* Anonymous photograph. (Dudley Library)

317 *Unemployed Dock Labourers waiting at the chain for work at the London Docks, 1901.* Anonymous photograph. (Mansell Collection)

320 *Demonstration by Unemployed Workers in Trafalgar Square, London, 10 October 1908.* Anonymous photograph. (Radio Times Hulton Picture Library)

323 *Navvy's Hut.* Photograph by S. W. A. Newton, c.1890. (Newton Collection, Leicester Museum)

Select Bibliography and Discography

An exhaustive bibliography would be well-nigh impossible and
I have therefore listed the rather heterogeneous collection of
works which I happen to have consulted.

Social History and Allied Subjects

GENERAL

E. W. Bovill, *The England of Nimrod and Surtees, 1815–1854*,
  Oxford University Press, 1959.
J. L. and B. Hammond, *The Rise of Modern Industry*, 1925.
C. Harvie, *et al.*, *Industrialization and Culture, 1830–1914*,
  Macmillan, 1970.
J. Warburg, *The Industrial Muse*, Oxford University Press, 1958.
H. Perkin, *The Origins of Modern English Society, 1780–1880*,
  Routledge & Kegan Paul, 1969.
C. S. Davies, *Living through the Industrial Revolution*, Routledge
  & Kegan Paul, 1966.
P. Lane, *The Industrial Revolution*, Batsford, 1972.
P. Lane, *The Victorian Age*, Batsford, 1972.
E. W. Bovill, *English Country Life, 1780–1830*, Oxford
  University Press, 1959.
E. J. Hobsbawm, *Industry and Empire*, Penguin, 1969.
E. P. Thompson, *The Making of the English Working Class*,
  Gollancz, 1965; Penguin, 1967.
C. Hill, *Reformation to Industrial Revolution*, Penguin, 1969.
T. S. Ashton, *The Industrial Revolution*, Oxford University Press,
  1948.
G. D. H. Cole and R. Postgate, *The Common People, 1746–1846*,
  Methuen, 1961.
J. L. and B. Hammond, *The Town Labourer, 1760–1832*, Guild
  Books, 1949.
J. L. and B. Hammond, *The Village Labourer*, Guild Books, 1948.
J. L. and B. Hammond, *The Skilled Labourer*, 1919.
W. E. Tate, *The English Village Community and the Enclosure
  Movements*, Gollancz, 1967.
J. L. and B. Hammond, *The Bleak Age*, 1934.
J. Laver, *The Age of Illusion*, Weidenfeld & Nicolson, 1972.
E. S. Turner, *Roads to Ruin*, Penguin, 1966.
W. J. Reader, *Life in Victorian England*, Batsford, 1964.

R. Hart, *English Life in the Eighteenth Century*, Wayland, 1970.

R. Hart, *English Life in the Nineteenth Century*, Wayland, 1970.

E. J. Hobsbawm, *Labouring Men*, Weidenfeld & Nicolson, 1964.

T. C. Smout, *A History of the Scottish People, 1560–1830*, Collins, 1969.

R. A. Buchanan, *Industrial Archaeology in Britain*, Penguin, 1972.

N. J. Smelser, *Social Change in the Industrial Revolution*, Routledge & Kegan Paul, 1959.

E. R. Pike, *Human Documents of the Industrial Revolution*, Allen & Unwin, 1966.

E. R. Pike, *Human Documents of the Victorian Golden Age*, Allen & Unwin, 1967.

A. Briggs, *The Age of Improvement*, Longman, 1959.

R. J. Cruickshank, *Roaring Century*, Hamish Hamilton, 1946.

J. Laver, *A Concise History of Costume*, Thames & Hudson, 1969.

J. J. Tobias, *Crime and Industrial Society in the Nineteenth Century*, Penguin, 1972.

J. Burnett, *A History of the Cost of Living*, Penguin, 1969.

B. Inglis, *Poverty and the Industrial Revolution*, Hodder & Stoughton, 1971.

K. Dawson, *The Industrial Revolution*, Pan, 1972.

A. Llewellyn, *The Decade of Reform*, David & Charles, 1972.

W. G. Hoskins, *The Making of the English Landscape*, Penguin, 1970.

T. H. White, *Farewell Victoria*, Penguin, 1963.

G. M. Trevelyan, *English Social History*, 4 vols, Penguin, 1964.

E. P. Thompson, 'Time, work-discipline and industrial capitalism', article in *Past and Present*, no.38, December 1967.

S. D. Chapman, *The Early Factory Masters*, David & Charles, 1967.

T. S. Ashton, *Iron and Steel in the Industrial Revolution*, 1924.

G. M. Young, *Victorian England*, 1936.

F. Klingender, *Art and the Industrial Revolution*, Paladin, 1972.

S. and A. Briggs, *Cap and Bell*, Macdonald, 1972.

D. Marshall, *Industrial England, 1776–1851*, Routledge & Kegan Paul, 1973.

J. F. C. Harrison, *The Early Victorians*, Paladin, 1973.

B. W. Beacroft, *The Cotton Industry and Factory System, 1750–1850*, Yendor Books, 1973.

TRANSPORT

J. Copeland, *Roads and their Traffic, 1750–1850*, David & Charles, 1968.

P. Smith, *The Turnpike Age*, Luton Museum and Art Gallery, 1970.

J. M. Thomas, *Roads before Railways, 1700–1851*, Evans, 1969.

S. and B. Webb, *TheStory of the King's Highway*, 1913.

C. Hadfield, *The Canal Age*, Pan, 1971.

P. Smith, *Waterways Heritage*, Luton Museum and Art Gallery, 1971.

H. Perkin, *The Age of the Railway*, Panther, 1970.

L. T. C. Rolt, *Isambard Kingdom Brunel*, Longman, 1957; Penguin, 1970.

T. Coleman, *The Railway Navvies*, Penguin, 1968.

R. Watson, *The Transport Revolution*, Longman, 1971.

W. O. Tristram, *Coaching Days and Coaching Ways*, 1893.

POPULAR SPORTS AND PASTIMES

A. Delgado, *Victorian Entertainment*, David & Charles, 1971.

M. Baker, *Discovering English Fairs*, Shire Publications, n.d.

A. Smith, *Discovering Folklore in Industry*, Shire Publications, 1969.

T. Langley, *The Tipton Slasher: His Life and Times*, Black Country Society, n.d.

R. Christian, *Old English Customs*, Country Life, 1966; David & Charles, 1972.

W. Addison, *English Fairs and Markets*, Batsford, 1953.

J. Ford, *Prizefighting*, David & Charles, 1971.

F. W. Hackwood, *Staffordshire Customs*, Lichfield, 1924.

G. Hardwick, *Traditions, Superstitions and Folklore*, 1872.

W. Hone, *The Everyday Book and Table Book*, 3 vols, 1838.

J. Laver, *English Sporting Prints*, Ward Lock, 1970.

J. Strutt, *The Sports and Pastimes of the People of England*, 1801.

A. Williams, *Round about the Upper Thames*, 1922.

A. R. Wright and T. E. Lones, *British Calendar Customs: England*, 3 vols, 1936–40.

R. Chambers, *The Book of Days*, 2 vols, 1863.

T. F. T. Dyer, *British Popular Customs*, 1876.

R. W. Malcolmson, *Popular Recreations in English Society, 1700–1850*, Cambridge University Press, 1973.

PUBLIC HEALTH AND HOUSING, EDUCATION, DIET

N. Longmate, *King Cholera*, Hamish Hamilton, 1966.

I. Martin, *From Workhouse to Welfare*, Penguin, 1971.

J. Burnett, *Plenty and Want*, Penguin, 1968.

H. A. Moncton, *A History of English Ale and Beer*, Bodley Head, 1966.

B. Harrison, *Drink and the Victorians*, Faber, 1971.

P. Davies, *Children of the Industrial Revolution*, Wayland, 1972.

V. E. Neuburg, *Popular Education in Eighteenth-Century England*, Woburn Press, 1971.

N. Longmate, *Alive and Well*, Penguin, 1970.

B. W. Beacroft, *Health and Housing in British Towns, 1800–1900*, Yendor Books, 1973.

M. Rochester and B. J. Smith, *Children in Industry*, University of Keele, 1973.

TRADES AND OCCCUPATIONS, CRIME AND PUNISHMENT, POVERTY

D. Bythell, *The Hand-Loom Weavers*, Cambridge University Press, 1969.

P. Quennell (ed.), *London's Underworld*, Spring Books, 1950 (selections from Henry Mayhew's *London Labour and the London Poor*).

T. Coleman, *Passage to America*, Hutchinson, 1972.

K. Chesney, *The Victorian Underworld*, Temple Smith, 1970.

R. Wood, *Law and Order, 1725–1886*, Evans, 1970.

J. Dorner, *Newgate to Tyburn*, Wayland, 1972.

A. G. L. Shaw, *Convicts and the Colonies*, Faber, 1971.

M. Clarke, *His Natural Life*, 1870; Penguin, 1970.

A. Babington, *The English Bastille*, Macdonald, 1971.

N. Edsell, *The anti-Poor Law movement, 1834–44*, Manchester University Press, 1971.

J. D. Marshall, *The Old Poor Law*, Macmillan, 1968.

M. E. Rose, *The English Poor Law*, David & Charles, 1971.

F. M. Eden, *The State of the Poor*, 3 vols., 1797; abridged edn, 1928.

J. Addy, *A Coal and Iron Community in the Industrial Revolution*, Longman, 1969.

B. Lewis, *Coal Mining in the Eighteenth and Nineteenth Centuries*, Longman, 1971.

M. Tomalin, *Coal Mines and Miners*, Methuen, 1960.

F. E. Huggett, *A Day in the Life of a Victorian Farm Worker*, Allen & Unwin, 1972.

R. Groves, *Sharpen the Sickle: the History of the Farm Workers' Union*, Porcupine Press, 1949.

G. Kent, *Poverty*, Batsford, 1968.

J. U. Nef, *The Rise of the British Coal Industry*, 2 vols, 1932; reprinted Cass, 1966.

R. L. Galloway, *A History of Coal Mining in Great Britain*, 1882.

G. I. H. Lloyd, *The Cutlery Trades*, 1913.

R. Challinor and B. Ripley, *The Miners' Association*, Lawrence & Wishart, 1968.

W. Felkin, *History of Machine-Wrought Hosiery and Lace Manufacture*, 1867.

P. Collins, *Dickens and Crime*, Macmillan, 1964.

P. F. Speed, *Police and Prisons*, Longman, 1968.

P. Shellard, *Factory Life, 1774–1885*, Evans, 1970.

H. and B. Duckham, *Great Pit Disasters*, David & Charles, 1973.

J. G. Rule, *The Labouring Miner in Cornwall, c.1740–1870*,
  Warwick University Press, Ph.D. Thesis.

R. Challinor, *The Lancashire and Cheshire Miners*, Frank
  Graham, 1972.

LUDDISM, CHARTISM, STRIKES, LOCK-OUTS AND TRADE UNIONS

H. Marsh, *Documents of Liberty*, David & Charles, 1971.

D. Liversidge, *The Luddites*, Watts, 1972.

M. I. Thomis, *The Luddites*, David & Charles, 1970.

J. Marlow, *The Peterloo Massacre*, Panther, 1971.

R. J. White, *Waterloo to Peterloo*, Penguin, 1968.

D. Thompson, *The Early Chartists*, Macmillan, 1971.

J. L. and B. Hammond, *The Age of the Chartists*, 1930.

M. Hovell, *The Chartist Movement*, 1920.

A. E. Musson, *British Trade Unions, 1800–1875*, 1972.

S. and B. Webb, *A History of Trade Unionism in England*, 1902.

P. Horn, *Joseph Arch*, Roundwood Press, 1971.

F. Peel, *The Risings of the Luddites*, 1895; reprinted Cass, 1968.

A. Aspinall, *The Early English Trade Unions*, Batchworth, 1949.

J. Marlow, *The Tolpuddle Martyrs*, Deutsch, 1971.

The History of the TUC, 1868–1968, TUC, 1968.

FURTHER SOURCE MATERIAL

J. Priestley, *Historical Account of the Navigable Rivers, Canals
  and Railways throughout Great Britain*, 1831; reprinted Cass, 1969.

S. Smiles, *Lives of the Engineers*, 1862.

M. Scrivenor, *History of the Iron Trade*, 1854.

J. S. Walker, *An Accurate Description of the Liverpool and
  Manchester Railway*, Liverpool, 1830.

J. C. Bourne, *Drawings of the London and Birmingham Railway*, 1839.

P. Lecount, *The History of the Railway connecting London and
  Birmingham*, 1839.

E. Chadwick, *Report on the Sanitary Condition of the Labouring
  Population of Great Britain*, 1842.

W. Greenwood, *There was a Time*, Penguin, 1967.

W. J. Marchant, *In Praise of Ale*, 1888.

H. Mayhew, *London Labour and the London Poor*, 1851–62.

H. Mayhew and J. Binny, *The Criminal Prisons of London and
  Scenes of Prison Life*, 1862.

A. Randell, *Sixty Years a Fenman*, Routledge & Kegan Paul, 1967.

J. Arch, *Life*, 1898.

C. Booth, *Life and Labour of the People of London*, 1891–1903.

A. Somerville, *The Autobiography of a Working Man*, 1848;
  reprinted MacGibbon & Kee, 1967.

J. Gutteridge, *Lights and Shadows in the Life of an Artisan*,
  Coventry, 1893.

T. Burt, *Autobiography*, 1924.

A Memoir of Edmund Cartwright, 1843; reprinted Adams & Dart,
  1971.

W. H. Barrett, *Tales from the Fens*, Routledge & Kegan Paul, 1963.

W. H. Barrett, *More Tales from the Fens*, Routledge & Kegan
  Paul, 1964.

W. Plomer (ed.), *Kilvert's Diary*, 3 vols, 1938–40.

W. Reitzel (ed.), *The Autobiography of William Cobbett*, Faber, 1967.

W. Hutton, *Life*, 1816.

G. Edwards, *From Crow Scaring to Westminster*, 1922.

E. Eden (ed.), *The Autobiography of a Working Man*, 1862.

W. F. Vance, *A Voice from the Mines and Furnaces*, 1853.

W. Lovett, *Life and Struggles*, 1876; reprinted MacGibbon & Kee,
  1967.

J. Brown, *A Memoir of Robert Blincoe*, Manchester, 1832.

G. J. Holyoake, *Sixty Years of an Agitator's Life*, 2 vols., 1892.

The Diary of John Ward of Clitheroe, Weaver, in Transactions of
  the Lancashire and Cheshire Historical Society, vol.105, 1954.

W. H. Barrett, *A Fenman's Story*, Routledge & Kegan Paul, 1965.

M. Thale (ed.), *The Autobiography of Francis Place*, Cambridge
  University Press, 1972.

LOCAL HISTORIES

E. Chitham, *The Black Country*, Longman, 1972.

F. A. Bruton, *History of Manchester and Salford*, 1927.

J. Simmons, *Life in Victorian Leicester*, Leicester Museums, 1971.

J. Sanders, *Birmingham*, Longman, 1969.

W. H. Thomson, *History of Manchester to 1852*, Sherratt &
  Hughes, 1967.

E. Midwinter, *Old Liverpool*, David & Charles, 1971.

R. Muir, *A History of Liverpool*, 1907.

M. Walton, *Sheffield*, Sheffield Telegraph, 1948.

S. Middlebrook, *Newcastle Upon Tyne*, Newcastle, 1950.

H. B. Philpott, *London at School*, 1904.

V. L. Davies and H. Hyde, *Dudley and the Black Country, 1760–
  1860*, Dudley Public Libraries, 1970.

M. H. W. Fletcher, *Netherton, Edward I to Edward VIII*, Dudley
  Public Libraries, 1969.

B. Gibbons, *Notes and Suggestions for a History of Kidderminster*, Kidderminster, 1859.

C. Gill, *Studies in Midland History*, 1930.

C. Hardwick, *History of the Borough of Preston*, 1857.

W. Harris, *History and Antiquities of the Borough and Parish of Halesowen*, 1836.

A. Hewitson, *History of Preston*, 1883.

R. Jenkins, 'Stourbridge and Dudley: a sketch of the industrial history of the district', in *Newcomen Society Transactions* vol.8, 1927–8.

J. A. Langford, *A Century of Birmingham Life*, 2 vols., 1868.

N. J. Frangopulo, *Manchester*, Blond, 1967.

E. A. Goodwyn, *A Century of a Suffolk Town: Beccles*, vol.1, (1760–1815), College Gateway Bookshop, Ipswich, n.d.

A. T. Patterson, *Radical Leicester, 1780–1850*, Leicester University Press, 1954.

J. Prest, *The Industrial Revolution in Coventry*, Oxford University Press, 1960.

M. I. Thomis, *Politics and Society in Nottingham, 1785–1835*, Blackwell, 1969.

S. Timmins (ed.), *The Resources, Products and Industrial History of Birmingham*, 1866.

J. Wilson Jones, *The History of the Black Country*, Birmingham, n.d.

R. E. Leader, *Reminiscences of old Sheffield*, 1876.

I. C. Ellis, *Records of Nineteenth-Century Leicester*, 1935.

J. D. Chambers, *A Century of Nottingham History, 1851–1951*, Nottingham University Press, 1952.

G. Barnsby, *The Dudley Working-Class Movement, 1750–1832*, Dudley Public Libraries, 1966.

W. H. B. Court, *The Rise of Midland Industries, 1600–1838*, 1938.

J. F. Ede, *History of Wednesbury*, Wednesbury Corporation, 1962.

W. G. Dimock Fletcher, *Chapters in the History of Loughborough*, 1883.

Folk Song and Allied Material

B. Copper, *A Song for every Season*, Heinemann, 1971.

F. Howes, *Folk Music of Britain and Beyond*, Methuen, 1969.

R. Nettel, *A Social History of Traditional Song*, Adams & Dart, 1969.

H. Anderson, *The Story of Australian Folk Song*, Oak Publications, New York, 1970.

C. Chilton, *Victorian Folk Songs*, Essex Music, 1965.

M. Pollard, *Ballads and Broadsides*, Pergamon, 1969.

E. MacColl, *The Shuttle and Cage*, Workers' Music Association, 1954.

R. Vaughan Williams and A. L. Lloyd, *The Penguin Book of English Folk Songs*, Penguin, 1959.

V. de Sola Pinto and A. E. Rodway, *The Common Muse*, Penguin, 1965.

A. L. Lloyd, *Come all ye Bold Miners*, Lawrence and Wishart, 1952.

A. L. Lloyd, *Folk Song in England*, Lawrence & Wishart, 1967.

R. Palmer, *Room for Company*, Cambridge University Press, 1971.

R. Palmer, *The Painful Plough*, Cambridge University Press, 1972.

R. Palmer, *Songs of the Midlands*, EP Publishing, 1972.

R. Palmer, *The Valiant Sailor*, Cambridge University Press, 1973.

R. Palmer, *Poverty Knock*, Cambridge University Press, 1974.

P. Seeger and E. MacColl, *The Singing Island*, Mills Music, 1960.

J. Ashton, *Modern Street Ballads*, 1888.

J. Bell, *Rhymes of the Northern Bards*, Newcastle, 1812.

M. W. Disher, *Victorian Song*, Phoenix House, 1955.

J. H. Dixon, *Ancient Poems, Ballads and Songs of the Peasantry of England*, 1846.

R. Ford, *Song Histories*, Glasgow and Edinburgh, 1900.

C. F. Forshaw (ed.), *Holroyd's Collection of Yorkshire Ballads*, 1892.

J. Harland, *Ballads and Songs of Lancashire*, 1875.

W. Henderson, *Victorian Street Ballads*, 1937.

C. Hindley, *Curiosities of Street Literature*, 2 vols., 1871; reprinted John Foreman, 1966.

C. J. D. Ingledew, *Ballads and Songs of Yorkshire*, 1860.

W. H. Logan, *A Pedlar's Pack of Ballads and Songs*, Edinburgh, 1869.

C. MacInnes, *Sweet Saturday Night*, MacGibbon & Kee, 1967.

E. D. Mackerness, *A Social History of English Music*, Routledge & Kegan Paul, 1964.

J. Ord, *The Bothy Songs*, Paisley, 1930.

L. Shepard, *The Broadside Ballad*, Herbert Jenkins, 1962.

L. Shepard, *The History of Street Literature*, David & Charles, 1973.

J. Bruce and J. Stokoe, *Northumbrian Minstrelsy*, 1882.

J. Stokoe and S. Reay, *Songs and Ballads of Northern England*, n.d. (1899?).

J. Wilson, *Tyneside Songs and Drolleries*, SR Publishers, 1970.

The Bishoprick Garland, 1834; reprinted Frank Graham, 1969.

G. and M. Polwarth, *Folk Songs from the North*, Frank Graham, 1970.

G. and M. Polwarth, *North Country Songs*, Frank Graham, 1969.

J. Freeth, *The Warwickshire Medley, or, The Convivial Songster*, 1780.

The Collected Writings of Samuel Laycock, 1900.

W. A. Barrett, *English Folk Songs*, 1891.

J. Freeth, *Political Songster*, 1790.

T. Wilson, *The Pitman's Pay*, 1872.

W. Thom, *Rhymes and Recollections of a Hand-Loom Weaver*, 1845.

E. Elliott, *Corn Law Rhymes*, 1831.

J. Mather, *Songs*, 1862.

I. Campbell, *Come Listen*, Ginn, 1970.

J. Raven, *Songs of a Changing World*, Ginn, 1973.

There are broadside collections in many libraries, including the following: British Museum, Bodleian, Cambridge University, Nottingham University, Newcastle Upon Tyne University, London University, Birmingham Reference Library, Society of Antiquaries, Norwich Public Library, Derby Public Library, Mitchell Library (Glasgow), Oldham Public Library, Manchester Central Library, Chetham's Library (Manchester), Vaughan Williams Memorial Library (Cecil Sharp House), Newcastle upon Tyne Public Library, Sheffield Public Library, Sheffield University, Hereford Public Library, Victoria and Albert Museum, Worcester Public Library. (I have personally used all these; I have no doubt that there are many others.) A number of county record offices also have broadside material.

Discography

Recordings of songs in this book (not always the same version)

Humphrey Hardfeatures' description: Waterloo–Perterloo, Argo ZFB68.

The Jolly Waggoner: The Watersons, Topic 12T142.

I can't find Brummagem: The Wide Midlands, Topic 12TS210.

The Dalesman's Litany: record of same name, Leader LER2029; *Roy Bailey*, Leader LER3021.

The Weaver and the Factory Maid: The Iron Muse, Topic 12T86.

Washing Day: Keep your Feet Still, Leader LER2020.

The Skeul-Board Man: Tommy Armstrong, Topic 12T122.

John o'Grinfield (under the title of *The Poor Cotton Wayver*): *The Iron Muse* (see above).

Birmingham Jack of all Trades: The Wide Midlands (see above).

Cowd Stringy Pie: Transpennine, Topic 12TS215.

Jim Jones: The Great Australian Legend, Topic 12TS203; *Ned Kelly and that Gang*, Leader LER2009.

Durham Goal: Tommy Armstrong (see above).

General Ludd's triumph: The Bitter and the Sweet, Topic 12TS217.

The Barnsley Anthem: Dave Burland, LER2082.

The Rambling Comber: Jump at the Sun, LER2033.

The Rest of the Day's Your Own: Good Mornin' All, Argo 2FB83.

Recordings (other than those listed above) which include material
to do with the social history of the nineteenth century

TOPIC RECORDS, 27 Nassington Road, London NW3 2TX
Northumberland for Ever, 12T186.
The Irish Country Four, 12TS209.
The Collier's Rant, TOP74.
Along the Coaly Tyne, 12T189.
Steam-Whistle Ballads, 12T104.
Chorus from the Gallows, 12T16.
The Manchester Angel, 12T147.
Oldham's burning Sands, 12TS206.
Jack of all Trades, 12T159.
Fair Game and Foul, 12T195.
Deep Lancashire, 12T188.
Owdham Edge, 12T204.
Men at Work, TPS166.
Canny Newcassel, 12TS219.
The frosty Ploughshare, 12TS220.
The painful Plough, ImpA103.
Room for Company, ImpS104

ARGO, 115 Fulham Road, London SW3 6RR
History reflected IV: Liberty, Equality, Fraternity, ZPR107/8.
History reflected V: the Great Exhibition, 1851, ZPR109/10.
Sweet Thames flow Softly, ZFB61.
The Female Frolic, ZFB64.
Kate of Coalbrookdale, ZFB29.

LEADER SOUND, 5 North Villas, London NW1 9BJ
Bob Davenport, LER3008.
Jack Elliott, LEA 4001.
High Level, LER2030.
A Song for every Season, LEA4046–9.

FOLK HERITAGE RECORDINGS, Camp Farm, Montgomery, Wales
The fine old Yorkshire Gentleman, FHR038.

TRANSATLANTIC RECORDS, 120 Marylebone Lane, London W1
The Elliotts of Birtley, XTRA1091.

Index of First Lines

	page
A boy to me was bound apprentice	154
Ally bally, ally bally bee	148
All you that are low-spirited, I think it won't be wrong	299
All you that delight in the railway making	42
All you that does in England dwell	156
A man that is born a husband to be	166
As old John Bull was walking one morning free from pain	88
A stands for alphabet, I've turned it to rhyme	270
A story I'm going to tell ye	188
Attend you blades of London and listen unto me	179
Cheer up, cheer up, you sons of toil and listen to my song	309
Come all sporting husbands, wherever you be	172
Come all you bonny boys	112
Come all you lads of high renown and listen to my story	105
Come all young men of learning and a warning take by me	242
Come all you young fellows that have a mind to range	240
Come one and all, both great and small	168
Come you cock-merchants far and near	123
Confound it, aw ne'er wur so woven afore	226
Each Monday morn before I rise I make a fervent prayer	144
Full twenty years and more have passed	78
Give attention to my ditty and I'll not keep you long	83
Good people all, both great and small, come listen to my rhymes	223
Good people all, give ear I pray	250
Good people all I pray draw near that in this country dwell	264
Good people all who hear my voice	110
Good people, come listen awhile, now	162
Good people I pray, now hear what I say	289
Gosh dang it, lads, I'm back again	68
Happy land! happy land!	318
Have you not heard the news of late	313
Here tradesmen, 'tis plain, at no roguery stop	175
I am a hand weaver to my trade	133
I am a jolly roving blade	210
I am a miner stout and bold	130
I am a navvy bold, that's tramped the country round, sir	40

I know a stingy fellow and his name is Farmer Grab	316
I'm a poor cotton weaver as many a one knows	207
In Manchester New Bailey we've got a new corn mill	254
It's hard when folks can't find th' work	71
It's of a buxom tally man who dwells in our town	190
It's of a football match, my boys, delightful to be seen	125
It's of a tradesman and his wife I heard the other day	183
It was on March the nineteenth day	306
I would take them into Cheshire and there they would sow	260
Kind friends, gather near, I want you to hear	324
Ladies and gentlemen all, I am ready at your call	95
Last New year's day eawr Nan hoo sed	34
No more chant your old rhymes about bold Robin Hood	286
Noo, O dear me, what mun aw dee, aw've nee pleyce noo ti play	120
Now there is a bloke whose name is Curly Williams	247
Of all the great wonders that ever were known	52
Of all the wonders of the age, there's nothing now so much the rage	59
Of hammers and files no more heard than din is	92
Oh listen for a moment, lads, and hear me tell my tale	244
Once on a time this good old town was nothing but a village	73
One day I got out on the spree – I fell out with my mother	135
One day when I was out of work a job I went to seek	236
One mornin' at half-past eight, aa sais te ma bit bairn	150
On the fourth day of July, I recollect well	46
Over in Yorkshire a farmer did dwell	234
Pay heed to my ditty, ye frolicsome folk	196
Rise, Britons, rise now from your slumber	296
Since cast-iron has got all the rage	31
That monster oppression, behold how he stalks	281
The road, the road, the turnpike road!	22
The scenes of Manchester I sing	62
The sky with clouds was overcast, the rain began to fall	142
The summer was over, the season unkind	274
This day for our new navigation	28
Through eating too much supper	321
To Hereford Old Town a new hero is come down	268
To mortals who genuine liberty prize	278
We're all dahn in't cellar 'oil	160

We're broken-hearted gardeners, scarce got a bit of shoe 230

What a row and a rumpus there is I declare 302

When first I went a-waggoning, a-waggoning did go 56

When I'd finished off my work last Saturday at neet 65

When I was a young man I lived rarely 138

Ye friends to Reform, prepare for good fun 294

Ye kind-hearted souls, pray attend to our song 204

Ye lads and lasses spruce and gay, attend unto my song 102

You Birmingham lads, come and listen awhile 50

You combers all, both great and small 200

You Englishmen where'er you be, come list to what I say 214

You lads and lasses blythe and gay 98

You'll all have heard of Durham Gaol 257

You working men of England one moment now attend 219

Acknowledgements For permission to use copyright material, acknowledgement i
made to the following: To the Cecil Sharp Estate for the tunes 'Rosetta', 'The Rigs o
London Town' and 'Sweet Kitty'; to The Three Candles Ltd for the tunes 'The Piper'
Tunes' and 'Dublin Jack of all Trades' from *Irish Street Ballads* by Colm O'Lochlainn
to Ascherberg, Hopwood & Crew for tune 'The Bold Trooper' from *English Peasan
Songs* by F. Kidson, for tune and words to 'Truro Agricultural Show' from *Cornis*
Dialect and Folk Songs by R. Dunstan and the tune 'John O'Grinfield' from *Garland* b
F. Kidson; to Mrs Ursula Vauthan Williams for the tune 'The Waggoner' from Vaugha
Williams ms Collection; to E F D S S for 'The Besom Maker', 'Lisbon', 'The Keepers &
Pouchers', 'Parker's Widow' and 'The Sailor's Frolic'; to E F D S S Publications fo
the tune 'The Dalesman's Litany'; to Duckworth for the words to 'The Football Match
from *Folk Songs of the Upper Thames* by Alfred Williams; to A. L. Lloyd for tune an
words to 'The Weaver and the Factory Maid' and 'The Best-Dressed Man of Seghill'
to Novello for the tune 'The Brisk Young Batchelor' from *English Folk Songs* by C
Sharp and tune and words to 'Rambling Comber' from *English Country Folk Songs* b
C. Sharp; to Norman Buchan and Collins for tune and words to 'Coulter's Candy' from
101 Scottish Songs edited by Norman Buchan; to Francis, Day & Hunter for tune and
words to 'The Rest of the Day's Your Own' from *Old Time Comic Songs No 1* by J. P
Long and David Worton; to George Ewart Evans for tune and words to 'Curly Williams'
to Harvard University Press for tune 'Kirtle Gaol' from *Ballads* and *Sea Songs from
Nova Scotia* by W. R. Mackenzie; to B B C for the tune 'The Sailor's Alphabet', collecte
by Peter Kennedy; to Pamela Bishop for the tune 'The Colliers' March'; to Sandra
Faulkner for the tune 'Striking Times'; to David Hillery for the tune and words o
'Cowd Stringy Pie'. The editor would also like to thank: Edward Thompson, Norman
Longmate and David Goodway for communicating material; Tony Wilson for hel
with elucidating North-eastern references; Sandra Faulkner for providing guita
chords for the great majority of the tunes; Katherine Thomson for chords for the
songs on pp.22 and 133; Pamela Bishop for chords for the tunes on pp.47, 142, 14
and 282; Edward Thompson for suggestions and advice on the text; Katherine Thomson
for suggestions and advice on the tunes; and the librarians and staffs of the librarie
listed on p.348 for their invaluable assistance.